# Worktime and Industrialization

*An International History*

LABOR AND SOCIAL CHANGE

*a series edited by*
*Paula Rayman and Carmen Sirianni*

# Worktime and Industrialization

## An International History

*Edited by*

## GARY CROSS

TEMPLE UNIVERSITY PRESS
*Philadelphia*

Temple University Press, Philadelphia 19122

Copyright © 1988 by Temple University. All rights reserved

Published 1988
Printed in the United States of America

The paper used in this publication meets the minimum requirements of American National Standard for Information Sciences—Permanence of Paper for Printed Library Materials, ANSI Z39.48-1984

Library of Congress Cataloging-in-Publication Data
Worktime and industrialization : an international history/ edited by
  Gary Cross.
    p.  cm.  —  (Labor and social change)
  Bibliography: p.
  Includes index.
  ISBN 0-87722-582-6 (alk. paper)
  1. Hours of labor—History.  2. Industrial relations—History.
I. Cross, Gary S.  II. Series.
HD5106.W67  1988
331.25′7—dc19

88-12173
CIP

# Contents

# List of Contributors

GARY CROSS, a historian at the Pennsylvania State University, is the author of *A Quest for Time: The Reduction of Work in Britain and France, 1840–1940* (University of California Press, 1989).

HOWARD ROCK, Chair of the Department of History at Florida International University, has written *Artisans of the New Republic: The Tradesmen of New York City in the Age of Jefferson* (New York University Press, 1979).

CLIVE BEHAGG, a historian based at the West Sussex Institute of Higher Education, has contributed articles to numerous social history journals and is completing a book focusing on informal patterns of workers' control among English artisans in the mid-nineteenth century.

TERESA MURPHY, a member of the Department of History at the University of Rhode Island, is completing a book presently titled, *Conversion, Pursuasion, and Politics; Evangelical Artisans in Antebellum America.*

STEWART WEAVER, a historian at the University of Rochester, is the author of *John Fielden and the Politics of Popular Radicalism, 1832–1847* (Oxford University Press, 1987).

KATHRYN KISH SKLAR of the Department of History at the University of California at Los Angeles has written *Catherine Beecher, A Study in American Domesticity* (Norton, 1976) and is completing a biography of Florence Kelley.

DAVID R. ROEDIGER, a historian at the University of Missouri, is co-author of *Our Own Time, A History of American Labor and the Working Day* (Verso/ Greenwood Press, 1988) and many other works.

WILLIAM CHASE, based at the University of Pittsburgh's History Department, has written *Workers, Society, and the Soviet State: Labor and Life in Moscow, 1918– 1929* (University of Illinois Press, 1987).

LEWIS SIEGELBAUM of the Department of History at Michigan State University is author of *The Politics of Industrial Mobilization in Russia, 1914–1917* (Macmillan and St. Martin's Press, 1983–84).

BENJAMIN KLINE HUNNICUTT, a member of the Department of Leisure Studies at the University of Iowa, has written *Work Without End: Abandoning Shorter Hours for the Right to Work* (Temple University Press, 1988).

# Worktime and Industrialization

*An International History*

# 1

## Worktime and Industrialization: An Introduction

### Gary Cross

I

WESTERN INDUSTRIALIZATION has been the cause and consequence of many things. Surely one of the most concrete changes occurred in the allocation of personal time. The shift from work toward family and leisure time was as central to the industrial era as the increase in consumption and investment. The division of the day was key to the social contest over the distribution of the economic fruits of increased productivity. Time might be called the ultimate scarce resource; its allocation influenced not only economic growth but the character of family life and leisure. Yet this theme has been strangely neglected.

Industrialization was impossible without a radical change in thinking about time. Historians have long stressed that time discipline (or the work ethic) and the temporal segmentation of work and leisure were culture prerequisites of industrial capitalism. The mechanical clock perhaps was as important as the steam engine in this process. The ability to measure time precisely was essential to the employers' quest to control and intensify the pace of work. The factory clock was both a symbol and a tool of the new work discipline. As duration was reduced to the regularity of the pendulum, costs and outputs could be estimated and customer flows accurately assessed. Economic theorists reflected this by defining value as abstract labor time.[1]

Insofar as industrialization meant the deskilling of labor, the wage earner increasingly experienced work as the marketing of minutes. What workers sold was the sacrifice of time; as employers seized control over the work process and as the hours of labor became a managerial prerogative, wage earners began to conceive of worktime as not their own. Gradually recognizing that employers bought working hours rather than merely skill, work-

3

ers began to place a higher price on their time. Simultaneously, wage earners became aware that time was a scarcity to be protected and liberated from work. The clock on and off the job had radically different meanings. As management expelled "life" from work, the duration of labor became central: For the employer, it indeed became money; for the laborer, it meant not only income but also a debit from life. In the long run, both had an incentive to segment work and leisure time. The struggle would be over the allocation.[2]

In the past few years, historians with widely ranging national, period, and thematic interests have begun to explore the linkage between time and industrial society. This emerging literature has reached the point where a collection of viewpoints concerning the varied but closely interrelated aspects of the history of worktime is in order. In an era of increasing global integration, such a collection on work and time should also be international. This perspective is warranted for historical reasons: Beginning in the 1830s, there was considerable cross-fertilization of ideas and strategies of labor, management, and reformers across the industrializing world. The political and economic impediments to the diminution of worktime were comparable. By the 1880s, the increasing integration of the world economy produced a movement for an international workday that culminated in the nearly universal eight-hour day after World War I. At the same time, national differences in work and leisure cultures, as well as political and economic structures, meant that there would be alternative paths to the modern allocation of time.[3]

Contemporary historians' understanding of the relationship between time consciousness and industrialization has been greatly influenced by E. P. Thompson's "Time, Work Discipline, and Industrial Capitalism." He argues that while employers learned to measure labor value in terms of time and sought to maximize profit by extending working hours and eliminating "gaps" in the workday, laborers were obliged to adapt to this new sense of time. Wage earners gradually discovered the relationship between time, productivity, and pay. When employers found ways of increasing hourly output, workers demanded a monetary share of increased productivity and insisted that worktime beyond a standard period of production be paid a premium or be abolished. Time had become a "currency," observes Thompson, to be "not passed but spent." He summarizes the history of industrial worktime:

The first generation of factory workers were taught by their masters the importance of time, the second generation formed their short-time committees in the ten-hour movement; the third generation struck for overtime and time-and-a half. They had accepted the categories of their employers and learned to fight back with them. They had learned their lesson, that time is money, only too well.[4]

Employers had undermined the "task oriented" work of the artisan and his "alternative bouts of intense labor and idleness" in favor of the work discipline inherent in "time oriented" labor. The worker accepted "barriers between work and life." In effect, according to Thompson, the laborer ceded control over his time at work in exchange for increasing both the price of that time and the hours of leisure apart from labor.[5]

Ironically, given Thompson's stress on the autonomy of workers' culture, this interpretation has encouraged a view of the worker as passively responding to the transformation of the labor process imposed by the employer. This analysis has dovetailed with the common assumption that after 1850, worktime became essentially a reformist issue. Labor, recognizing that it could no longer hope to shape the economy in its own image, capitulated to the logic of capitalism by trading off control over worktime to management in exchange for extended consumption time. Freedom became privatized experience to be enjoyed only "after hours" and beyond the factory gate.[6]

Also ironically, this analysis has largely coincided with modernization theory: With industrialization, workers learned to adapt to clock discipline, developed instrumental attitudes toward their jobs, and abandoned traditional leisure patterns. They relinquished their preindustrial proclivity to work only as long as necessary to maintain customary living standards (working few hours or days if wages rose or food prices declined). Instead, workers began to prefer income to leisure time. The wage earner was transformed into an "economic man."[7]

So persuasive have these arguments been that they have unwittingly choked off research into the question of worktime for almost a generation. Both American and European historians of early industrialization have embraced Thompson's linkage of time, work discipline, and economism. And the view that time had became money for most workers has been reflected in the tendency of late-nineteenth- and twentieth-century labor historians to associate worktime with wages. Movements for shorter hours have even been linked with reformist manipulation of working-class militancy.[8]

Recent research has revised this interpretation in two directions: Historians have questioned and refined Thompson's image of early industrialization (ca. 1800–1850). Others have begun to revise the linkage of reformism, economism, and short-hour movements after 1850 (especially between 1890 and 1940). Despite many differences, these historians have recognized the essentially radical and positive meaning of the reduction of worktime.

The burden of this collection is to provide a forum for new research in the relationship between industrialization and worktime. The chapters in this volume focus on two essential periods in the process: 1800–1850 and 1890–

1940. The collection is also international, at least in an effort to provide a balance of American and European perspectives on this common problem.

## II

For the historian of early industrialization, the question of when and where modern time consciousness emerged is being revised. Recent research has shown that a regular workday predates the mechanized factory. The image of the porous day of labor in the preindustrial artisan's workshop is now recognized as a stereotype, at least in England. Moreover, fresh investigations have revealed that the struggle over the allocation of time was hardly an invention of the nineteenth-century hours movement. While few artisans directly challenged the "traditional" and sometimes irregular workday, the number of days that artisans and even servants were willing to work varied with the season and wage levels. As Michael Sonenscher suggests for eighteenth-century France, artisans usually viewed wage work as a supplement to other sources of income (e.g., farming). Thus, when employers found them inconstant laborers, they were, in fact, modulating wage work with time devoted to these income alternatives. In contrast, the hours of wage work demanded by employers were less dictated by the sun and temperature (as commonly assumed in "preindustrial theory") than by the costs of maintaining inventories and interest charges on raw materials. Masters often had an incentive to increase the workday during rush periods to get the goods out and then to lay off labor or reduce hours in the dead season. The ancien régime French state sided with the employer in this conflict over worktime by imposing the labor passport, or *livret,* on workers and legally obliging them to "work"; this tended to limit the mobility of labor, and, of course, it did not guarantee regular employment.[9]

As Howard Rock shows in Chapter 2 of this collection, New York City artisans in the early American republic were not entirely disinterested in the question of worktime. Their perception of time, however, was shaped by the structure of their work and social life. Some craft workers were less concerned with the length of the workday than with the opportunity to gain free time by graduating to the status of master. Long and regular workdays could be seen (as they were for the journeyman printer Benjamin Franklin) as an investment in a future life of independence, a degree of prosperity, and even leisure. Other artisans, less affected by this prudential work ethic, preferred to interrupt the workday by the rituals of foot ales, long and frequent meal and drinking breaks, and spontaneous gatherings for sport, gambling, and conversations. They too were relatively indifferent to the length of the day. The same was probably true of women workers whose productive tasks were interspersed with the nursing of babies or tending to children (even in workshops). Students of early factory work are impressed by the "leisurely" pace of the machines.[10] A customary day from sunup to sundown or even of several hours of work by candlelight was acceptable, at least in periods of rushed work.

This, however, hardly suggests a passivity toward time among the preindustrial workforce. To be sure, when the eighteenth-century English employer attempted to break these work and leisure patterns, the length of the workday was not the first issue. Rather, it was the piece rate. Still, these struggles emerged as conflicts over the workweek. As often noted, employers advocated reducing piece rates (as well as raising food prices and expanding the labor supply) as a means of obliging independent artisans to labor longer. In effect, this forced craftsmen in cottages and workshops to commit longer weekly periods to wage work.[11] Moreover, even as employers gradually sought to impose time discipline directly through the central management of labor in the factory, workers often succeeded in preserving their customary daily gaps in the work routine, irregular workweeks with "Saint Mondays," and seasonal holidays. They defended these "bits" of free time from wage work.[12]

As Clive Behagg shows in Chapter 3, the early industrial struggle over time was symptomatic of a quest for control over work and its product. Despite the obvious linkage between piece rates and time wages and the decline of skill, early-nineteenth-century English workers were loath to recognize the contract as embodying simply the sale of labor time. Instead they clung to their identity as independent contractors selling finished goods; workers believed that, during their jobs, they controlled the product and thus the time required to complete their tasks. The objective was to preserve autonomy in a small work group, whose independence was defined by its ability to set its own schedule.

Despite the nineteenth-century trend toward a "regular workday," historians have uncovered plenty of evidence in the early twentieth century of workers retaining a preference for the seasonal workyear (e.g., among dockers) and the informal observance of wakes, "Saint Monday," and other traditional punctuations of work regularity. At most recent scholarship has stressed, the pace of mechanization was far slower than is painted in the textbook picture of the "Industrial Revolution." Working hours, except for the small number of workers in the textile mills, did not increase, at least not in Britain.[13]

Nevertheless, the question remains: When and how did artisans and factory workers become sensitive to duration of daily labor, abandon the ancient traditions of the natural workday from sunrise to sunset, and tolerate or even embrace life sharply segmented from work? Although Thompson and others have done us a great service in raising these questions, they have tended to stress the passive role of labor—adapting or capitulating to the imposition of new clock-centered work rules and mechanization. Yet historians have also begun to recognize a more active and positive quest for reduced labor time. Of course, the work process was key to the transition in time consciousness. Yet this change was also a function of wider political and cultural factors that gave expression to new quests for autonomy.

Clearly, mechanization gave employers a means of regulating the pace of work. As Marx stressed, the machine obliged the worker—as a condition of employment—to submit to the hours and intensity of work dictated by the employer. Deprived of the means of production, the wage earner had no choice. Yet it was less the machine than the centralized workplace that gave employers control over worktime. Especially in unmechanized firms, the only way of increasing surplus value was to extend the workday.

Again, as Behagg and Rock note, employers found a variety of ways of imposing regularity on the workday. For example, laws could be used to enforce punctuality and reduce absenteeism. Another means was modifying the pay system—especially by ending a guaranteed workday in order to force labor to absorb the costs of ebbs in production or by manipulating piece rates or changing to day wages when it was to the employers' economic advantage.[14]

In all these ways, workers were obliged to adapt to changes with a new tactic: a reduction in daily working hours. This demand had a variety of intents. Shorter hours might mean a decrease in the use of machines and thus the rate at which the textile industry accumulated glut-creating inventories; reduction of worktime was also an attempt to extract from employers a larger share of the economic gains of increased productivity by placing a higher price on an hour of work in overtime; and fewer daily hours would reduce seasonal employment by obliging capital to extend work over a longer period. These and other responses show that worktime was a complex factor in the struggles over the distribution of industrial productivity.

New views of time were also adaptations to changes in the organization of work. The gradual purging of play from work obliged workers to reclaim leisure "after hours." The employers' onslaught against "Saint Monday" required the compensation of the Saturday half-holiday. The separation of work and domestic life resulting from the removal of materials and machines from the cottage redirected workers toward embracing a clear segmentation of work and "life" as the only practical defense of family interests. The option of withdrawing the mother from wage work was only a partial solution. The gradual end of the tramping system and the diminishing opportunities for farm or part-time self-employment made the seasonal workyear far less attractive; it increasingly meant regular joblessness rather than a respite from a daily routine. The demand for a uniform workday, stretched out over the whole year, was an adaptation to an increasingly urbanized economy. Not only was there a desire for a shorter workday but, with it, the quest for a regular and predictable separation of work and "life."[15]

Yet it would be wrong to see these changes as mere accommodations to employer initiatives or the imperatives of industrial organization. In fact, hours movements were seldom associated with "modern" economic sectors during early industrialization. They more frequently appeared in trades where labor was organized and during periods when workers were part of wider political movements. The relationship between the rise of short-hour movements and the quest for political rights has been observed in the history of early American Republican ideology and in English Chartism. Less research has been done on the linkage between short hours and the French and German revolutionaries of 1848. The quest for individual dignity—expressed in the right of political participation—was paralleled by the demand for the right to control one's own time. Historians of feminism have observed the ties between "political" and personal liberty in periods of liberal ferment. The claim for personal time in revolt against the patriarchal domestic economy and the protest against "wage slavery" appeared in the same context as did political radicalism. Struggles over the length of the workday in retail shops, for example, were attempts by workers to gain freedom from the master's nearly unlimited access to their time. It paralleled the long quest for the liberty of living away from the master's shop. Efforts to reduce worktime were broadly political; they expressed, as an individual right, the control over how much time the worker would sell—the only thing that distinguished the worker from the slave. One important meaning of Republican and Chartist ideology was that the state should protect that right.

In Chapter 5, Stewart Weaver especially addresses this political dimension in his critique of interpretations of the ten-hour movement that focus on the elite origins and conservative results of the Factory Act of 1847. He finds the source of the short-hour struggle in the textile community and the Chartist/radical movements. The quest for a ten-hour law was a means of asserting workers' control over the operation of machinery and an attempt to redistribute the wealth created by mechanization; but, even more, it was an assertion of freedom from work and liberty for self-expression, a *sine qua non* of participation in society. The ten-hour movement was as much a value for the skilled outworker and artisan, who supported it in an effort to prevent the general lengthening of the workday.[16] The underlying ideal was a citizenship right to equal access to leisure—apart from the economists' estimation of the productivity of labor time or the claim that the state should "protect" only the dependent child and mother. Ultimately, by gaining a regular short workday, wage earners took away the employer's control over the worker's life. The ten-hour movements of the 1820s through 1840s were not only a defense against the onslaught of industrialization but also a positive claim to personal time and privacy.

Teresa Murphy makes this point in her chapter on the culture and religion of New England workers in the 1830s and 1840s. What linked textile laborers with construction workers was a common identity with an ideal of religious "perfection"—a self-initiated moral ideal that required cultivation in time free from toil. This reversal of the traditional Calvinist association of salvation with work temporarily united workers in disparate trades. It challenged, rather than succumbed to, middle-class ideological hegemony.

The transition to a modern consciousness of time was complex. It may have been an adaptation to the end to the tramping system, but it was also a quest for the right of permanent settlement and predictable work. Probably it was induced by the decline of household production and the intermingling of work and life, but the desire for predictable and regular time free from care and employer control also played a role. Surely the rising demands of coordinated work in the factory required fixed hours, but so also did the workers' desire for "common enjoyment" with family and friends. The short-hour movements may have been an adaptation to the separation of work and life (home) in order to fulfill family responsibilities, but what about the obvious quest for a new definition of family built less around economic exchange than a morality of childrearing and reciprocal affection? New attitudes toward time may have been a response to the attempt of management to shift the cost of seasonal production onto the worker; it also gave form to the workers' drive for a regularity in life—to end to the roller-coaster ride of overwork and underwork, of wageless leisure and debt-driven toil. Short-hour movements may have originated in the effort of masters to control the culture and process of work; still, it was the workers who sought independence from the paternalism of the domestic economy. Should we find the demand for a reduced and regular workday to be simply a compensation for the loss of autonomy during work? In many ways, the decline of self-management was a lamentable change. But such a view obscures the fact that time had a social meaning outside of work in new (and sometimes perhaps even more satisfying) patterns of family and leisure life.

Laborers' changing attitudes toward time correlate with the advance of these modern industrial labor relations—the intensification of work, time-cash accounting of employment, and the separation of worker from master. Yet, as Thompson reminded us over twenty years ago, it also has to do with the initiative of worker movements and, we must add, the positive embrace of new notions of autonomy, organized around a new allocation of time.

## III

Perhaps the most troublesome implication of the time- and work-discipline analysis is that it tends to reduce the struggle over time after 1850 to a *fait accompli* or reformism. Yet the later reductions of the workday were neither by-products of industrialization nor booby prizes conceded to stabilize industrial relations. They were perhaps the most difficult of concessions won by workers in both the nineteenth and twentieth centuries.

First, employer resistance to short hours was almost always more stiff than it was to higher pay; the two were related only in limited ways. As M. A. Bienefeld has shown, for the worker to set the "normal day" was to take away part of the manager's authority over the workforce and to limit his ability to master his own enterprise. The economic benefits of the regular workday were often greater for the laborer than for the employer; in many trades, capital had an incentive to maintain an irregular workday (usually under the form of a long "regular day"). It was to the employer's advantage to have at his disposal the worker's time until 7:00 or 8:00 P.M. in order to meet the demands of an unanticipated order or expand output to meet demand during a boom or seasonal rush. A shorter workday had many potential harmful effects: It could raise wage costs (either in overtime rates or simply in higher labor prices when growth reduced the jobless rate); it could force employers to buy expensive machinery, accumulate inventories (in anticipation of later sales), and thus tie up capital. In contrast, the longer workday allowed the employer to avoid these costs during expansions while imposing the economic effects of reduced product demand on labor through short-time and layoffs. Whereas wage increases could be easily reversed in response to prices (at least in the nineteenth century), employers feared that this would not be possible with hours. A shorter workday, then, threatened to slow the turnover of capital and inventory and to choke off profits and accumulation.[17]

At the same time, workers were seldom able to reduce hours. During economic downturns, when they had an incentive to share jobs through shorter regular hours, they lacked bargaining power. During economic booms, they had the advantage of a tight labor market, but many individual workers preferred to accumulate (and replenish income lost during the last recession) by working overtime. The incentive of job sharing was missing. Only during upswings in labor demand or in skilled trades were workers able to win worktime reductions. Yet even these conditions, especially if immediately preceded by recession, were hardly guarantees of an hours movement and certainly not of a successful one. It is thus hardly surprising that hours demands were usually on the back burner of the workers' stove.

Competition also dissuaded individual employers from "unilaterally" reducing hours in any market. And as the market widened (especially with technological transfers), regional or even national collective bargaining agreements were inadequate guarantees that an improved hours standard would not price a trade out of national and world markets. As a result, scholars who look exclusively at the struggle in the workplace or even trade will have the impression that worktime was of little concern to the late-nineteenth- and twentieth-century worker. This was far from the truth.

The essential point is that worktime could not be effectively addressed at the level of the enterprise or industry. Except in extraordinarily well placed trades—for example, in construction, where international competition was insignificant, or in privileged labor and commodity markets such as English metal goods in the late 1860s—it was impossible for unions to impose shorter regular hours on employers.[18] The partial result was that worktime was reduced in highly discontinuous patches (e.g., 1847–1850 and 1918–1920).

Perhaps more amorphous, but no less real, was the reluctance of elites to agree to shorter hours for fear of the cultural consequences—more working-class leisure and perhaps an undermining of work discipline. The anxiety caused by the portent of male free time was especially evident in the political opposition to including men in the factory acts of the mid-nineteenth century in Britain and a generation later in France. It still animated opposition to the "three-eights" (the equal division of the day between work, sleep, and leisure) in the 1890s.[19]

Thus the worktime issue inevitably became political, at both national and international levels. In many cases, only a law could "even the field" between labor and management and, equally important, eliminate the threat of standard-breaking employers who would gain an economic advantage over the more humane (or better capitalized) firm by raising hours. These dynamics were recognized as early as 1815 in Robert Owen's proposal for an international hours standard at the Vienna peace conference. These problems brought together the International Working Man's Association in 1864, and they were a central theme of the Second International in 1889.[20] From the perspective of the historian of workers' control and the labor process, this may appear as reformism—the abandonment of the autonomy of the workplace for the accommodation to the formality and authoritarian structure of collective bargaining and to protective labor legislation. Students of consumer society might even interpret these hours movements as unintentional steps toward the segmentation of life unto unfree work and the false liberation of manipulated mass consumption.[21] Yet these approaches largely misunderstand (or ignore) the dynamics of the hours movement and the problems and objectives behind them.

This is not to suggest that "reformists" were not part of the equation: Barring a successful revolution, labor leaders were inevitably obliged to embrace consensus positions, compromises to build coalitions between the disparate goals of workers and to win a middle-class voting public. Even in the United States, where trade unions usually opposed maximum-hour laws, at least for adult males, these same difficulties obliged them to seek support beyond the workplace and even to participate (although reluctantly) in international conclaves that promoted transnational worktime standards.[22]

In Chapter 6, Kathyrn Sklar reviews this problem in the United States from the 1840s through World War I. She shows why and how women were at the forefront of the legal struggle for reduced working hours. Despite the common thesis that legislative protection sprang from paternalistic motives, legal action was the only possible means of expressing the worktime goals of women in factories and sweatshops. Gender was often a surrogate for class legislation.

This movement often created strange bedfellows: In Britain in 1890, eight-hour demonstrations encompassed Tory-voting skilled artisans, the newly enfranchised unskilled docker, the voteless female matchmaker, as well as conservative trade union officials, young New Model Unionists, Marxists, and Fabians. The call for the eight-hour day surely obscured the specific needs of the workplace, yet it provided a rallying cry that periodically united an otherwise dispersed and impotent working-class movement.[23] The loose front for shorter hours soon included traditionalist religious communities endeavoring to "protect" working mothers and children, proponents of fatigue science, and even progressive businessmen who found profit in a more compressed and thus more efficient workday. The language of middle-class reform frequently permeated into the discourse of organized labor. In France, "Taylorism," as uniquely defined by labor leaders, became an argument for shorter hours; lack of economic modernization, they argued, alone held back the social good of the eight-hour day.[24]

As David Roediger shows in Chapter 7 of this volume, these groups were not always effective. American labor leaders widely praised "Fordism," which promised to pass the benefits of the assembly line on to operatives in the form of an eight-hour day and, later, a forty-hour week. Yet he also shows that in the 1920s, few businesses followed this model of progressive capitalism by linking leisure with productivity and consumption. Despite labor's abandonment of the radical tradition of Ira Stewart, management refused to accept a tradeoff of free time for the intensification of work. One might argue that businessmen have frequently been unwilling to follow their long-term interests. Yet the simple economics of competition and increased costs per hour more easily explain this resistance. In any event, business reformers were unreliable allies. Moreover, the voluntarism and narrow craft unionism of the American Federation of Labor produced insufficient pressure on employers to force hours reductions in the 1920s.

The question remains, When and why did worktime diminish? Surely the militancy and perhaps independence of the labor movement had something to do with this process. The more moderate American unions were unable to gain a national eight-hour standard until 1938, nearly twenty years after it became common in Europe. Indeed, while the "American standard" of wages and hours was the envy of Western European labor in the late nineteenth century, the American leisure norm fell behind the Europeans in the 1920s. And if European trade unions admired the high wages in American auto factories, they ignored the unregulated conditions of southern textile workers.

Yet, as I argue in Chapter 8, the reduction of worktime was also a product of political crisis. The sort of reformist coalition that failed in the United States after World War I was relatively successful in Europe. The difference can only partially be attributed to the factor of trade union leadership. Probably more important was the relatively greater effect of the postwar crisis in Europe. There, virtually every instance of hours reduction was a product of *both* an insurgency from below and a penetration of a network of reformers from above into the state apparatus. The international context of this dual pressure for change only reinforced the impact at the national level. In this period of discontinuity, the "normalcy" of industrial competition and the market bias against hours reductions were reversed.

Yet the attempt to reallocate time did not occur everywhere within the context of reform. In Russia, it was the consequence of the Bolshevik Revolution. Yet, as the chapter by Lewis Siegelbaum and William Chase shows, this took place within a similar historical context as did the hours movements of the West. It was part of the global struggle for time in the 1890s; and, again as in the West, it peaked during the upswing of political activity in the late 1890s and in 1905. Further, the eight-hour day became the first concession to the crisis of the world war. Indeed, the example of the November 1917 eight-hour decree in Russia stimulated a westward-moving wave of worktime insurgency that climaxed only in the spring of 1919. Like the French labor movement, the Bolsheviks linked work efficiency (identified with Taylorism) to shorter hours. New work methods were both to raise output and to free time for social and cultural goals. A productivist optimism ran across the ideological barrier between the communists and Western European socialists.[25]

Yet, of course, the Russians faced problems unknown in the more developed capitalist West. The Soviets experienced a dilemma in attempting to industrialize and, at the same time, fulfill the Western European vision of the "normal day." This was concretely revealed in the difficult experiments with shorter hours in Soviet industry during the interwar period. Chase and Siegelbaum offer an original treatment of this unexplored terrain. The Soviet challenge was to increase productivity in the wake of the destruction of the civil war and the shortage of skilled manpower. At the same time, the Soviets tried to hold to the advanced standard of an eight-hour day. They faced an insuperable task: to draw into the factory a largely peasant workforce expected to adapt immediately to a work discipline that took generations to inculcate into the Western European worker. After 1927, the inadequacy of the machine stock and industrial organization frustrated planners' efforts in introducing a seven-hour shift. This chapter explores the difficulties of Soviet efforts to create a more "rational" use of labor time. Again, as in the West, for social reasons men and women resisted the introduction of shift work.

The limits of the nineteenth-century vision of a reallocation of time are analyzed in a quite different way in Benjamin Hunnicutt's chapter. He asks a crucial question: Why did the historic trend toward the reduction of worktime practically end in the 1930s in the United States? His answer affects our understanding of changing attitudes toward time (or leisure) and income (or work), and it sheds light on the contemporary difficulties in further reducing worktime. Hunnicutt focuses on the critical failure of a bill introduced in 1933 in Congress for a thirty-hour week. The victory of opponents, within both business and the New Deal administration, signaled the end of the linkage between economic progress and the diminution of worktime. Instead, economic progress thereafter was almost exclusively associated with the growth in economic activity and job security. Central to Hunnicutt's analysis is the context of the Great Depression, which shaped the decision to abandon the idea of job sharing for a Keynesian model of economic expansion. His analysis suggests an important change in thinking about how to allocate productivity between leisure and income.

The defeat of a broad-based forty-hour movement in Europe paralleled the American struggle. An international coalition of reformers and workers was beginning to form in 1932. In many ways, it was similar to the group that emerged in 1919. Yet the spread of fascism, the dominance of economic nationalism, and the impotence of labor assured defeat of a worktime remedy to the economic crisis. While the French Popular Front introduced a forty-hour week on a strictly national basis in 1936, the inability of others to win hours reduction and the drift to war assured the failure of this experiment. Ever since, the forty-hour week has had a bad press in European (and especially French) economic theory. To be sure, the mid-1930s brought the near-universal entitlement to the annual paid vacation, a benefit broadly extended in the prosperous 1950s and 1960s at least in Europe. By the early 1960s, the forty-hour standard had become common in Europe. Yet this expressed an extremely small share of the increased productivity of the last fifty years. Even when early retirement and late job entry are added into the equation, the predominant distribution of efficiency has gone to consumption rather than free time. The era of the progressive reduction of worktime, at least for now, has come to an end.[26]

# IV

This collection is not meant to present a "school" of research. Indeed, there are many implicit and sometimes open disagreements between the contributors. I doubt that any of the authors would not take exception with my argument presented here. Our differences in part reflect the particularities of our disparate regional and period specialties, as well as the biases of our different approaches—social, political, or cultural. This diversity, of course, is by design. It may help stimulate new questions. At least we are talking to one another.

Yet these differences also reflect the sadly narrow boundaries of modern historical specialization. Several obvious gaps remain. For example, despite many pious words about comparative history, we remain largely ignorant of the similarities and differences between the United States and Western Europe (or East Asia) in the transition to a "regular" workday. What would such a comparison say about the "exceptionalism" of American industrial relations? The rich literature of the early-nineteenth-century specialist is still largely separated from the less developed social history of the twentieth-century researcher. Part of this problem is temperamental. The early industrial historian often sympathizes with the artisan culture with its intermingling of work and "life," while the late modernist historian may be more likely to embrace the individualistic world of segmented work and leisure. Still, the transition from one phase to the other is a weak link.

A third question comes to mind. Is there any future for a short-hour movement? Authors in this text and elsewhere might well give contrary answers that would reflect the trajectories of their research. One might argue that if there has been an end to short hours, it is because of a cultural shift away from the preference for leisure and toward a gospel of work and economic growth. Another might counter that because of change in free-time preferences, a new age has emerged in which time schedules have become highly individualized and in which the old "standards" (e.g., the eight-hour day) no longer appeal to workers. Another still might claim that the prognosis for winning further time from work is limited until organized labor is able to strengthen its base and develop a clearer focus on the value and even necessity of working shorter hours. Finally, another might argue that the present weakness of both labor and reform coalitions reflects an absence of an international conjuncture appropriate for reform.

Yet each of the contributors to this book offers a perspective on the linkages between industrialization and the political economy of worktime. In different ways and across the boundaries of period and region, they address this basic question.

## NOTES

1. Nels Anderson, *Work and Leisure* (London, 1981), pp. 52, 71; Lewis Mumford, *Techniques and Civilization* (New York, 1934), p. 14; Werner Sombart, *Der Moderne Kapitalismus* (Leipzig, 1919), pp. 809, 828–831; Carlo Cipolla, *Clocks and Culture: 1300–1700* (London, 1967); David Landes, *Revolution in Time: Clocks and the Making of the Modern World* (Cambridge, Mass., 1983); and Jacques Attali, *Histoire du temps* (Paris, 1982).

2. For the classic exposition of this, see Karl Marx, *Capital* (New York, 1967), I:235–256. Note also Wilbert Moore, *Man, Time, and Society* (New York, 1963), pp. 8–68.

3. I develop this theme in chapter 8.

4. Edward P. Thompson, "Time, Work-Discipline, and Industrial Capitalism," *Past and Present* 38 (1967): 86.

5. Ibid., pp. 57, 61, 94. See also Nicole Samuel, *Le Temps libre. Un Temps social* (Paris, 1984), pp. 9–10.

6. Note, for example, Donald Reid, "The Decline of St. Monday," *Past and Present* 71 (May 1967): 57–97; William Reddy, *The Rise of Market Culture: The Textile Trade and French Society, 1750–1900* (Cambridge, 1984), pp. 136–137; Eric Hobsbawm, *Labouring Men* (London, 1964), pp. 371–386; G. Stedman Jones, *The Language of Class* (London, 1983), pp. 235–238; Michelle Perrot, *Les Ouvriers en grève,: France, 1871–1890* (Paris, 1974), I:184, 260–263; and Peter Stearns, *Lives of Labor* (New York, 1976), pp. 208–209, 250–251.

7. Lujo Brentano, *Hours and Wages in Relation to Production* (London, 1898), popularized these ideas. They were developed, of course, in such works as Reinhard Bendix, *Work and Authority in Industry* (New York, 1956), Chap. 5, 7; and Clark Kerr and John Dunlop, *Industrialism and Industrial Man* (Cambridge, Mass., 1964), p. 219 especially.

8. For example, Charles Tilly and Edward Shorter, *Strikes in France* (New York, 1974), pp. 66–68, 190; Peter Stearns, "Measuring the Evolution of Strike Movements," *International Review of Social History*, pt. 1 (1974): 153–156: and E. H. Phelps Brown, *A Century of Pay* (London, 1968), p. 208.

9. M. Harrison, "The Ordering of the Urban Environment: Time, Work and the Occurrence of Crowds, 1790–1835," *Past and Present* 110 (1986); Steven Kaplan, "Reflexions sur la police du mode du travail," *Revue historique* 529 (1979): 17–37; Michael Sonenscher, "Work and Wages in Paris in the Eighteenth Century," in *Manufacture in Town and Country Before the Factory*, ed. Maxine Berg, Pat Hudson, and Michael Sonenscher (Cambridge, 1983), pp. 162–167; and Reddy, *Rise of Market Culture*, Chap. 1.

10. Tom Dublin, *Women at Work* (New York, 1979), pp. 72–73. See also David Brody, "Time and Work during Early American Industrialism," paper, March 1987.

11. The classic exposition of this thesis is E. A. Furniss, *The Position of Labor in a System of Nationalism* (New York, 1919), pp. 118–154, 233–335.

12. Jeffrey Kaplow, "La Fin de la Saint-Lundi: Etude sur le Paris ouvrier au xix⁰ siècle," *Le Temps libre* 2 (1981), pp. 107–118; and Reid, "Decline of St. Monday," pp. 56–97.

13. Eric Hopkins, "Working Hours and Conditions during the Industrial Revolution, a Re-appraisal," *Economic History Review* 25 (February 1982): 52–67.

14. The example of these tactics used in English construction is in Richard Price, *Masters, Unions and Men: Work Control in Building and the Rise of Labour* (Cambridge, 1980), pp. 38–39, 158, and Chap. 3.

15. I develop these themes in my *Quest for Time: The Reduction of Work in Britain and France, 1840–1940* (Berkeley, 1989), especially Chaps. 2, 3.

16. Craig Calhoun, *The Question of Class Struggle: The Social Foundations of Popular Radicalism during the Industrial Revolution* (Chicago, 1982), pp. 191–196.

17. M. A. Bienefeld, *Working Hours in British Industry: An Economic History* (London, 1972), pp. 143–148, 162–179, 194–197. See also John Owen, *The Price of Leisure* (Rotterdam, 1969), Chaps. 2, 3; and John Owen, *Working Hours, an Economic Analysis* (Lexington, 1979).

18. For example, on the British nine-hour movements of the late 1860s and early 1870s, see John Burnett, *The History of the Nine Hours Movement at Newcastle and Gateshead* (London, 1872); Monica Hodgson, "The Working Week in Victorian Britain, 1840–1900," master's thesis, University of London, 1974, pp. 39–53; and Price, *Masters, Unions, and Men*, pp. 45–52. Parallel movements in America are noted in David Montgomery, *Beyond Equality, Labor and the Radical Republicans, 1862–1872* (New York, 1967).

19. Examples of this hostility are William Shaxby, *The Case Against Trade Union and Legislative Interference* (London, 1898), pp. 11–12, 22–23; and Yves Guyot, *La Tyrannie socialiste* (Paris, 1893); pp. 5, 114–115, 121–122. See also my *Quest for Time,* Chap. 3.

20. Note, for example, Benoit Malon, *Le Socialisme integral* (Paris, 1894), 2:82–85; Parker Moon, *The Labour Problem and the Social Catholic Movement in France* (New York, 1921), pp. 123–138; Maurice Dommanget, *Histoire du Premier mai* (Paris, 1953), Chaps. 1–2; and Steven Bauer, *Der Weg zum Achtstudentag* (Zurich, 1919), Chap. 1.

21. Stuart Ewig, *Captains of Consciousness* (New York, 1976), pp. 24, 30.

22. See David Roediger and Philip Foner, *Our Own Time; American Labor and Working Hours* (Westport, Conn., 1988).

23. Eric Hobsbawm, *The Turning Point of Labour,* 2nd ed. (London, 1977), p. 111. See also Alexander Trachtenberg, *The History of May Day* (New York, 1935); William E. Murphy, *History of the Eight Hours Movement* (Melbourne, 1896, 1906); and Dommanget, *Histoire,* pp. 121–131.

24. Roediger and Foner, *Our Own Time,* Chap. 8; and A. E. P Duffy, "The Eight-Hour Movement in Britain, 1836–1893," *Manchester School of Economics and Social Studies* 36 (1968): pp. 203–222, 345–363. On the growing role of fatigue science in the generation before World War I, see Anson Rabinbach, "The European

Science of Work: The Economy of the Body at the End of the Nineteenth Century,'' in *Work in France,* ed. Steven Kaplan and Cynthia Koepp (Ithaca, N.Y., 1986), pp. 475–513. On the role of Taylorism in the French labor reformism, see my ''Redefining Workers' Control: Rationalization, Labor Time, and Union Politics in France, 1900–1928,'' in *Work, Community and Power: The Experience of Labor in Europe and America, 1900–1925,* ed. James Cronin and Carmen Sirianni (Philadelphia, 1983), pp. 143–172.

25. Examples of the Western European socialist infatuation with work efficiency are Henri de Man, *Joy in Work* (New York, 1929); William Watson, *Men and Machines* (London, 1935); and Jules Moch, *Socialisme et rationalisation* (Paris, 1927).

26. Some post–World War II studies are Anne Lapping, *Working Time in Britain and East Germany, a Summary* (London, 1983); Sue Roger, *Vers une société du temps libre* (Paris, 1981); Ronald Ehrenberg, *Longer Hours or More Jobs* (Ithaca, N.Y., 1982); and Fred Best, *Flexible Life Scheduling* (New York, 1980). See also the forthcoming anthology on the sociology of worktime edited by Carmen Sirianni for Temple University Press.

# Independent Hours: Time and the Artisan in the New Republic

## Howard Rock

### I

WHILE MUCH has been written about the changing concept of time in the period of the Industrial Revolution, particularly in Great Britain, the culture of worktime has been largely unexplored within the life of the early American artisan.[1] This chapter is an incipient effort to fill this gap using the experience of the New York City artisan as an example. Following a discussion of the meaning of work and the nature of the workplace for the colonial craftsman, I analyze the impact of the economic and political revolutions of the late eighteenth and early nineteenth century. To some extent, traditional values had already been displaced by the late colonial era. Yet the time consciousness that E. P. Thompson describes for eighteenth-century England was often slow in coming in nineteenth-century America. Profound changes regarding hours devoted to both work and leisure were part of the new world of the early Republic, but these changes were very much within an American context.[2]

New York was one of four major colonial cities. It was well behind Philadelphia in growth, but with 21,000 inhabitants in 1770, it had overtaken Boston. Located on an excellent natural harbor, it served as an entrepot for imports and exports. Artisan enterprise was oriented to mercantile trade. Bakers, for example, supplied local inhabitants and produced large quantities of hardbread for ocean voyages. The city's prosperity lived and died with trade. The mercantile elite was at the top of the social structure, but the bulk of the inhabitants were artisans, or mechanics, as they were commonly called. Below them were unskilled laborers, mariners, and finally slaves, who composed up to 15 percent of the city's population.[3]

The world of the colonial artisan was largely that of the master, and

21

worktime must be considered within that context. Mobility was such that most craftsmen could expect to complete their apprenticeship (sometimes before the age of twenty-one), spend a few years as journeymen in New York and other seaport cities, and move on to become small-scale entrepreneurs. All trades were not alike, and an artisan in one of the more prestigious and lucrative crafts (e.g., a silversmith or clockmaker) was of different means than a mechanic working in the more plentiful trades (e.g., shoemaking and tailoring). The latter often lived fairly close to the edge, depending on the work of their family and, optimally, an apprentice or two and a journeyman to supplement their income. Masters generally labored in their own shops or lodgings. A small shoemaker might take in work for a merchant, finish it at his home or garret, and then return it to the merchant for sale. A prominent saddler or cabinetmaker would likely have a store and workshop in the front and living quarters in the back.[4]

The colonial master worked in a world that retained a number of preindustrial traits. First, most craftsmen were task oriented. They worked their own hours in their own homes to finish a chair, table, shoe, or waistcoat. Second, most goods were "bespoke," or made to order at a customer's request and specifications. Third, although masters put in a long day, traditionally from sunup to sundown, the divisions of the day were up to them and included various breaks for meals and other needs. Fourth, corporate values remained in the community. The price of bread was regulated so that the needs of the people were met before the profit of the farmer, baker, or merchant; cartmen were carefully supervised to prevent a monopoly of the critical supply of firewood. Finally, uncertainties of weather, ignorance of markets, the length of travel, and the difficulty of communication caused frequent interruption in the work schedule. Periods of intense work alternated with days of little labor.[5]

Yet, while preindustrial customs and conditions were present, the eighteenth-century artisan did not live in a quiet, backward world. Britain was the most aggressively commercial and consumer-oriented nation in the West, and despite English mercantile policy that intended America for a less prominent role in the manufacture of goods, this entrepreneurial spirit was present among American artisans. Toward the end of the colonial era, the presence of thousands of British troops caused an influx of capital and an increased demand for goods and services. Mobility, in turn, became more common, and in the more lucrative crafts a number of artisans attained merchant standing. Craftsmen saw greater opportunity, and their plans expanded proportionately. As Carl Bridenbaugh has noted, eighteenth-century colonial artisans were "men of ambition; they were consciously on the make. To raise themselves and their families above their present level . . . was their goal." Time was far too valuable to waste on unproductive pastimes. There is little evidence that "Saint Monday" ever existed in America. Indeed, ambition even touched crafts under municipal regulation. A cartman, for example, was required to own his own cart for fear of creating monopolies by merchant proprietors. Yet this safeguard made these men independent entrepreneurs with enhanced respect and, despite strictly set prices, considerable ambition and esprit de corps.[6]

Another critical aspect of a modern work environment common in colonial America was the work ethic. Once a Puritan religious ideal but now a secular standard as well, it was, when coupled with growing ambition, a powerful force. Its greatest advocate, Benjamin Franklin, who lived in the colonial era and the early years of the Republic, was successful both in the workshop and the public arena. The Philadelphia printer was a teacher and role model for urban artisans throughout America. Craftsmen bought and read his almanacs, and in later years named their trade societies after him. He represented the accomplishments possible with the diligent use of labor.[7]

Time was central in Franklin's work ethic. His pseudonym, "Poor Richard," admonished craftsmen to be frugal and rigorous and to allow no wasted moments to interfere with their progress: "Dost thou love life, then do not squander time, for that's the stuff life is made of." Minutes given over by the industrious artisan to useless frivolity or extra slumber could never be recalled. "There will be sleep enough in the grave," he cautioned, for life was finite and "lost time is never found again." At stake was the industrious craftsman's business, his success. As the 1751 *Almanac* cautioned, "he that is prodigal of his time, is, in effect, a Squanderer of Money. . . . *Time is Money.*"[8]

Franklin poses the life of the industrious, independent, middling sector, the artisan community, as the ideal. This was in stark contrast to the long-standing tradition that held craftsmen to be men who, because they labored with their hands, were of inferior standing and limited public awareness. Even the printers, the most educated of colonial craftsmen, had to accept that "in the eyes of their neighbors they were by training mechanics, without full legitimacy as men of independent intellect and creed." To Franklin, quite the opposite was true. Poor Richard counseled that "he that hath a Calling, hath an office of Profit and Honour"; industry gave "Comfort and Plenty and Respect." An enterprising and hard-working craftsman who carefully husbanded his time would find economic success; that, in turn, would lead to public and private esteem. The craftsman community listened carefully to this lesson.[9]

## II

The War of Independence established a new American republic based on participatory government. New York City artisans, who had a limited though significant role in colonial politics during the Revolution, moved into the center of action. Sharing power and governance with the merchants, the mechanics espoused a radical Paineite program demanding immediate independence and popular ratification of the new state constitution. After the Revolution, mechanics became a constituency that was critical to the success of the two rival parties: the Hamiltonian Federalists and the Jeffersonian Democratic–Republicans. In the 1790s, allegiance shifted to the Jeffersonians, whose egalitarian republicanism offered, together with legislative nominations and tariff advocacy, an ideal compatible with artisan revolutionary aspirations. First, it recognized mechanics' desire for (and it granted them) a measure of civic respect, particularly in the face of continued contempt and deferential expectations from the mercantile elite. Second, Jeffersonian republicanism promised a new and seemingly unlimited horizon for entrepreneurial ambition. The lifting of British mercantile restraint foretold a free and growing market in an independent and prosperous nation where industrious artisans would prosper as autonomous capitalists.[10]

While some progress was made in the early national era toward enhanced political recognition, the fulfillment of financial ambitions remained elusive. For the postrevolutionary period ushered in a second upheaval, a transformation of the American economy that Thomas C. Cochran has termed the "business revolution," which profoundly affected New York's craftsmen. Expanding foreign and national trade, a growing urban and rural population, better transportation, together with an imaginative, venturesome, and capital-rich mercantile sector, made large-scale production both possible and potentially highly profitable. The more populous of the mechanic trades (printing, shipbuilding, tailoring, shoemaking, masonry, cabinetmaking, and carpentry) were much altered. Shoemakers now produced large numbers of footwear for sale to slave markets in the West Indies and the South. Tailors assembled more ready-made "slop" clothing as well as made-to-order items. Cabinetmakers manufactured large numbers of chairs for local and export markets. New and complex construction, both commercial and residential, proceeded apace to keep up with the expanding population.[11]

The capital necessary to become independent in these expanding trades was beyond the reach of most craftsmen. Consequently, entrepreneurial independence was no longer common or certain. Moreover, large-scale production demanded a subordinate and often less skilled labor force. The proportion of journeymen to masters increased dramatically. In the new marketplace, less than one in four journeymen would attain master standing. Too, relations between masters and journeymen became much less familial. The new economy meant a cost-conscious, competitive market in which masters were concerned primarily with the balance sheet: obtaining the most work for the least cost. Dealings with employees were more formal and adversarial than before.[12]

For some masters, the new marketplace meant opportunities for profits and advancement well beyond colonial possibilities. Others found themselves in less secure situations. Intense competition, debt, and high capital costs were constant threats to their livelihood. Still, the possible rewards of success and the increased difficulty in achieving independence made the position of master craftsman an all the more coveted standing. Too, Jeffersonian republicanism considered financial independence a prerequisite to full citizenship. Consequently, those able and willing to aspire to master status seldom lost sight of their goal. As Stephen Allen, a craftsman who began his career as a journeyman sailmaker after the Revolution, attaining first economic prosperity and then political success as mayor of New York, recalled of his early career: "Progress toward independence [was] always uppermost in my thoughts . . . which determination was one of my principle stimulants to my exertions." [13]

Like their colonial predecessors, early national masters usually worked long days. This was often necessary to keep up with the competition and ensure that all work was performed adequately and on schedule. Stephen Allen recalled his hours in the sail loft when he would arrive before both his journeymen and the sun, working with the aid of a lantern. He would often remain well after dark, retiring around 9:00 P.M. In a significant shift, masters also had to spend more time out of the shop, gaining customers or dealing with merchants and banks for marketing and credit. It was not unusual for a master to hire a foreman to oversee his employees, increasing even further the distance between himself and his journeymen. [14]

Whatever the length of their workday, masters considered themselves in charge of their hours. They determined when they arrived and left and how they ran their business. This sense of control was critical. The masters were the proprietors, leaders, and protectors of their crafts. It was from their organization, the General Society of Mechanics and Tradesmen, that Independence Day orators were chosen. It was they who reminded their fellow craftsmen of the sacrifices of artisans in bringing liberty to the country and who declared the centrality of the role of the mechanic in the continued prosperity and endurance of the Republic. It was they who represented the entire mechanic constituency in resentment toward banks that disdained dealing with or making loans to craftsmen, or of the wealthy in not paying their bills on time, or in appealing to Congress for protection of their manufactures. They knew best how their time and that of their employees should be spent. [15]

The situation of the journeymen in this era was quite different from that of their masters, and the meaning of worktime for these craftsmen reflected that fact. Unlike previous generations in New York, when the two were nearly "indistinct from each other" and, indeed, "journeymen as a class had virtually ceased to exist,'' wage-earning craftsmen were now part of a growing labor pool that included immigrants and mechanics who had migrated to New York City from other areas of the state and New Jersey. They had stronger affiliations with one another than with their bosses, and generally lived separately. Married journeymen found shelter in rented rooms and single men in boardinghouses in the outer wards. Only 2 percent owned real estate and only 8 percent possessed even $150 worth of personal property, as compared, respectively, to one-fourth and three-fourths of the masters.[16]

Most journeymen were paid either according to piecework or by daily rates. Although occasional instances of long-term labor contracts can be found in court records, they are rare.[17] Shoemakers, printers, cabinetmakers, tailors, and most other indoor craftsmen trades receive wages according to the amount and quality of the goods they produced. Printers, for example, were paid for setting type at 25 cents per em (30 cents for foreign-language type). Journeymen cabinetmakers could find their allotments in a *Book of Prices* in which the various jobs involved in making furniture were listed. A plain chest would cost the master $6.50 in labor, while a library case required $20. Shoemakers were paid either according to the task, such as binding, or for producing finished goods such as boots and shoes. Bespoke, or personally ordered, footwear carried a higher price than that made for general sale. Craftsmen working out-of-doors, especially carpenters, masons, and shipwrights, who together composed over one-fourth of journeymen craftsmen, were paid a daily wage. The rate varied from 10 to 16 shillings per day ($1.25 to $2) in the early nineteenth century. Shipwrights received a few shillings per day less than carpenters and masons. A few indoor mechanics received such compensation as well. Newspaper employees, for example, received $9 per week on a morning daily and $8 per week on an evening publication.[18]

Hours of labor varied greatly. For craftsmen working at piecework, there was no set time to report or leave. Many labored in their homes, while others shared a garret or else toiled in the workrooms of the master, who supplied the raw materials and was in charge of marketing the finished wares. Despite the lack of specific working hours, the workday of a craftsmen in piecework was long, often twelve to fourteen hours. Artisans receiving a daily wage worked established hours. During the summer, shipbuilders put in a fourteen-hour day, from 4:00 A.M. to 7:00 P.M. with an hour off for breakfast at 8:00 A.M. and two hours off for lunch at noon. Masons and carpenters worked a thirteen-hour day with three hours off for meals.[19]

Indoor journeymen craftsmen who worked for daily or weekly wages also worked set hours. Part of the year they were required to work late by candlelight At other times, should they labor after 8:00 P.M., they received ''overtime'' pay. A journeyman bookbinder, John Bradford, published a song to the tune of "Yankee Doodle," celebrating the Tenth of March, "The Night on Which Journeymen Mechanics Cease Working by Candlelight."

> For five months every night we were
> Obliged to work till eight, sirs,
> But lamp and candlesticks now are
> Till October out of date, sirs.
>
> Though if at night to work we stay
> You know as well as can be,
> For each hour we'll get the pay,
> Yankee Doodle Dandy.
>
> Now let's be jovial, douse the glim;
> Extinguish every light, sir,
> Tis seven months ere again we'll trim
> Our lamps to work by night sir.[20]

What were the major differences in worktime for these journeymen in comparison to their colonial predecessors? Both labored long hours. Piecework wages were also common to both periods. The hours of out-of-doors craftsmen, too, with long meal breaks, had traditional roots deriving from centuries-old English practice.[21] What was dramatically altered was the framework of these prices and hours. When mobility between journeyman and master status was common in both directions, and work was carried on in familial settings, the pace and hours of the two were nearly identical, and the price of piecework could be informally fashioned. In the postrevolutionary economy, as the responsibilities and relations between journeymen and masters became strictly that of employer and employee, these arrangements took on a different complexion. A shoemaker, for example, might work long hours in Jeffersonian New York, as had his counterpart a generation or two before. But this shoemaker was not working for himself, nor had he any expectations that he would be soon. The labor he put in was for the benefit of the master, with whom he maintained strictly a business connection. Consequently, he had to focus on the rate of compensation he received.

Formal agreements to the wages and hours described above were the logical result of this situation. Journeymen organized craft societies that, along with establishing death and disability benefits, strove for leverage in the marketplace. In the piecework trades, they bargained over rates. Instead of loose arrangements reached in a peerlike setting within the confines of the master's shop, citywide prices were formally negotiated and their final version published. Many settlements required long and sometimes difficult hours of negotiation. In 1809, for example, the printers consented to a com-

promise set of prices only after long hours of discussion whose "eloquence
. . . would have graced a senate house."[22]

Not only the journeymen preferred formal arrangements regarding wages
and hours. Seeking greater efficiency and cost savings, masters too preferred
established schedules. In some instances, this brought them to the bargaining table. In other situations, considering themselves the guardians of their
crafts, they preferred to set the rates themselves. This was true in 1802 when
the master cabinetmakers unilaterally promulgated a new *Book of Prices*.
Similarly, master masons and carpenters met each spring to determine what
rate they would give. Reliability was also important to employers, and a
broadside published in 1805 by the master builders is exemplary. Complaining of the "irregularity and confusion" that existed because of a lack of
"uniform regulation," the masters announced the precise hours journeymen
were to be on the job. Work was to begin at 6:00 A.M. from March through
November and at 7:00 A.M. in the fall and winter. Depending on the season,
journeymen received an hour for breakfast and one to two hours for lunch.
From November through March, the slack season of cold weather and limited daylight, only a nine-hour day was demanded. The masters in this instance were not attempting to deny journeymen their traditional breaks or
lengthen the workday, but within that framework they wanted their men on
the job every minute to which they were entitled.[23]

The early national era was the first period in American history to see
major labor unrest. When journeymen trade societies were unsuccessful in
bargaining, they often turned to more coercive measures. At one time in
1809, almost all building in New York came to a halt as the carpenters
engaged in large-scale work stoppages that resulted in violence, threats, and
the use of strikebreakers. That same year, the shoemakers' society was prosecuted for a criminal conspiracy for attempting to institute a closed shop.
Cabinetmakers and tailors set up their own journeymen enterprises in disputes over the prices to be paid for work and over the use of women in the
trade, while printers walked out on employers a number of times as they
strove to increase daily wages for newspaper employees and piece rates for
other typographical labor.[24]

Time was a factor in labor conflict, although the problems of seasonality
were often of as much importance as the length of the workday or workweek. New York's masons and carpenters, the largest out-of-doors professions, already possessed (when breaks are considered) the ten-hour day—
something fellow laborers in other cities would not attain for many years.[25]
They were more concerned with the many days they were unable to work
because of inclement weather or slack demand. During a walkout in 1819,
the journeymen masons argues that such conditions allowed them to work

an average of only 213 days per year. That meant about 100 days, or about four months out of twelve, in which they were unemployed. They demanded that their wages be set at a rate that would allow them to recover at least part of the lost time.[26] That same year, the city's tailors abandoned their employers over a similar concern with "dead time." These artisans were bitter over their employers' practice of using women workers to perform tasks traditionally done by the journeymen, thus forcing them into many days—up to six months—of unemployment. The tailors contended that inherently unqualified laborers were taking hours of work that rightfully belonged to them.[27]

The length of the workday was a factor in walkouts by a number of indoor craftsmen. These were not factory-oriented disputes, however, since there were very few factories in New York in this era, and those that were initiated were not successful.[28] Nevertheless, trades such as shoemaking, tailoring, and cabinetmaking were in the process of developing sweatshop conditions in which the amount offered for a particular job, whether it was veneering a cabinet or stitching a boot, forced journeymen into situations in which they were forced to work inordinately long hours in order to make a decent or, sometimes, even a subsistence wage. In 1802, the cabinetmakers argues that even before the masters decided on an "imposition" that would lower their wages by 15 percent, their wage was "barely sufficient to maintain the most industrious mechanic, provided he had a family." At a trial for criminal conspiracy, William Sampson, the noted Irish émigré and counsel for the journeymen cordwainers, declared that with "a leather apron and a strap, a last, a lap-stone and a hammer," the shoemaker would "peg and stitch from five in the morning till eight in the evening." Yet, even with such hours, he was barely able to "feed and educate his family." Other witnesses testified to even longer hours.[29] Consequently, although the price per piece was the central issue discussed at the bargaining table, when weighing a proposed settlement, most journeymen considered just what that price meant when applied to the number of hours they were willing or able to put in and that they considered to be appropriate for a skilled journeyman mechanic.

Strikes and walkouts also carried a political dimension that included worktime. Journeymen were unwilling to concede that they lacked the requirements for full citizenship, even though they lacked the financial independence that orthodox republicans considered necessary for such standing. Political equality could still be secured if they at least retained a wage commensurate with their skills and place in society. They contended that the Revolution guaranteed a craftsman in his prime, whose "labor constituted the great wealth of the country," the hours of contentment at work due "men professing an ingenious art." In retirement it promised him hours free of want and anxiety, similar, perhaps, to the productive years of retirement of their hero and role model, Benjamin Franklin.[30] As one journeyman carpenter proclaimed in the midst of a walkout:

Among the inalienable rights of man are life, liberty and the pursuit of happiness. By the social contract every class of society ought to be entitled to benefit in proportion to its qualifications. Among the duties which individuals owe to society are single men to marry and married men to educate their children. Among the duties which society owes to its individuals is to grant them just compensation not only for current expenses of livelihood, but to the formation of a fund for the support of that time of life when nature requires a cessation of work.[31]

Even with the powerful capitalist ambition generated by the American Revolution thwarted, the legacy of 1776 could still be preserved if journeymen mechanics upheld their dignity during hours of work against greedy employers who would become "merciless tyrants" at their expense. Clearly reminding themselves and the public of the revolutionary struggle, journeymen commonly used military allusions in declaring their intent to contend with their employers.[32] Despite their increasingly permanent standing as wage earners, they were still entitled to independent hours.

## III

If the issue of worktime divided masters and journeymen at the workplace, the opposite was true within New York City society where both were identified as part of the mechanic class. In the face of continuing contempt from, and expectations of deference to, the mercantile community, artisans responded with arguments that their hours were much the more valuable to the new nation than those of either the more or, for that matter, the less fortunate.

Craftsmen's collective attitude toward time must be seen in the light of their republican quest for full participation and self-respect in the body politic. Jeffersonian New York, unfortunately, offered all too few signs of success. Differences between merchants and artisans, if anything, grew wider. Residential areas were increasingly distinct, while economic stratification rose markedly. Living in elegant town homes and dressing in silk waistcoats and well-coiffured wigs, the city's gentry continued to hold themselves above the leather-apron-clad mechanics. In partisan politics, the merchant-dominated Federalists claimed that artisans, because of the nature of their work and training, especially their long hours spent at manual rather than intellectual education, were incapable of holding high public office. They should willingly defer to the choices of their superiors.[33]

The mechanics' response was a defense of the manner in which they spent their hours and a condemnation of the use to which other segments of society put their time. No group, they maintained, contributed as much to society as the productive classes. Stephen Allen, for example, criticized those who achieved independence other than with diligent labor. Attaining wealth through inheritance or gift was often a "curse" rather than a blessing, for it usually led the recipient to "excess and extravagance, frequently to dissipation, and in such cases, render[ed] the life, one of misery, instead of happiness." Only when wealth was earned "through a long course of industry and attention to business" did it afford real satisfaction and happiness.[34]

The *Independent Mechanic,* the only newspaper in this era written for mechanics, was equally intent on demonstrating that artisans put their time to greater and more valuable use than others in the society.[35] The disparity between the lives of the elite and artisan classes, so apparent on the streets of New York City, was a common theme in its columns. One series of articles, by "Censor," described groups of young men known as the "bloods." These youths, who through the "indulgences of their parents" possessed numerous idle hours, used that time to wander around the city, bothering and often frightening the women in their paths. Other juveniles of similar background, if not as violent as the "bloods," were equally useless to society. They stood ostentatiously in the streets, endlessly staring at pieces of paper. One mechanic who followed one of these lost souls for an hour and a half noticed that the "letter" he held consisted of only five lines. Time would not permit this craftsman more minutes for investigation. How "ridiculous" were the moments wasted by this "class of young men" when compared to the industrious work habits and "honest, blunt and unaffected manners of a young mechanic."[36]

Similar scorn was directed at the adult wealthy, whose daily routines differed as much from that of the artisan as did their style of dress and housing. While a merchant typically breakfasted at 8:30, spent a couple of morning hours on the wharves, followed by a similar stay in the counting house, retiring to dinner at 4:00 and a late supper at 11:00, artisans worked their ten- to fourteen-hour day.[37] Parodying and exaggerating these hours and the style of luxury and greed they represented, the *Mechanic* depicted the hours of a "glutton." Rising at 11:00 in the morning, "after many efforts" he dressed in order to begin his "important business." This took place in the tavern, where he drank a pot of ale and smoked a half dozen "segars." By then it was 3:00 P.M. and time for a dinner of perhaps four pounds of beef. This lasted until 8:00 when beer and mutton were demanded. Next it was off to the theater to be seen by the "ladies," another tavern, and finally, at 3:00 in the morning, home with the support of the watchmen. (Constables in New York were often former mechanics.[38])

The idle poor were objects of similar rebuke in the *Mechanic*. The weekly was contemptuous of the "littleness and languor" with which the "unoccupied idler carries on a weary life." Rather than work, of which they were clearly capable, they preferred to waste their hours in drink. When money for liquor was wanting, they chose not to beg but to steal, threatening the livelihood of the hard-working artisan. Advocating a strict law-and-order policy, including a "workhouse" to instill "industry" as a "cure for poverty," the paper declared that there was no question that, compared to the *"real* pleasure which the industrious mechanic enjoys, as the evening sun sets on a well spent day," the behavior of the poor was a civic disgrace.[39]

Echoing the Franklin work ethic common in the eighteenth century, these articles argue that the productive hours of the humble craftsman were more valuable to the community than the time logged by other classes. In addition, in the early national era they have a republican political context. The essays parallel the Fourth of July orations that praised artisans as the "axis of society" in whose hands the "palladium of [American] liberty" rested. As a single group, the mechanic constituency was ever conscious of its place and purpose in the new Republic. Unlike the worktime of many other professions, without the useful hours of the craftsman, American liberty was doomed.[40]

## IV

Hours of rest and leisure in the new Republic reflected both traditional customs and the new sense of republican spirit. There is no question that longstanding diversions remained popular in New York. Drinking was no doubt the favorite of these: the number of small groceries and taverns that served liquor numbered over 2000 by 1817, part of what one historian has termed the "alcoholic republic." Also common were gambling and blood sports. Shortly after the Revolution, a bull-baiting rink seating 2000 was erected in the city.[41]

It is difficult to know to what extent the craftsman community participated in these customary forms of leisure. No doubt many of the unemployed and underemployed found an outlet in the grocery or tavern, as did many a tired journeyman after working a long day or week. Apprentices, too, while fewer in number, less constrained, and more intent on gaining a cash wage than their colonial predecessors, still found time for traditional pranks and rowdiness, as did some of the semiskilled workers doing labor formerly performed by apprentices and skilled journeymen. Nor was it uncommon in some crafts to have regular breaks in the workday for drinking. Both printers and shipwrights regularly interrupted labor at 11:00 in the morning to "jeff" for beer.[42]

Opposition existed within the artisan community to these forms of indulgence, especially when they tended to excess. They were deemed contrary to the republican spirit that saw the craftsman as the guardian of American liberty. Too, they were incompatible with the work habits of an industrious master trying to make it in a competitive marketplace or to journeymen attempting to gain leverage in a crowded labor pool. It is not surprising that the *Independent Mechanic,* whose editor was an aspiring master filled with republican zeal, devoted numerous articles to descriptions of the dire consequences resulting from hours wasted on spirits and gambling. For example, the paper told of one lad who, falling in with the "bloods," became entrapped in a life of drinking and gambling and ended a suicide. Gambling as well was termed a depraved and sinful practice. More, it was a "laborious" trade, since its victims "toil day and night at it, and do not allow themselves that remission, which the laws, both of God and man, have provided for the meanest mechanic." When traditional forms of leisure deprived craftsmen of their industry and judgment, they were unacceptable to the republican-minded sector of the artisan community.[43]

Popular forms of leisure that had traditional roots but were yet compatible with republican ideals and marketplace demands attracted New York mechanics. One such significant haven from work was the fraternal society. The same craft organizations that craftsmen formed for trade leverage provided regular occasions for camaraderie, craft pride, and participation in patriotic celebrations and parades. Local volunteer fire companies, too, were a favorite outlet for artisans. At washing days, weekly meetings, and fires, these craftsmen found time for fraternity while fulfilling a civic duty.[44]

Leisure, finally, provided outlets in which artisans could find relaxation and refuge. This was especially true on the Sabbath, a day of quiet equality. Few carriages appeared on the streets, and some churches even blocked the highways with chains. Craftsmen joined other New Yorkers in family outings to the circus, gardens, or, most commonly, the Battery. From a haughty, genteel point of view, not untypical of the city's elite, Washington Irving recalled that park where "the gay apprentice sported his Sunday coat, and the laborious mechanic, relieved from the dirt and drudgery of the week, poured his weekly tale of love into the half averted ear of the sentimental chambermaid."[45] To the artisan, however, the peace and family harmony that a craftsman found on his Sunday walk or at his fireside was equal to, or greater than, that attained by the wealthy merchant. A poem by "Journeyman Mechanic" entitled "Saturday Night" offered such a message:

Six days I've toil'd and now we meet
To share the welcome weekly treat
Of toast and tea, of rest and joy,
Which, gain'd by labour, cannot cloy.

. . .

Of rich and poor the difference what?—
In working or in working not,
Why then on Sunday we're as great
As those who own some vast estate.

For on to-morrow's happy day
We shall work less, perhaps, than they;
And though no dainties it afford
What's sweet and clean will grace our board.[46]

The greater sense of industry and usefulness to which the craftsman dedicated his time made the Sabbath a day of sweet contentment. Those who employed their hours less productively seldom found such peace.

The Sabbath, too, was a time for churchgoing and reflection about the broadest meanings of time and the common lot of mankind. Many articles in the *Mechanic* counseled a religious outlook, in view of the "rapid tide of time" that carried men on, soon to their death. Another essay, a reminiscence of childhood, described the relentless passage of years and the peace and quiet of childhood days. An "extract on nature" lamented the "ephemera" that was mankind's lot, "how trivial all his great operations." It was incumbent to spend one's days without affectation, in the exercise of "industry, patience and contentment." Pondering man's few moments on earth, the writer of "Reflections in a Grave-Yard" exposed the utter equality of all who lay in repose, and the visions of providence and eternity beyond.[47]

## V

It is clear that the modern work ethic was present in the colonial era and continued to thrive after the Revolution. Too, traditional small enterprises, so common in the eighteenth century, were still to be found in early national New York. But the American Revolution and the business revolution had made some real alterations in artisans' conceptions of time. With the widening difference in role between master and journeyman, the kind of work that each man did during his workday was less and less similar. The master tended to be more concerned with credit and marketing, while the journeyman remained tied to manual labor. Too, journeymen had to struggle to maintain their republican respect as skilled craftsmen, employing tough collective action to ensure that their hours were compensated in a manner befitting skilled republican artisans in a democratic society. The mechanic community as a whole engaged in a continuing struggle for political and social recognition. More than ever, mechanics were conscious of the virtues of the manner in which they spent their time, particularly in contrast to the other, less productive segments of the community. As the guardians of the new republican state, the manner in which they devoted their minutes, hours, and days was critical to the success or failure of American independence.

## NOTES

1. For the English experience, see E. P. Thompson, "Time, Work-Discipline and Industrial Capitalism," *Past and Present* 38 (1967): 58–97; Douglas Reid, "The Decline of St. Monday," *Past and Present* 71 (1976): 75–101; David S. Landes, *Revolution in Time: Clocks and the Making of the Modern World* (Cambridge, Mass., 1983), Chap. 14; and M. Harrison, "Time, Work and the Occurrence of Crowds, 1790–1835," *Past and Present* 110 (1986).

2. Late American preindustrial work habits are discussed in Bruce Laurie, "Nothing on Impulse: Life Styles of Philadelphia Artisans, 1820–1850," *Labor History* 15 (1974): 337–366; Herbert G. Gutman, "Work, Culture and Society in Industrializing America, 1815–1819," *American Historical Review* 78 (1973): 533–588; and Eric Foner, *Tom Paine and Revolutionary America* (New York, 1976), pp. 48–56.

3. Gary Nash, *The Urban Crucible: Social Change, Political Consciousness, and the Origins of the American Revolution* (Cambridge, Mass., 1979), *passim;* David T. Gilchrist, ed., *The Growth of the Seaport Cities, 1790–1820* (Charlottesville, 1967).

4. Nash, *Urban Crucible,* pp. 16–17, 258–263; Jackson T. Main, *The Social Structure of Revolutionary America* (Princeton, 1965), pp. 79–84; Paul Zankovich, "The Craftsmen of Colonial New York," Ph.D. dissertation, New York University School of Education, 1956; Samuel McKee, Jr., *Labor in Colonial New York, 1664–1776* (New York, 1934); and Billie G. Smith, "The Material Lives of Laboring Philadelphians, 1750–1800," *William and Mary Quarterly* 38 (April 1981).

5. Carl Bridenbaugh, *The Colonial Craftsman* (New York, 1950); Peter J. Parker, "The Philadelphia Printer: A Study of an Eighteenth Century Businessman," *Business History Review* 40 (1966): 24–46; Howard B. Rock, *Artisans of the New Republic: The Tradesmen of New York City in the Age of Jefferson* (New York, 1979), p. 184; Graham R. Hodges, *New York City Cartmen, 1667–1850* (New York, 1986), Chaps. 2–4; and Nash, *Urban Crucible,* pp. 10, 12.

6. Bridenbaugh, *Colonial Craftsman,* p. 165; Nash, *Urban Crucible,* p. 12, Chap. 12; Hodges, *New York City Cartmen,* pp. 42–49; Sharon V. Salinger, "Artisans, Journeymen, and the Transformation of Labor in Late 18th Century Philadelphia," *William and Mary Quarterly* 40 (1983).

7. J. E. Crowley, *This Sheba Self: The Conceptualization of Economic Life in Eighteenth-Century America* (Baltimore, 1974), pp. 83–84 *et passim;* and Nash, *Urban Crucible,* p. 328.

8. Benjamin Franklin, *The Autobiography and Other Writings,* edited by L. Jesse Lemisch (New York, 1961) pp. 188–197; *Almanac* quoted in Thompson, "Time, Work-Discipline and Industrial Capitalism," p. 73.

9. Stephen Botein, " 'Meer Mechanics' and an Open Press: The Business and Political Strategies of Colonial American Printers," *Perspectives in American History* 9 (1975): 136, 157–158; Bridenbaugh, *Colonial Craftsman,* p. 155; and Franklin, *Autobiography,* p. 73.

10. Staughton Lynd, "The Mechanics in New York City Politics, 1774–1785," *Labor History* 5 (1964): 215–246; Alfred F. Young, "The Mechanics and the Jeffersonians: New York, 1789– 1801," *Labor History* 5 (1964): 247–276; Rock, *Artisans of the New Republic,* Chaps. 1, 2, 5; Joyce Appleby, *Capitalism and the New Social Order: The Republican Vision of the 1790s* (New York, 1984); Joyce Appleby, "The Social Origins of American Revolutionary Ideology," *Journal of American History* 64 (1978): 935–958; and Gordon S. Wood, "Interests and Disinterestedness in the Making of the Constitution," in *Beyond Confederation: Origins of the Constitution and American National Identity,* ed. Richard Beeman *et al.* (Chapel Hill, N.C., 1987), pp. 77–81.

11. Thomas C. Cochran, *Frontiers of Change: Early Industrialism in America* (New York, 1981); and Rock, *Artisans of the New Republic,* Chap. 9. Real property value in New York City rose 741 percent (to $4,275,000), and personal property rose by 1208 percent (to $2,322,000). Edmund P. Willis, "Social Origins and Political Leadership in New York City from the Revolution to 1815," Ph.D. dissertation, University of California—Berkeley, 1967, pp. 97–98, 113, 119.

12. Rock, *Artisans of the New Republic,* pp. 239–257, 264–273. Not all craftsmen took part in the "business revolution." As much as any, the early Republic was an age of transition. There remained many small craft shops, often in the more specialized areas (goldsmithing, umbrella making, and the like); within the growth trades, too, a small-scale independent worker might yet find a niche. Nevertheless, the most important crafts, employing the bulk of the city's journeymen, were affected.

13. James C. Travis, ed., "The Memoirs of Stephen Allen, 1767–1852," typescript, New York Historical Society, 1927, p. 49.

14. Ibid., pp. 40–44.

15. Thomas Earle and Charles T. Congdon, *Annals of the General Society of Mechanics and Tradesmen of the City of New York* (New York, 1882); Sean Wilentz, *Chants Democratic: New York City and the Rise of the American Working Class, 1788–1850* (New York, 1984), pp. 61–76, 87–97; and Rock, *Artisans of the New Republic,* pp. 128–143, 162–169, 171–178.

16. McKee, *Labor in Colonial New York,* p. 22; Rock, *Artisans of the New Republic,* pp. 242–243, 248–257.

17. In 1790, a suit was brought in Mayor's Court by Samuel Allinson, Jr., against Abraham Wilson, claiming that Allinson had been contracted to work for Wilson for twenty-six weeks at 36 shillings per week. When slack periods arose, Allinson demanded that he be compensated, since his employer had told him that "you are in my employ and shall not be a loser." Wilson only offered him a "Crank

and wheel hands'' as payment. The court found for the plaintiff and awarded Allinson £13. An ad in the *Evening Post* requested three coopers to engage for a year to make barrels. Payment was to be made by the barrel, however. Mayors Court Minutes, June 20, 1790, New York Public Library; *Evening Post,* July 14, 1803.

18. Charles F. Montgomery, *American Furniture: The Federal Period, 1788–1825* (New York, 1966), pp. 20–26; Estelle M. Stewart, *The History of Wages in the United States from Colonial Times to 1928* (Washington, D.C., 1929), pp. 109–110; Victor S. Clark, *History of Manufactures in the United States* (New York, 1949), 1:390–391; *Evening Post,* November 13, 1816; *Columbian,* December 9, 1813; *American Citizen,* December 1, 1803; Richard C. McKay, *Some Famous Sailing Ships and Their Builders* (New York, 1928), p. 5; John R. Commons *et al., A Documentary History of American Industrial Society,* 10 vols. (Cleveland, 1909–1911), 3:86–87; "To the Master Printers of New York" (broadside), New York Historical Society; Rock, *Artisans of the New Republic,* pp. 248–250.

19. McKay, *Sailing Ships,* p. 6; Master Builders of New York, Broadside, New York Historical Society, 1805; Commons, ed., *Documentary History,* 3:121.

20. John Bradford, *The Poetical Vagaries of a Knight of the Folding Stick of* PASTE CASTLE (New York, 1813).

21. David Roediger, " 'Liberty of Leisure,' Colonial Realities, Revolutionary Citizenship and the Beginnings of the American Artisanal Movement for a Shorter Working Day,'' paper delivered at International Conference of the Centre de Recherches sur L'Histoire des Etats-Unis, June 1987, pp. 4–5.

22. George A. Stevens, *New York Typographical Union Number Six* (Albany, 1912), pp. 51–57; for a discussion of the various societies, see Rock, *Artisans of the New Republic,* pp. 272–274.

23. *Morning Chronicle,* December 31, 1802; Master Builders, Broadside.

24. Rock, *Artisans of the New Republic,* Chap. 9; and Paul Gilje, *The Road to Mobocracy: Popular Disorder in New York City, 1763–1834* (Chapel Hill, N.C., 1987), pp. 175–202.

25. See David Roediger and Philip S. Foner, *"Our Own Time": American Labor and the Working Day* (forthcoming, 1988).

26. *Evening Post,* May 31, 1819.

27. *Evening Post,* July 13, 1819.

28. On the creation of sweatshop conditions in the artisan trades, see Wilentz, *Chants Democratic,* Chap. 3. One attempt was made to form a textile mill in early New York. John Barrow & Sons purchased 2 spinning mules and 5 jennies to go with 16 looms in the production of broadcloth. The firm hired 37 men, 4 women, and 18 boys, but failed because of high costs and harsh times. The same fate awaited another enterprise that intended to hire 400 women and girls in needlework. A hat-making business employing 50 men, 10 women, and 15 boys managed to stay afloat, as did the Lorillard tobacco manufactory with 30 men and 50 to 60 boys. These were major exceptions to the rule of moderately sized but still market- and cost-conscious craft enterprises that usually contained from 10 to 20 employees. Federal Manufacturing Census, 1820, Nos. 1317, 1321, 1270, 1279, microfilm, National Archives.

29. *Evening Post,* November 24, 1804; *American Citizen,* December 22, 1802; *Morning Chronicle,* January 1, 1803. Commons, ed., *Documentary History,* 3:279.

30. Commons, ed., *Documentary History,* 3:180; Journeymen Cabinetmakers of New York City, *Book of Prices* (New York, 1796), p. 3.

31. *American Citizen,* April 10, 1809.

32. Howard B. Rock, "The Mechanics of New York City and the American Revolution: One Generation Later," *New York History* 57 (1976): 388–390.

33. Wilentz, *Chants Democratic,* pp. 24–35; Christine Stansell, *City of Women: Sex and Class in New York, 1789–1860* (New York, 1986), pp. 3–10; Rock, *Artisans of the New Republic,* pp. 1–4, Chap. 2; and *American Citizen,* November 7, 1810. See also Roediger, "Liberty of Leisure," pp. 8–13.

34. Travis, ed., "Memoirs of Stephen Allen," p. 93.

35. The printer and editor Joseph Harmer, having just left journeyman status, noted that mechanics did not have the time to read the dailies (and often not the money to buy them). This weekly, appearing each Saturday evening, would provide the artisan community the news and information it required. *Independent Mechanic,* April 6, 1811.

36. *Independent Mechanic,* May 18 and 25, 1811.

37. John Bernard, *Retrospections of America, 1797–1811* (New York, 1811), p. 52.

38. *Independent Mechanic,* February 15, 1812.

39. *Independent Mechanic,* August 3, 1811, and May 30, 1812.

40. John T. Irving, *An Oration* (New York, 1809), pp. 10–11; and Rock, *Artisans of the New Republic,* pp. 135–143.

41. W. J. Rorabaugh, *The Alcoholic Republic* (New York, 1979); Michael and Ariane Batterberg, *On the Town in New York: A History of Eating, Drinking and Entertainments from 1776 to the Present* (New York, 1973), p. 43; Report of Committee of the Common Council, City Clerk Filed Papers, Box 3181, March 8, 1816; Sidney I. Pomerantz, *New York: An American City, 1783–1803* (New York, 1938), pp. 485–588; and Rock, *Artisans of the New Republic,* pp. 296–300.

42. Herbert G. Gutman, "Work, Culture and Society in Industrializing America, 1815–1919," *American Historical Review* 78 (1973): 544, 566–567; Thurlow Weed, *The Autobiography of Thurlow Weed,* edited by Harriet Weed (Boston, 1883), p. 54; W. J. Rorabaugh, *The Craft Apprentice from Franklin to the Machine Age in America* (New York, 1986), pp. 3–56; and Gilje, *The Road to Mobocracy,* p. 191. For a description of typical colonial apprenticeship customs, see Alfred F. Young, "George Robert Twelves Hewes (1742–1840): A Boston Shoemaker and the Memory of the American Revolution," *William and Mary Quarterly* 38 (1981): 563–570.

43. *Independent Mechanic,* August 17 and 31, 1811; November 30, 1811; July 27, 1811.

44. Wilentz, *Chants Democratic,* pp. 87–97; and Rock, *Artisans of the New Republic,* pp. 128–143.

45. *Independent Mechanic,* June 13, 1812; and David T. Valentine, ed.,

*Manuals of the Corporation of New York City* (New York, 1842–1868), 5:156–161. Irving quoted in Rodman Gilder, ed., *The Battery* (Boston, 1936), p. 128.

46. *Independent Mechanic,* June 15, 1811.

47. *Independent Mechanic,* June 1, April 6, May 18, and November 23, 1811.

# 3

# Controlling the Product: Work, Time, and the Early Industrial Workforce in Britain, 1800–1850

## Clive Behagg

## I

TWENTY YEARS ago, Edward Thompson utilized the notion of time to explore what he saw as a new set of relationships created by the Industrial Revolution.[1] He concluded that by a variety of means, a new work discipline was imposed on the men and women who worked in British industry in the early nineteenth century. His findings were complemented and extended by Pollard's work on "factory discipline," and by Reid's research into the decline of "Saint Monday."[2] Here, the relationship between the factory, mechanization, and a new spirit of regularity within the workforce was made explicit. All of this was contrasted with the often irregular nature of the workforce before steam and the extended division of labor constrained the work routine. More recent work, however, has suggested that a regular working day and week preceded these developments. Mark Harrison, in particular, addresses this issue; the occurrence of crowd activity in Bristol, largely outside of work hours, suggests to him that the early industrial workforce operated on the basis of regularity rather than caprice. There was "a recognisable working day," and "Saint Monday" was simply part of an accepted working week that ran from Tuesday to Saturday.[3] Hopkins offers an alternative critique of Thompson's analysis, arguing that working hours in the late eighteenth century were long, hard, and often irregular, but that little had changed by 1850. Using a local study of an area whose workshop structure made it a typical work location, he concludes: "It certainly does not appear that new labour habits were being formed or that a new time discipline was being imposed in Birmingham and the Black Country."[4]

Thus, Thompson's original hypothesis has been qualified by the suggestion that he underestimated the regularity of the worker in the early industrial period and overestimated the intensification of work subsequently. More important, his emphasis on discontinuity has been challenged, at least implicitly, by a plethora of research on the labor process itself, stressing the continuities in productive relations through early industrialization. The new orthodoxy holds that the predominance of the small-scale, unmechanized unit of production and the persistence of subcontracting until well into the nineteenth century meant that where change did occur, it was not perceived in the simple class terms that Thompson suggests. "Factory discipline" was inappropriate to small-scale production where employer and employee might be drawn together by the smallness of the enterprise; "here was an ethos that reconciled," argue Sabel and Zeitlin of workshop centers that relied on skilled labor.[5] Even within the factory, the argument goes, employers eagerly accepted labor's structuring of work through the subcontract as a convenient means of organizing production.[6]

There are, however, two levels at which the debate over time use and workplace authority has proceeded on the basis of an incomplete appreciation of the nature of work. First, to see employers' attempts to control time through labor discipline primarily in terms of the mechanized workplace is to miss the pervasive nature of capitalist production. As Marx pointed out, in unmechanized industry the control of workers' time constituted the only way to extend the rate of surplus value.[7] We equate time control with machinery only because these were areas where capital was often triumphant and paraded its success ostentatiously. In fact, time usage was a bone of contention wherever work was reoriented to meet market needs, and conflict around this issue preceded mechanization rather than, as Reid seems to suggest, being contingent on it.[8]

Second, the debate has revolved around very specific issues: hours of attendance, levels of remuneration, and the pragmatic difficulties of organizing large numbers of workers to perform a series of interconnected productive processes. This chapter argues for the existence of an additional layer of complexity: We need to assess not only the quality of the relationship between employer and employee but also the way this relationship was mediated through a series of attitudes to the product. Throughout the early stages of capitalism, this tripartite relationship—between employer, employee, and product—involved competing notions of ownership, control, and authority, notions that remain to be examined. Marx observed that the employer owned the product partly because he also owned the labor time that went into its creation: "such as a horse he had hired for the day."[9] In the early stages of industrialization, of course, this was by no means a straightforward transaction, since most workers were paid by the piece; they produced goods and then "sold" them to their employers. Thus it was the product and not labor time that was apparently exchanged. Marx's analysis holds good, but early industrial workers attempted to reverse its internal logic by arguing that since they "owned" (or "co-owned") the product at the point of sale, this gave *them* the right to control labor time. Close examination of the British experience would seem to verify the broader point, which Marx subsequently made in his chapter on piece wages, that in terms of exploitation and the expropriation of surplus value, "the piece-wage is nothing but a converted form of the time-wage." [10] It is clear that by the early decades of the nineteenth century, there was little actual substance to the notion of the worker as independent producer, [11] but the notion *was* reflected in work organization, and this was used by workers to underpin their claim to autonomy over labor time.

It is argued here, therefore, that labor legitimated its authority over time in the workplace through an assumption of "co-ownership" of the product during the process of production. Such co-ownership was reflected in the work group's temporary possession of the product during its construction, within the territory of the workplace. Thus we are concerned not simply with the hours of labor but also with the issue of who owned the time spent at work; not only with the size and nature of the workplace but also with whose workplace it was considered to be. Worker attitudes, highlighted by the exploration of these themes, represent rather more than the defense of "traditional" work practices. They demonstrate a particular perception of how production ought to take place and an attempt to operate an alternative political economy on the part of the workforce.

## II

The intensively competitive nature of nineteenth-century industry was often justified through a meritocratic ideology that locked large- and small-scale production into an organic continuum. The large had once been small, but had grown with hard work applied within the structure of the market economy. The "rags to riches" myth is so central to individualism that it has proven highly resilient to the findings of empirical research. Certainly there is ample evidence to suggest that the factory, where it appeared in the textile and metalworking trades, represented a shift from a circulating to a fixed capital commitment rather than the organic growth outward from the workshop of the small producer. Despite this, the small producer was equated with independence and economic possibility, and one of the difficulties of analysis within this area lies in contextualizing the class-specific language of the dominant discourse. For example, in 1866 a large-scale manufacturer of pearl buttons in Birmingham, J. S. Wright, applauded the opportunities for advancement afforded by the predominantly small-scale nature of his trade:

All that is needed for a workman to start as a master is a peculiarly shaped bench
and a leather apron. . . . With these appliances and a steady hand, he may produce scarf-pins, studs, links, lockets, etc. etc. for all of which he will find a ready
market on Saturday among the numerous factors.[12]

Yet, only a few years earlier, Wright had pointed an accusing finger at small
producers in his trade during a dispute over declining prices. He explained
that in his opinion, "much of the evil complained of was caused by small
manufacturers, *part of the men,* who sold their work at a reduction because
they could not get full price and thus damaged the trade of the capitalist."[13]
He was not as ambiguous about small producers as might be thought by a
casual comparison of these statements. By the middle of the century, the
rules of economic competition were laid down by large-scale capital concerns. Small-scale production continued to thrive, but its role was largely to
service the needs of the larger unit, either as a variable outworking penum-
bra around the factory or by providing goods that were unsuitable for mass
production.[14] The small unit depended on the large one for credit and marketing facilities, and this relationship of dependence kept the small concern
small. Wright objected to small producers only when they were "part of the
men," and when they refused to accept the rules of the market game. In
this event, they expressed a heterodox approach to the economy through an
attempt to undersell Wright. In 1833, James Morrison had noted the loaded
way in which the rules of competition were being established:

The competition of the wealthy man, then, who by the weight of his capital can
bear all before him, can drive out the smaller master by lowering prices; . . . this
competition then is fair and honourable. But let it be opposed by the less important
manufacturer . . . and his competition becomes "unlawful, unnecessary and un-
feeling."[15]

Large manufacturers came to speak of the "legitimate trade," and *legitimacy* was defined by an acceptance, through practice, of the logic and morality of the market and the primary role of large capital within that sphere.

Nevertheless, large numbers of producers stood aside from the "legitimate trade," and for them was reserved the full force of mid-Victorian moral
polemic wherein economic heterodoxy was equated directly with immorality.[16] "Outwork industries" were particularly susceptible to this form of
attack. John Rogers, a Nottingham hosier, was happy that the managerial
role in production be played by a middleman between him and the worker:
"We are rather jealous of the journeymen generally, they have got into such
loose and abandoned habits that we are very jealous of taking them on."[17]

Similarly, in Birmingham, outworkers were seen to be beyond rational control. As one manufacturer put it in 1851, "There are many trades in which the workmen are very intemperate. These are principally the trades in which the work is given out and no factory discipline is observed."[18]

It has been difficult for historians to stand aside from the pejorative force of such statements. In fact, they hinged as much around the issue of the control of work as they did on the definition of respectability. By 1850, the small producer was more likely than not to be a petit-bourgeois reflection of his larger counterpart and similarly engaged in imposing work discipline on his workforce. In this sense, the term "factory discipline" really is misleading. Yet, earlier in the century, the position of the small producer was more ambiguous. Workers themselves drew a distinction between "honorable" and "dishonorable" masters, while to be an "honorable" master often meant leaving the "legitimate trade" for a business practice approved of by labor. There were a variety of ways in which an employer might be called on to act "honorably." At its most extreme, this can be seen in the involvement of small masters in strike activity in the early nineteenth century. "There has not been a strike but what some masters were at the bottom of it," complained one West Country woolen manufacturer to the Home Office in 1825.[19] During a strike in 1837 in Birmingham, Robert Basford, described in the local press as a "master-manufacturer," was arrested along with some of his women workers for an affray outside the factory of a large-scale manufacturer named Weaver. In sentencing him to three months at hard labor, the magistrate admonished him that "he ought not to have encouraged them to acts of violence, which, but for his example, they might not have attempted."[20] When Nassau Senior investigated trade-based organizations for Melbourne in 1831, he found it necessary to advise the Home Secretary that "we should recommend the infliction of very severe pecuniary penalties upon any masters encouraging combinations to the annoyance of any other masters."[21] Only two years later, the *Pioneer* urged its readers to "declare to existing masters that you are willing to admit them to your union if they choose to enter themselves as workmen."[22]

In the first half of the nineteenth century, small producers were invited to run their businesses according to mutually hostile models of operation suggested by labor and capital: either to be an "honorable" master and all that term implied or to be a part of the "legitimate trade." That most small producers moved into the orbit of capital is not in itself surprising given the broad constraints of a ruthlessly competitive economic universe. Nevertheless, there clearly was an approach to production approved of by labor, and it may be possible to reconstitute this from the glimpses of it we are able to gain. Within this mode, it would seem that the employer's role was to initiate the process of production and market the finished goods. What came between, the nature and pace of work, determining how and when an article was made, was properly the province of labor.

The persistence of subcontracting in British industry has been seen by some to emphasize the continuity of productive relations through the process of industrialization. Often referred to as "co-exploitation," or "co-domination," it has been interpreted as reflecting the willingness on the part of employers to take advantage of the workers' inclination to exploit one another.[23] Yet, as far as the labor force was concerned, the utility of such a system was that it allowed authority to be retained within the work group. By offsetting responsibility for organization to the work group, the employer was kept physically distant from the product during the process of production. Thus, subcontracting was the organizational mode for the ethos of production outlined above. Of course, the system varied in its nature. In Birmingham alone, subcontracting units were referred to as *gangs, chairs, sets, shops,* or *crews* according to the trade involved, and nationally the terminology was wider. Also, it should be noted that the recent emphasis on continuity through subcontracting has underestimated the pressures on the system to change its form significantly.[24] The working-class view of the ideal "gang" was of perhaps half a dozen people, headed by a skilled person who "sold" the finished product to the employer and passed the money on to the work group. Employer pressure after about 1830 seems fairly universal to have pushed for larger gangs. Skilled labor remained central to production, but a large gang increased the supervisory role of the skilled worker and his social distance from the less skilled. Thus we need to identify not only the survival of subcontracting but also the form it took, how it operated, and, above all, the point at which control of production within the work group became supervision on behalf of the employer.

At the heart of labor-oriented notions of appropriate production lay the idea of laborers as independent producers, either on their own behalf or as part of a small, collective unit. However far such a notion might have been from reality, it was still an important element in justifying particular approaches to work. It may be that this was a "traditional" approach to work, the anachronistic throwback to eighteenth-century forms that modernizing contemporaries always portrayed it to be. But compared with the outwork system, the movement to larger units of production often involved a loss of control over the product for the employer. John Ward Belper, partner in a Derby firm hiring out 4000 stocking frames, reverted from large shops to decentralized forms of production for precisely this reason. In the large shops, he explained in 1845, "the hands did more what they liked; they would not do this, nor would they do that; they would raise a quibble upon every alteration made, and we had more frequent turn-outs through it."[25] Similarly, William Shaw of Nottingham felt that the larger unit transformed labor in unacceptable ways: "Many before entering large shops are very different men to what they are after they have been in a while by reading bad books, inculcating bad principles and so on." [26] One Lancashire manufacturer, with whom Senior corresponded in 1831, was prepared to place the advent of recalcitrant labor in a more exact chronology: "Ten years ago workmen were the servants, now they are the masters. They dictate rules, regulations, and prices of labour and who must and must not be employed." [27] Clearly, workers often found that in larger units of production, "traditional" modes of organization could be consolidated and extended to command the time and space of the workplace.

Overall, the situation in industry up to 1850 is far too complex to allow a simple linear analysis. In some instances, workers retained their role as outworkers to avoid the employer discipline of the factory; elsewhere, the reverse took place. Sometimes, subcontracting was a function of employer authority; in other examples, the opposite was true. Thus the equation of either factory or subcontracting with capital's ability to mediate production severely underestimates the nature of the contest taking place in the early industrial workplace. Whatever the variety of experience, however, labor-oriented approaches to production appear to have been fairly universal, and the twin notions of time and territoriality might be used to explore this area.

## III

The self-image of the worker as independent producer operated in a variety of ways in both large- and small-scale units of production in the first half of the nineteenth century. The organization of production presupposed a control over time as a variable factor. Harrison has argued that in this period, work routines were already formulated into a recognizable working day and week. [28] This is clearly true; employers were hardly surprised each week when their workers did not show up on a Monday. In Birmingham, "Saint Monday" had the legitimizing force of local law behind it; a test case in 1780 found that employees could not be prosecuted under master-and-servant legislation for this kind of absenteeism. [29] Similarly, when Feargus O'Connor addressed a huge Chartist rally at Holloway Head in August 1838, he clearly felt that this was an audience for whom the regular working day was a substantial reality. Speaking on a "Saint Monday," he announced that "his political creed was 'a good day's wages for a good day's work.' " [30] In a similar vein, Thomas Winters assured a select committee in 1856 that the major objective of the National Association of United Trades (NAUT) "to secure for each member . . . a fair compensation for their industry, ingenuity and skill or as it is more generally understood 'a fair day's wages for a fair day's work.' "[31] Although he spoke as corresponding secretary of the NAUT, Winters's personal experience lay in the small workshops of the Leicester gloving trade where it might be expected that endemic irregularity would obscure the existence of a readily defined working day.

Clearly by the 1830s, not only was a "working day" recognized as a measurement of input and reward, but it has also been politicized so that it carried specific notions of fairness both within and outside the workplace. Of course, the universality of the term "a fair day's work" belies the vast range of actual experience within the workforce, and however it seems to echo later statements relating to regularity of attendance, it is unlikely that the term here means much more than (as Rule puts it) a "quota of work."[32] A Leicester wool comber, interviewed in 1850, argued that "we work what hours we please, but the shop is open for us from five in the morning until nine at night, upon Fridays until ten and upon Saturdays up to any hour we choose to stay. The pot is never extinguished from Sunday to Sunday."[33] In the same way, London cooperages often remained open from 3:00 A.M. to 9:00 P.M. The flexibility of the working day, and the value judgment inherent in the idea of "a fair day's work," underpinned workers' control of the product during production. Employers wishing to supervise the operations of the comb shop or the cooperage would have to match the range of hours of their workforce. In practice, this was unlikely; in Kidderminster, carpet weavers frequently carried their masters' keys in order to open and close the shop as work began and finished.[34] The heavy drinking and all-night partying that Charles Shaw so deplored in the potteries reflected the low profile adopted by his employers: "I am not sure if the employers knew of these proceedings. One of them was rarely seen at work. The other used to come about ten o'clock in the morning in a carriage and pair; and stay half an hour or an hour. I never saw him in a workshop."[35]

However much Shaw may have disapproved of the lively workplace culture that such an approach allowed, he was not averse to organizing his work so that he might have an afternoon's birdnesting in fine weather.[36] Dyke Wilkinson, in a Birmingham rule shop in the 1840s, read Burns, Shakespeare, and Goldsmith as he worked at his bench. He and his fellow workers felt so certain of their right to organize their worktime that they happily thwarted their employer's attempt at surveillance by "shying at him rotten potatoes, stale bread and . . . on occasions things of a worse description."[37] It was, therefore, not simply that the "working day" marked a flexible approach to work attendance but also that the intensity of work when it did take place was variable. This is the point that the "hours of attendance" debate, as enunciated by Harrison and others, tends to miss.

Within labor's territory of the workplace was a network of tacit agreements and informal rules by which work was conducted. Whatever the internal discords of the work group, they were outweighed by a common belief in the right of labor to organize the product at this stage. This was expressed most clearly over the issue of time and its use within the working day. James Hopkinson writes of the many interruptions to worktime in the Nottingham cabinet trade created by workplace activities such as workers' trials. He argues that his master did not object because they were pieceworkers, but he adds, "They were such an independent lot of men that they would not have cared much if he had."[38] The custom of "footing" took place at important points in the life of the individual (apprenticeship, marriage, and so on), but it was also used to underpin the collectivity of the work group by identifying significant moments in its creation and development. Metalworkers changing rooms (and thus work groups) in the same factory paid the "shifting shilling," and textile workers paid anything up to 10 shillings. In addition, as one observer in 1840 put it, "these footings fines are exacted from each other on all imaginable occasions." The printers covered not only the obviously significant but also the incidental, thus "going on a journey, 1s; when wife first comes to office, 6d; speaking to a female in the street, 1s; coming of age, 1s; first time of a youth being shaved, 1s."[39] Such activities represent rather more than the persistence of an eighteenth-century penchant for combining working and drinking on the part of the workforce. They were an expression of the right, claimed by labor, to organize time at the point of production.

This was a right protected and nurtured by the often fierce collectivity of the work group. To see labor's intervention in the workplace in this period as a function primarily of an incomplete formal trade union movement is to miss the major role taken by informal organization.[40] Thomas Winters, speaking of the trades of Leicestershire in 1856, explained that "there are no societies there now: there have not been for many years but there are strikes almost every week of the year." A similar point was made in 1845 by William Felkin, referring to the Nottingham silk trades: "General strikes have scarcely ever occurred . . . [but] strikes against particular masters are, even now, very common."[41] Even where formal organization existed, its effectiveness depended on the informal understandings of the work group. The London coopers, for example, had two sets of rules, one written and published and a second, unwritten, "for the good order of shops." When coopers' leader Robert Raven was asked how it was known when a rule had been broken, there being nothing to refer to, he argued that "among twenty or thirty of us someone would recollect what was the rule."[42]

This emphasis on informality had two advantages. First, the possession of certain forms of knowledge could be used to demark the outer boundary of the working community. Second, the understandings governing the use of worktime could be adapted to meet the specific situation confronting the work group. For example, by 1850 about a third of the pits in the Northumberland and Durham coalfield were unofficially restricting output through the control of time at work. As the *Morning Chronicle* correspondent observed, this regulation was "a rule among the men themselves" rather than a union direction. One hewer, asked to justify this intervention, demonstrated how traditional notions of a "quota of work" could be related to the changing economic context of a particular industry:

The restriction is fixed at what we consider a fair day's work for a man, with ordinary powers and endurance engaged in the toilsome and exhausting labour of hewing. . . . We know that there are more men in the trade than are requisite to raise the coal required for average vend: but by restricting each individual's work we compel masters to employ all or nearly all of us, and thus bring into operation what under the competing system would be the surplus labour. . . . But we also have this reason—we think . . . that this restriction limits the quantity of coals brought to the market; and in our opinion if the quantity be limited prices will rise and wages will—or at all events ought—tc rise with them.[43]

It may be that in constantly using the word "traditional" to describe the attitudes to worktime and workplace practices of early industrial labor, we have overlooked the way these were changed and adapted as time passed. This crucial area is one being opened particularly by feminist historians concerned to chart the changing nature of patriarchy. Sonya Rose, looking at the Nottingham hosiery industry, for example, argues that the particular construction of masculinity that became a feature of the workplace in this period was an adaptation and extension of traditional forms within a specific context.[44] In this sense, the changes that took place through the process of adaptation may have been at least as significant as the strands of continuity with the past. The development of gender differentiation is, of course, also important in reminding us that, whatever its commitment to libertarian politics, the community of work was not a community of equals.

Any employer wishing to commoditize labor more effectively by a control of time at work would have to breach the informality of the work group's internal agreements and thereby assert control of the product during the labor process. In market terms, this was a crucial issue, as the hewer quoted earlier obviously appreciated. Where workers set the pace of work, the manufacturer was always uncertain as to the final nature of the product, and the farther away from the labor process he was, the more imprecise would be his projection of product volume. For example, gun manufacturer John Goodman found that his subcontracting, decentralized workforce was capable of producing 1755 guns per week. Their lowest weekly total, however, when worker-initiated stoppages (excluding strikes) were at their highest, was a mere 93 guns.[45]

Clearly, the work group's ability to control time at work was neither constant nor uniform. It was, however, strongest at periods of high demand, precisely the moments when employers most needed to gauge accurately the nature of potential product volume. Physically excluded from the direct supervision of work, employers sought to impose a work rhythm externally through their only real points of contact with the "independent producer": the initial contract of employment and, at the other end of the process, the point of "sale." Thus the mode of intervention was, in large part, determined by the position adopted by the work group.

Recent work on the contract of employment by Adrian Merritt has argued that master-and-servant legislation developed "in a period of nascent capitalism" as a way of extending the managerial prerogatives of the employer. In cases fought out in nineteenth-century courts are seen "the conflict between the workers' attempt to retain the rights of independent contractors and the employers' insistence on their subjection to restrictions previously imposed on servants."[46] Master-and-servant legislation, while it perpetuated the notion that workers were independent producers free to enter into agreements on the basis of mutuality, at the same time locked them into a dependent and subordinate relationship with their employers. This mostly hinged around the issue of worktime and its use. Woods found that nearly 60 percent of prosecutions directed at workers in the Black Country under this legislation involved some notion of misuse of time within the contractual relationship ("leaving work without proper notice," "neglect of work," or "unlawful absence from work.").[47] In the small metal trades of the West Midlands, workers often bound themselves for one or two years to a particular employer, induced by a loan of a few pounds, which was later retrieved from the prices paid at the point of "sale" between employer and worker. A typical contract, drawn up under 4 Geo IV, cap 34, (1823), makes quite clear where authority is to lie during the process of production. During a three-year term, "the said CD shall and will diligently, well and faithfully serve the said AB, and also shall and will regularly attend in his manufactory or workshops at Wolverhampton aforesaid during the usual hours of work, and in all respects conform himself to his directions therein."[48] Even in trades where the hours of work were more firmly established, the employment contract was used by employers attempting to control what went on within that time. In the glass trade, where work proceeded in blocks of six hours, a typical glassworker's contract, cited in 1848, stated that "the said person shall do execute and finish, such a quantity of work during six hours as the master shall require."[49] Nevertheless, the issue of work pace remained a significant area of conflict, with the employer's economic viability dependent on the ability to enforce contracts over work practice. In the 1840s, Birmingham glass manufacturers lamented that, whereas in

Manchester a glassworker could press 290 sugar bowls in six hours, in Birmingham the figure was 260.[50] In 1858, the Midland glass manufacturers challenged and defeated their workers by means of a concerted lockout. As George Lloyd of *Lloyd and Summerfield* explained, this action has been necessary because "they found they were not the rulers in their own shops."[51] In the same way, the coal masters of Aberdare, having successfully terminated a strike over the employer's right to control the size of the labor force, took the opportunity to introduce, for the first time, a very detailed contract of employment. This covered not only the prices to be paid for the coal cut (the "sale") but also a clause concerning time use. This stipulated that the employee "was to do and perform when required . . . a full day's work in each and every working day or such quantity of work as shall fairly be deemed equal to a day's work and not leave their work until such day's work is fully performed."[52]

This contract was one of a range of attempts made to control worktime in a trade where control of the product was notoriously difficult for employers. Rule has shown, in the case of the Cornish mines, that the custom of contracting for work in a particular part of the mine clouded the issue of precise ownership of the mineral extracted at all stages before the pithead.[53] Similarly, in coal the workers generally assumed an autonomy over the coal mined commensurate in many important aspects with the independent producer. John Evans, of Dowlais Iron Works, explained the system in South Wales in 1854:

If a man commences a stall he has the advantage of it; if he should choose to leave the works he can always sell it for what it is worth. If the company chooses to open an air course through some of the stalls which prevent their getting that aircourse, they buy the pillar.[54]

The Lynvi Vale Iron Company, operating in the same area and employing both colliers and ironworkers, experimented with the point of "sale" as a device for intervening in the labor process. It found that the weekly pay on a Friday night interrupted the management pattern: "The work of Saturday was most unprofitable to us," the chairman, Alexander McGregor, explained, "from a want of sufficient combination in the different departments of the works." Payment on a Saturday simply shifted the problem to a Monday, and so the "long pay" (i.e., monthly payment) system was adopted after an unsuccessful strike passed the initiative to the company. The shift to a monthly pay converted weekly irregularity to a monthly phenomenon.[55] Other ironworks and collieries operated a six- to seven-week interval between pay periods for the same reason.

By the 1860s and 1870s in the mines of this area, however, the regulation of worktime by devices external to the labor process had been replaced by direct intervention through work restructuring. After a bitter series of strikes, the longwall method of coal extraction which reduced the autonomy of the work group, was introduced. Allied with the double-shift system, this severely undercut the miner's control of work and went some distance toward resolving the issue of product ownership at the point of extraction.[56]

Innovations of this nature generally followed decisive workplace encounters in the form of strikes or lockouts. Nevertheless, it is obvious that the notion of worker as independent producer exercising co-ownership of the product at work always had drawbacks for the workforce, and this became increasingly apparent as time passed. As industrialization developed, the "sale" to the employer was made under circumstances that were more clearly disadvantageous to the work group. In the small metalware trades, a discount of anywhere from 5 to 50 percent was deducted from prices paid by employers, according to the state of trade.[57] Hand weavers and stockingers had to put up with (among other things) the iniquities of manufacturers who measured their work with a 37-inch yardstick. Even where the conventional 36-inch stick was used, manufacturers, as Amos Cowgill explained, "did it in the mode of measurement in the swing of the arm."[58] Hewers might lose a full tub of coal at the pithead under the system of "laid out" and "set out" coal if the employer's checkweighman divined that too much stone or small coal was present.[59] The contract of sale, like the contract of employment, was a bargain of unequal parties, particularly in circumstances of overstocked markets and intense competition. In this way, the worker as independent producer was, in many trades, eventually debased into a sweated outworker.

The emergence of a work routine more clearly structured to the needs of capital rather than labor was often a recognition of this process of debasement on the part of the workforce. By the third quarter of the nineteenth century, small-scale industry operated more as a service sector for larger units of production than had been true previously, and it reproduced the work discipline of the larger unit. In addition, the small gang, which involved a particular relationship between skilled and unskilled workers, was distorted into a more evidently supervisory role for a small number of skilled workers. Joyce dates the advent of the working-class "overlooker" in the cotton mills from the late 1840s and significantly relates this to the decline of working-class politics with a defeat of Chartism.[60]

Thus the significance of paternalism among "new model" employers in the second half of the century is often misconstrued. When a formal scheme was introduced, whatever the apparent benefit to the workforce, it invariably replaced an informal arrangement that was more obviously the property of the workforce. "Saint Monday" exchanged for a Saturday half-holiday is a good example.[61] Similarly, insurance schemes often asserted the employer's rights over the time and territory of work. This point is perhaps illustrated by Robert Whitfield's explanation of how the Provident Club, which he introduced into his brassworks in 1847, operated: "Every man above 21 years of age . . . is compelled to contribute 2s 6d as entrance money, which sum is considered as paid instead of the usual "foot ales" or drinking money."[62] Replacing "foot ales" with workers' insurance undoubtedly gave the workforce greater sercurity; it also gave the employer greater control over work. In a similar way, Huntley and Palmer allowed each worker to take home a pound of broken biscuits each week; on the face of it, a good paternalist measure.[63] Yet if, as seems likely, this arrangement was designed to replace an informally exercised belief, common among workers in such trades then and now, that what was broken belonged to nobody and could therefore be taken, then this would have to be seen as part of a broader assertion of employer control over the product within the workplace. A formal arrangement, formally enforced, might ensure that workers were less "butter-fingered" on the production line.

By the middle of the century, it is possible to identify, in a number of trades, workers in a transitional state somewhere between "independent" production and wage labor. In the factories of the Nottingham lace trade in the 1850s, for example, alterations to machine patterns could take anywhere from three days to two weeks. In some factories, workers bore the cost of time lost, receiving an advance from the employer while "standing for alteration"—an advance that had to be repaid on a weekly basis once production began again. In other factories, workers continued to receive a (reduced) wage during the nonproductive period that was not repaid.[64] The point relates less to the generosity of particular employers and more to the relationship between authority and the ownership of the productive time lost. In turn, the issue of whose time it was related directly to whose workplace it was.

In fact, the 1860s and 1870s saw fairly widespread agreements on the formal working day. The Saturday half-holiday and nine-hour movements emerged alongside the development of formal trade unions with an accredited workplace role verified by law. Whatever was gained by the working community in this process, the increasingly hollow notion of the autonomous producer was being lost. When workpeople argued for a limitation of worktime within a formalized working day, they frequently did so by adopting the terms of the dominant discourse, whereby irregular work, facilitated by "independent" production within the workplace, was equated with immorality. Joiner George Potter, speaking for the nine-hour day in 1860, put it as follows:

Generally, when men are allowed to work piece-work, I believe that it encourages them to leave their work and go and have their beer and so on whereas the men working day-work cannot leave the shop; *where a man is his own employer,* and gets a job to do when he likes it encourages him to go away from his work and waste his time.[65]

For agreement to be reached, it was only necessary that this apparent consensus on the moral dimensions of the debate dovetail with the pragmatic considerations of the market economy. Leading the local employers in Birmingham on the issue of a nine-hour day, Richard Tangye later confided to readers of his autobiography that "we had long noted the fact that the energies of the men were expended before the close of the day, and that comparatively little work was done in the last hour, when of course more gas was used than during any other part of the day, and the cost in coal and wear and tear on machinery was no less."[66]

Formal agreements of this nature reflected an acceptance that the work relationship would be different from what it had been formerly. We should not make the mistake, however, of assuming that agreement over the rhythm of work reflected an unyielding complicity on the part of the workforce. Young W. G. Riddell, presenting himself for his first day at a Glasgow engine works, shortly before World War I, found the factory deserted. "I did not know," he explains, "that the men never started work after holidays on the appointed day." And he later discovered: "At some places they used to assemble at the gate and throw a brick in the air: if the brick stayed up they started work, but if it came down again they went for a drink."[67]

Patterns of informality relating to worktime still operated, despite the fact that the agreed-upon rules of the employer—employee relationship constrained them in ways that had previously been less evident. Tamara Hareven has shown in her study of factory workers in New Hampshire that submissiveness "was part of a strategy of accommodation that often involved play-acting," and the work of Peter Bailey would seem to support this notion.[68] What appears to have changed by the late nineteenth century, however, was that there was an acceptance, by increasing numbers of workers, that they were selling labor, rather than the product of that labor, to the employer. This was a very different kind of bargain from the one entered into earlier in the period. And it carried with it the implicit assumption that the employer had the right to supervise labor during worktime.

## NOTES

1. E. P. Thompson, "Time, Work Discipline, and Industrial Capitalism," *Past and Present* 38 (December 1967).

2. S. Pollard, *The Genesis of Modern Management* (London, 1965); and D. A. Reid, "The Decline of St. Monday," *Past and Present* 71 (May 1976). See also M. A. Bienefeld, *Working Hours in British Industry: An Economic History* (London, 1972).

3. M. Harrison, "The Ordering of the Urban Environment: Time, Work and the Occurrence of Crowds, 1790–1835," *Past and Present* 110 (February 1986).

4. E. Hopkins, "Working Hours and Conditions during the Industrial Revolution: A Re-Appraisal," *Economic History Review* 35, no. 1 (1982).

5. C. Sabel and J. Zeitlin, "Historical Alternatives to Mass Production," *Past and Present* 108 (August 1985). For a more detailed critique of this view, see C. Behagg, "Myths of Cohesion: Capital and Compromise in the Historiography of Nineteenth Century Birmingham," *Social History* 11, no. 3 (October 1986).

6. W. Lazonick, "Industrial Relations and Technical Change: The Case of the Self-Acting Mule," *Cambridge Journal of Economics* 3, no. 3 (1979).

7. K. Marx, *Capital* (Harmondsworth, England, 1976), 1:292, 326. The point is explored in M. Holbrook-Jones, *Supremacy and Subordination of Labour* (London, 1982), p. 11.

8. Reid, "Decline of St. Monday."

9. Marx, *Capital,* 1:292.

10. Ibid., 1:693.

11. For an analysis of this debasement in one area, see C. Behagg, "Custom Class and Change, the Trade Societies of Birmingham," *Social History* 4, no. 3 (October 1979). For an overview, see R. Price, *Labour in British Society. An Interpretive History* (London, 1986), pp. 156–48.

12. S. Timmins, ed., *Birmingham and the Midland Hardware District* (London, 1866), p. 454.

13. *Birmingham Journal,* September 22, 1849.

14. See, for example, on the ribbon trade of Coventry, P. Searby, "Weavers and Freemen in Coventry 1820–1861. Social and Political Traditionalism in an Early Victorian Town," Ph.D. dissertation, University of Warwick, 1972, pp. 108–109. The theme is more fully explored in C. Behagg, "Masters and Manufacturer: Social Values and the Smaller Unit of Production in Birmingham, 1800–1850," in *Shopkeepers and Master Artisans in Nineteenth Century Europe,* ed. G. Crossick and H. G. Haupt (London, 1984).

15. *Birmingham Labour Exchange Gazette,* January 26, 1833.

16. See, for example, on the views of employers in Kidderminster, L. Smith, "The Carpet Weavers of Kidderminster 1800–1850" Ph.D. dissertation, University of Birmingham, 1982, Chap. 3.

17. British Parliamentary Papers, *Report of the Commissioners Appointed to Inquire into the Condition of the Framework Knitters,* Pt. 2, 1846, xv.

18. *Morning Chronicle,* January 6, 1851.

19. Quoted in A. M. Urdank, "Custom, Conflict and Traditional Authority in the Gloucester Weaver Strike of 1825," *Journal of British Studies* 25 (April 1986): 213. Urdank's analysis is rather different from the one offered here.

20. *Birmingham Journal,* October 7, 1837.

21. Report on Combinations by Nassau Senior, Esq., and Thomas Tomlinson, Esq., Home Office Papers 44/56.

22. *Pioneer,* September 7, 1833.

23. E. J. Hobsbawm, *Labouring Men* (London, 1974), p. 299; and C. R. Littler, *The Development of the Labour Process in Capitalist Societies* (London, 1982), p. 78. See also Marx, *Capital,* 1:695.

24. See, particularly, Littler, *Development of Labour Process.*

25. Parliamentary Papers, *Royal Commission on Framework Knitters,* Q4727.

26. Ibid., Q1331.

27. Report on Combinations.

28. Harrison, "Ordering of Urban Environment."

29. R. Burn, *Justice of the Peace and Parish Officer* (1830), 4:391.

30. *Birmingham Journal,* August 11, 1838.

31. British Parliamentary Papers, *Report from the Select Committee on Masters and Operatives (Equitable Councils of Conciliation),* 343, 1856, Q6.

32. J. Rule, *The Experience of Labour in Eighteenth Century Industry* (London, 1981), p. 59.

33. J. Ginswick, ed., *Labour and the Poor in England and Wales 1849–1851. The Letters to the Morning Chronicle,* 2:197.

34. Smith, "Carpet Weavers," p. 227.

35. C. Shaw, *When I Was a Child* (London, 1903), p. 51.

36. Ibid., p. 81. Whipp notes that "many pot banks did not possess an office even in 1921." R. Whipp, " 'The Art of Good Management,' Managerial Control of Work in the British Pottery Industry, 1900–1925," *International Review of Social History* 29 (1984): 370.

37. D. Wilkinson, *Rough Roads. Reminiscences of a Wasted Life* (London, 1912), p. 30. The theme of territoriality and the workplace is explored in C. Behagg, "Secrecy, Ritual and Folk Violence: The Opacity of the Workplace in the First Half of the Nineteenth Century," in *Popular Culture and Custom in Nineteenth Century England,* ed. R. D. Storch (London, 1982).

38. J. Hopkinson, *A Victorian Cabinet Maker* (London, 1968).

39. British Parliamentary Papers, *Report from the Assistant Handloom Weavers' Commissioners,* pt. 5, 639 (xxiv), 1840, 58.

40. This area is well explored, for the building trades, in R. Price, *Masters Unions and Men* (Cambridge, 1980).

41. British Parliamentary Papers, *Select Committee on Masters and Operatives,* Q463.

42. British Parliamentary Papers, *Report from the Select Committee on the Combination Laws Particularly as to 5 Geo IV c95,* 437, 1825, 47–52.

43. Ginswick, *Labour and the Poor,* p. 68.

44. Sonya O. Rose, " 'Gender at Work': Sex, Class and Industrial Capitalism," *History Workshop Journal* 21 (Spring 1986): 113–32.

45. British Parliamentary Papers, *Report of the Select Committee on the Manufacture of Small Arms,* 12 (xviii), 1854, Q336.

46. A. Merritt, "The Historical Role of Law in the Regulation of Employment—

Abstentionist or Interventionist?'' *Australian Journal of Law and Society* 1, no. 1 (1982): 82.

47. D. C. Woods, "The Operation of the Master and Servant Act in the Black Country, 1858–1875," *Midland History* 7 (1982).

48. *Morning Chronicle,* February 3, 1851.

49. *Birmingham Journal,* June 24, 1848.

50. Ibid.

51. R. F. to H. Martineau, August 15, 1859. Martineau Papers, University of Birmingham.

52. Ginswick, *Labour and the Poor,* 3:129.

53. J. Rule, "The Labouring Miner in Cornwall c. 1740–1870" Ph.D. dissertation, University of Warwick, 1971.

54. British Parliamentary Papers, *Report from the Select Committee on the Payment of Wages Bill and the Payment of Wages (Hosiery) Bill,* 382, 1854, Q6068.

55. Ibid., Q5811–5911. See also W. R. Lambert, "Drink and Work—Discipline in Industrial South Wales c. 1800–1870," *Welsh Historical Review* 7 (1975).

56. J. H. Morris and L. J. Williams, *The South Wales Coal Industry* (Cardiff, 1958), pp 60–63, 258–269. See also M. J. Daunton, "Down the Pit," *Economic History Review* 24 (1981): 578–97.

57. Behagg, "Custom Class and Change."

58. British Parliamentary Papers, *Select Committee on Combination Laws,* 141.

59. Ginswick, *Labour and the Poor,* 3:52–53.

60. P. Joyce, *Work, Society and Politics* (Brighton, 1980), p. 103.

61. Reid, "Decline of St. Monday."

62. *Morning Chronicle,* January 6, 1851. For a less critical analysis of industrial paternalism, see D. A. Reid, "Labour, Leisure and Politics in Birmingham c. 1800–1875," Ph.D. dissertation, University of Birmingham, 1985.

63. S. Yeo, *Religion and Voluntary Organisations in Crisis* (London, 1976), p. 100.

64. Ginswick, *Labour and the Poor,* 2:153.

65. Parliametary Papers, *Select Committee on Masters and Operatives,* Q989.

66. R. Tangye, *One and All* (Birmingham, 1889), p. 116.

67. W. G. Riddell, Adventures of an Obscure Victorian (London, 1982), p. 11.

68. T. K. Hareven, *Family Time and Industrial Time* (Cambridge, 1982), p. 135; and P. Bailey, " 'Will the Real Bill Banks Please Stand up?' Towards a Role Analysis of Mid-Victorian Respectability," *Journal of Social History* 12, no. 3 (Spring 1979).

# 4

## Work, Leisure, and Moral Reform: The Ten-Hour Movement in New England, 1830–1850

### *Teresa Murphy*

### I

STRUGGLES FOR a shorter workday, at first for ten hours and later for eight, were at the heart of much of the labor unrest throughout the nineteenth century. Like the process of industrialization, the gains (and losses) in the United States, at least in the antebellum period, were often made in piecemeal fashion, the result of collective bargaining in individual trades rather than any meaningful legislation at state and national levels.

In New England, the struggle to reduce hours was particularly long and frustrating. Housewrights in Boston struck for a shorter workday in 1825. Machinists, carpenters, and shipwrights led the way in a regionwide movement during the early 1830s, creating an organization that united industrial workers with artisans in traditional trades, under the banner of the New England Association of Farmers, Mechanics and Other Workingmen. In the mid-1840s, the movement gained new impetus as factory operatives joined in the struggle and formed the New England Workingmen's Association. The movement was concentrated in mill villages, although it was sometimes led by skilled craftsmen from such traditional trades as carpentry.[1] The leaders created an organization that not only brought semiskilled factory workers under the same umbrella as skilled artisans but welcomed the participation of women. Yet, despite a broadening basis of support, their attempts met with failure during this period. New England mechanics would finally achieve a ten-hour day in the 1850s, but factory operatives would have to wait until the 1870s for meaningful legislation to be passed.[2]

Historians who analyze these movements face a series of perplexing questions, not only about why they failed, but about their general character. The regional associations of the 1830s and 1840s, which grew to embrace

skilled and semiskilled industrial workers as well as traditional artisan, operated more as reform movements than as recognizable trade union activity.
Masters were invited by journeymen to join local organizations, which, except in the large towns of Providence and Boston, were organized by community rather than trade. Strikes for shorter hours were rare in New England,
and by the 1840s, even condemned by many workingmen. They increasingly cast their criticism in moral and religious terms, as the issue of long
workdays was transformed from one of simple economic exploitation to one
of perfection and salvation.

What are we to make of these developments, particularly in view of the
research that has tied nineteenth-century Protestantism to the creation of
middle-class hegemony? Paul Johnson has argued effectively that evangelical Protestantism in the early nineteenth century, with its emphasis on free
moral agency, legitimated the economic domination of capitalists who employed wage labor. Workingmen who joined churches in later revivals, Johnson
suggests, probably did so under pressure from their employers. Anthony
Wallace, in studying the mills outside Philadelphia, contends that evangeli-
calism led manufacturers to acts of benevolence (including the passage of a
weak ten-hour law) that had the effect of pacifying employees in their mills.[3]
From perspectives such as these, nineteenth-century Protestantism subdued
unruly workers and became one of the defining characteristics of the bourgeois mentality.

Other historians have felt less comfortable ceding Protestantism solely to
the middle class. Both Bruce Laurie and Sean Wilentz, studying antebellum
working people in Philadelphia and New York, have noted that during the
1840s, evangelical workers incorporated a critique of their working conditions into their religious perspectives. Those who demanded a shorter workday in Philadelphia might be deferential to their employers, but they were
also vigilant parents, concerned about the plight of their children in the
mills. In New York, the Order of United American Mechanics, a Protestant
(and nativist) labor organization that rose to prominence after 1845, and the
Mechanics Mutual Protection Association, which established a branch in
New York City in 1846, were more than outposts of ethnic bigotry or religious enthusiasm. The Order of United American Mechanics opposed immigration because it drove down wages, and the Mechanics Mutual
championed higher wages for artisans and a ten-hour day for factory workers
as critical for a Christian Republic.[4]

Even as they make their arguments about workers in the 1840s, however, Wilentz and Laurie acknowledge the limits of religious inspiration and
the close connection between Protestantism and middle-class hegemony.
Wilentz prefaces his discussion of the mechanics' movements by pointing
out that until 1845, Protestantism was "an article of entrepreneurial faith"

that "dulled class antagonisms" with assertions of cultural superiority. Despite their economic critiques, the nativism of the American Mechanics and the opposition of the Mechanics Mutual to strikes and unions undercut the class consciousness of the 1830s. In fact, the importance of these groups lies in their function as a bridge to the future, a bridge that evangelical workers traveled to reunite with those radical workers from whom they had been estranged during the previous decades.

Laurie's workers appear even less militant than those in New York. He notes that while religiously inspired workers might petition for a ten-hour day, they would not strike for one, for that "was tantamount to acknowledging class polarities and denying the social fluidity that was the ideological keystone of revivalism."[5] We are left to wonder if these ten-hour advocates in Philadelphia were simply subscribing to the philosophy of the middle class. Did religion provide them with any kind of lens for viewing themselves as workers in opposition to employers, or was it a perspective that essentially denied the notion of opposition? Were particular values being asserted by working people that were not shared with their employers, especially when it came to issues of time?

What I argue in this chapter is that the Protestant religion in New England provided an important intellectual resource for working people in developing a critique of emerging usages of worktime. As such, it was also an important vehicle for creating working-class unity during the 1830s and 1840s. Both points are important to keep in mind as we try to evaluate the meaning of the struggle for a shorter workday. On one level, the movement for a ten-hour day was simply a bread-and-butter issue, an attempt to improve working conditions. But the implications of this struggle broaden once we look beyond the workplace to the larger movement that was being created.

## II

Individual trades in New England might strike over questions of wages, methods of payment, and apprenticeship, but the issue of time united them. Levels of skill clouded the problem of differentials in wage rates both across and within trades, thus limiting the ability of the wage issue to unite broad segments of the working class; there was also tremendous variety in methods and frequency of payment. But most workers in New England had to contend with steady increases in the length of the workday throughout the early nineteenth century, increases that were made both openly and surrepitiously. "Lighting up" mills in the winter extended the length of short workdays, while factory and shipyard clocks were purposely slowed down to keep workers at their tasks past normal quitting time. Workers in the building trades might be pushed to extend their day's labor during the summer months, only to face layoffs in the winter.[6] Time was thus an issue around which workers could coalesce in protesting exploitative working conditions.

By tying criticisms of lengthy workdays to demands for a particular number of hours, instead of protesting the more specific abuses, such as "lighting up," workers developed a strategy that could unite people from diverse trades. No doubt this was one reason machinists in Providence, in the course of their meetings during 1831, altered their critique of long hours. Their original protest challenged the practice of working by candlelight, a human intervention into the natural workday that stretched the notion of "a day's work" to provide greater profits for employers. Demanding instead a day more closely attuned to natural rhythms, they resolved to work only from sunup to sundown. Such a workday was probably especially appealing to the many factory workers who had migrated from rural New England to find work and who still felt an affinity to the agricultural work cycle, but it would have little appeal in the building trades where the cold and dark of outdoor winter work made "lighting up" unfeasible. Not surprisingly, the machinists altered their stance a few weeks later, adopting the ten-hour day as their cause.[7] Substituting their man-made timetable of ten hours for that of either their employers or the agricultural cycle, they were able to attract workers from the building and maritime trades to their cause, providing the impetus for the formation of the New England Association of Farmers, Mechanics and Other Workingmen during the early months of 1832. In this instance, at least, the demand for ten hours was not only the result of negotiations with employers or an acknowledgment of factory discipline but was part of an attempt to create broad working-class support beyond the factory walls.

The coalition failed to institute a ten-hour day in the factories and workshops of New England that spring. Many workers refused to strike; those who did strike were sometimes replaced by scabs from the country. Local auxiliaries of the association began to investigate cultural and political solutions during the next couple of years, but by 1835, the organization had faded. Nevertheless, it appears to have inspired the Boston Trades Union, which was formed in 1834. The union launched another ten-hour drive in 1835, a struggle that would end in failure for the Boston workers but that galvanized workers around the country.[8] Long workdays, along with virtually all forms of labor activism, evaporated during the depression that followed the Panic of 1837. According to Thomas Dublin, mills in Lowell not only lowered wages but ran on part-time schedules.[9] Those who had jobs hardly felt secure enough to demand better working conditions, let along build a coalition of workers throughout the region. This did not mean that working people abandoned a critique of worktime, however.

As business improved in 1843, so too did the amount of work required of many laborers and the length of their workdays. Thus Dublin points out that between 1842 and 1843, an increase in the number of looms tended by operatives boosted productivity by 70 percent, while their earnings increased only 16 percent. Paul Faler, examining what scanty evidence is available for shoemakers in Lynn, suggests that by the 1840s, cordwainers had to work a fourteen-hour day to get only a slightly higher wage than they would have received with a much shorter workday in 1830.[10] What both studies suggest is that with the business upturn in the early 1840s, many wage earners in New England were able to maintain, or even slightly improve, their wage situation (compared to the early 1830s), but only at the expense of their leisure time. As mechanics and operatives began to resurrect their labor organizations in the early 1840s, they did so with an acute consciousness of this problem, as well as with a renewed commitment to a broadly based labor movement.

The cordwainers of Lynn were organizing for higher piece rates and the reform of apprenticeship rules when representatives of the ten-hour movement attended their convention in 1844. Since both demands would have the effect of reducing the length of the workday, the shoemakers gave their support to the movement and prepared a ten-hour petition. Operatives in places such as Lowell and Andover also got behind the drive for a ten-hour day, as the speed-up and stretch-out in textile mills took their toll. In the machine shops, the pace of work probably was not as grueling, and the pay was certainly better, but the days were still long, as machinsts in Worcester and Lowell would attest.

Skilled artisans in factory towns also felt the pressure of long days. Carpenters in Fall River, who led the ten-hour drive in 1844, condemned the corporations as the greatest enemies of local mechanics. They claimed that many boss carpenters, under pressure from the mills, refused to sanction a ten-hour day for their men. Micah Ruggles, one of the major factory owners (as well as an antislavery Quaker), refused to hire masons on a ten-hour system. A mechanic identifying himself as "P" wrote later that mill owners would not grant mechanics a ten-hour day because the "factory help" would make a similar demand.[11] No doubt carpenters in Worcester felt similar pressure, for they were quick to join the machinists there over the issue of time.

All these groups, from factory workers to skilled artisans, joined together in the New England Workingmen's Association. The road to such unity, however, was not always smooth or even well-traveled, as some local problems demonstrate. Skilled artisans were sometimes reluctant to join forces with the unskilled (especially if the latter happened to be women), even when they recognized that their problems had a common economic source. As a result, Mary Blewett points out, male cordwainers in Lynn failed to gain much support from female shoebinders during their struggles of the 1840s. Similarly, carpenters in Fall River were unsuccessful in their attempts to gain support from textile operatives during this period.[12] Failures such as these no doubt weakened local movements, but they also served to underscore the extraordinary accomplishment of the New England Workingmen's Association in uniting such a diverse body of workers throughout the region.

The alliance of traditional artisans with new industrial workers was particularly important in New England. The fact that they shared common bosses may have encouraged unity. Capitalists there constituted a much more unified elite than they did elsewhere in the United States. Merchants were often mill owners, and mill owners were often large landowners, so that workers in shipyards, factories, and construction sties might share the same employers.[13] If the workers themselves were not originally aware of it, the capitalists made the point. Merchants had been quick to intervene in conflicts between masters and journeymen during the 1830s, just as factory owners in Fall River had dictated hours in the building trades during the 1840s. In Boston, in particular, merchants and capitalists repeatedly interfered in struggles between masters and journeymen over the length of their workday, supporting longer hours for carpenters in 1825 and for shipwrights and caulkers in 1832. Providence workingmen complained in 1832 of a manufacturer who had taken it upon himself to enter a carpenter's shop, a bleach house, and a machine shop to tell owners and agents that if they did not follow his instructions for employment, he would use his influence to destroy their businesses.[14]

Thus it was not simply the issue of mechanization that propelled debates over the length of the workday. Deteriorating conditions in a variety of trades, propelled by an obviously interlocking capitalist structure, confronted both skilled and unskilled workers in new and traditional occupations, particularly in factory towns. In response to these economic conditions, a movement for a ten-hour day emerged. But the movement was shaped, particularly in the 1840s, by the logic of the religious and moral reform ideologies that were of central importance in the debates between working people and their employers.

## III

Of course, moral reform was not the only argument used for a shorter day. New England workers, like those elsewhere in the United States, also demanded time to develop as citizens, and republicanism was an ever present part of their discourse. The preamble to the constitution of the New England Association of Farmers, Mechanics and Other Workingmen began

with a discourse on the ways in which moneyed aristocracies perverted republican principles and the natural equality of men before going on to demand the right of workers to control the length of their workday. An editorial
in the *Mechanic* a decade later urged support for a shorter workday because
of the "necessity of promoting that independence, intelligence and virtue of
the laboring class which will enable them to wield the powers with which
they are vested, with wisdom."[15] As a resource in the struggle of workers
for their rights, republicanism has received important attention from scholars.[16] It was a language shared by workers and their employers that opened
the way for debate on the meaning of equality, as well as the rights and
duties of citizens.

Emphasis on the need for virtue among a republican citizenry also provided an important means for linking religion and morality with the demands
of republicanism.[17] But the uses of morality as a shared language of wage
earners and their employers are less obvious, particularly because moral
questions could be so much more divisive among workers. Conflicts among
drinkers and nondrinkers, believers and nonbelievers, and Catholics and
Protestants are only a few of the rifts among workers that were related to
moral concerns. Both Laurie and Wilentz, for example, note the way in
which moral commitments often served to undercut, rather than promote,
alliances among workers in Philadelphia and New York.

In New England as well, these divisions were apparent, as "professors"
sought out those of a similar inclination in mill towns and bemoaned their
contact with the rougher sort. Matthias Haines, a pious youth from New
Hampshire, lasted only a week at a Dorchester furniture factory, where his
roommates kept him up until the wee hours of the morning playing cards.
"No sleep for poor me," he confided in his diary. "I had to lay and endure
the noise but this I could have borne very well but to hear the language they
uttered was enough to sicken any one."[18] Charles Metcalf, who had arrived
in Lowell from Maine to train as a machinist, wrote of similar concerns to
his mother: "I come in contact with and necessarily hear persons use pro-
fane language every day," he complained, "and I feel that there is danger
of the moral sensibilities becoming blunted with contact with vice of any
kind."[19] Clearly, such men might have difficulties discussing shared problems of exploitation with their earthier colleagues, let alone acting on them.

Morality also presents problems because it was used by capitalists and
employers to implement their new work regimen and lengthen the workday.
As Paul Faler has detailed for us in Lynn, this new industrial morality emphasized "self-discipline, industry, sobriety, self-denial, and respect for authority," traits that are more or less necessary to survive the early stages of
industrialization in any economic system.[20] Thus it does not seem to provide
the same promising intellectual resources for challenging labor exploitation

that a republican ideology might. The respectability created by this new moral code would seem more likely to promote ties with employers than oppose them.

But a commitment to Protestant moral reform issues might not have the same divisive effects in New England that it would elsewhere. Workers in New England were far more ethnically homogeneous during the 1830s and 1840s than were workers in New York and Philadelphia. While impoverished English and Irish immigrants were streaming into New York and Philadelphia at the end of the eighteenth century and the beginning of the nineteenth century, relatively few found their way to the ports of Providence and Boston. An analysis of the records of the Hamilton Manufacturing Company in Lowell revealed that 96 percent of the operatives working there in the middle of the 1830s were from the Untied States, as were 92 percent in the middle of the 1840s. If they did not come from Massachusetts, they came from New Hampshire, Vermont, or Maine. Not until the end of the 1840s did large numbers of Irish begin taking positions in the mill. Waltham seems to have echoed this situation, having only 8 Irish households in 1840, but 163 Irish households in 1850, a figure that then constituted almost one-quarter of the town's population. In Lynn, over 80 percent of the population of 1870 had been born in the United States, with population growth there still linked primarily to rural migration.[21]

This ethnic homogeneity may be one important reason the criticisms of moral reform activities and Protestantism that surfaced in New England were far less frequent and more muted than those that occurred in New York and Philadelphia. Many workers in New England ignored the moral reform movements of the time, but they seem to have been less offended by these activities than were workers elsewhere. This would be an important factor as workers debated issues of morality with employers.

Many employers in New England aggressively promoted the morality of long workdays, a stance that demanded a response from their workers. In part, employers believed their own rhetoric, and in part they meant to legitimate their positions of authority. But what they also did was to open their behavior to moral judgment, and to introduce morality as one of the central terms in their debates with workers. Morality was not simply a value that employees shared with their employers; rather, it was an important focus of conflict between the two groups, a contested terrain.

Boston housewrights challenged their wages and long workdays as unfair in 1825 and confronted masters who defended long days as the basis for Boston's reputation as the city "of early rising and industry." Moral problems would proliferate if apprentices and journeymen were left to their own devices, seduced from industry and exposed to temptation. "That we consider idleness as the most deadly bane to usefulness and honorable living," they argued, "and knowing, (such is human nature) that where there is no necessity, there is no exertion, we fear and dread the consequences of such a measure upon the morals and well being of society." Their sentiments were echoed by the capitalists funding the building trades, who felt that shorter days would open "a wide door for idleness and vice."[22] This argument still surfaced in the debates of the 1840s. Jonathan Ware, a Unitarian minister in Fall River, opposed a ten-hour day because it struck "at the root of a habit which is wealth to the working man. I mean early rising." Ware had heard that men working on a ten-hour day were not rising before breakfast, and concluded, "We shall deteriorate sadly if early rising be neglected."[23]

These assertions of moral responsibility by employers (and those who supported them) are important for several reasons. First, they suggest a commitment to a patriarchal religious order that was eroding under the impact of evangelical religion. Within this patriarchal order, it was expected that human beings would be sinful and that they could be held in check by a stable and hierarchical society led by ministers, merchants, and masters. Religious revivals and moral reform movements, however, had resulted in a growing emphasis on individual conscience rather than patriarchal responsibility, either at home or in the workplace. The free moral agency described by Johnson, which absolved employers of any feelings of obligation toward their employees, also rendered arguments of moral responsibility increasingly hollow.

The breakdown of patriarchal religious authority, as Mary Ryan has pointed out, not only took place in economic relationships but within the middle-class home as well. Artisans and farmers increasingly found themselves unable to provide for their children with a family business or farm, and were forced to release their offspring into the wage labor force. As a result, evangelical mothers sought to instill internalized restraints in their children, as a defense against the moral temptations they might face. In so doing, they further subverted the traditional family structure in which men had been the moral focus.[24]

The work by Johnson and Ryan has been tremendously important in helping us to understand the creation of the middle class in the early years of the nineteenth century. Viewed from a slighty different perspective, however, their work can help us explain why the Protestant religion appealed to working people as well.

The breakdown in patriarchy, for example, was hardly confined to middle-class families. The young men and women flowing into the textile factories and machine shops of New England had clearly declared their economic independence from their parents.[25] Even in textile mills run on the family system of labor, there can be little doubt that traditional forms of patriarchal authority were subverted. Jonathan Prude has shown how Samuel Slater's mill in Webster, Massachusetts, separated parents and children during the workday, and how children over the age of fourteen received their own wages and sometimes even their own lodgings. As Prude concludes, "Management's intrusions forcefully and directly challenged received notions of parental authority and responsibility."[26] In Lynn, shoemaking has been a family operation, with women engaged in shoebinding. But, as Mary Blewett argues, this process had changed by the late 1830s, as manufacturers, rather than husbands or fathers, dealt directly with female shoemakers.[27]

With economic changes such as these, many working people also became interested in developing voluntaristic moral restraints. They joined churches, attended lectures, and participated in temperance societies; they became respectable. But this respectability did not lead to acquiescence. Instead, it allowed working people to spot quickly the limits of arguments put forth by their employers from a patriarchal perspective.

When masters and capitalists created a debate that spotlighted the issue of morality and their ability to foster it within the workplace, they advanced a theory that was, in fact, crumbling before them. This was one of the central contradictions in the middle-class quest for moral hegemony. Employers were attempting to be paternalistic at the same time that they were encouraging behavior that would undermine a paternalistic outlook. Rational recreation, in the form of temperate behavior, educational pursuits, and religious commitments, was put forth by its advocates as an alternative to the "vices" of the working class and wealthy alike. Many of the same employers who condemned the idleness of workers outside the workplace promoted temperance societies and other moral reform organizations, as well as funded religious groups. In addition to promoting values that employers sincerely cherished, rational recreation held the additional attractions of creating for employers an increased sense of moral virtue, and perhaps a more disciplined workforce.[28]

For workers migrating to factory towns, these new forms of leisure were often an important lure, providing excitement and sociability that were not available in rural hamlets. Lowell was particularly famous for its lectures and churches, but other mill towns offered opportunities for socializing and improving as well. Still, these activities demanded a lot of time. The pious machinist Charles Metcalf wrote to his mother soon after arriving in Lowell, "It is said, as you are aware that there are great privileges in Lowell, tis true they are . . . but after the toils of the day, and week are over *I* for one feel unfitted to enjoy those privileges."[29] Although Metcalf said nothing of the labor unrest going on around him, the letter was dated June 2, 1844, at a high point of agitation for a shorter workday in Lowell.

Early on, New England workers demonstrated both a commitment to moral reform and an acute sensitivity to the logical weakness of opponents who argued for the moral benefits of a long workday. When the New England Association of Farmers, Mechanics and Other Workingmen consolidated around the issue of a ten-hour day in 1831, they stipulated in their constitution that anyone who worked longer should be paid overtime, indicating an understanding that time had become money. But they linked the issue of time and morality through their criterion for membership: Anyone of good moral character could join, regardless of whether employer or employee. The New Bedford local elaborated on the point by stating that "as a society we want to improve our moral condition—we want to increase the boundary of our knowledge and understanding—we want to have sufficient opportunity each day to perform the duties enjoined on us by our Maker and by mankind."[30]

Morality thus became an issue of individual control, not an employer's responsibility; it was achieved in the world of leisure rather than the world of work. Here, workers could establish autonomy and limit the power of employers in their lives. Workers, not employers, pushed for a radical disjuntion between the worlds of work and leisure, worlds of discretely banded lengths of time.

The criterion for membership in the New England societies, which was linked to morality rather than wage-earning status, baffled workers from other areas. But within the context of struggle in New England, it made tremendous sense. Working people had defined their goal as a shorter workday, and any employer acquiescing to this demand would be welcome to join. By stating the criterion of membership as moral character, however, working people were claiming the moral mantle for themselves and leaving those who equated virtue with long hours (as did most employers) out in the cold.

In addition, many workers were well aware of the way in which leisure institutions supported by employers could be instruments of domination. Thus they created their own organizations. Both the Boston and New Bedford locals of the New England Association of Farmers, Mechanics and Other Workingmen, for example, launched their own lyceums in the 1830s, to provide alternatives to those of masters and gentlemen, places that encouraged self-loathing and ridicule among workingmen. As the *New Bedford Workingmen's Press* pointed out in an article describing their new lyceum:

It is an incontrovertible fact, that the non-producers assume a feeling of superiority over the producers. The former, having more time for study, become the most intelligent, and when associated with the latter professedly for improvement, are too apt to take advantage of honest error, and by means of *satire* to destroy their confidence and kill their ambition; thereby subverting the very purposes for which they associated.[31]

Taken out of context, these lyceums might be viewed as simple attempts at self-help; viewed within the context of a struggle with capitalists over leisure, they emerge as a clear and self-conscious appropriation of territory that the bourgeoisie had claimed as its own. Another, more colorful example of this phenomenon would develop in the 1840s with the creation of the Washingtonian Temperance movement in which many of the local societies and many of the national speakers, who were reformed alcoholics, were of decidedly plebian backgrounds.

This contest would be carried even further in the struggle for shorter hours during the 1840s. The workers who led the movement pushed their arguments over morality and time to more radical conclusions than had developed in the 1830s. The idea of working longer hours, even for extra pay, receded as the concept of leisure became increasingly inalienable. After the economic hard times of the late 1830s and early 1840s, working people were no doubt particularly conscious of the need for more jobs—jobs that might be created if the length of the workday was shortened. But more important, these labor struggles were taking place in the context of a moral reform movement that had moved toward concepts of perfectability in the 1840s, and in which religious salvation had become more closely intertwined with issues of morality. The theological revolution that placed a growing emphasis on individual conscience had spawned a variety of movements predicated on the potential of human beings to do good and perfect society. Perfectionism shaped the antislavery and temperance movements, and inspired even more radical positions, such as nonresistance. But when used by working people to assess their conditions of labor, perfectionism reinforced the demand for a ten-hour day as a starting point, if not the goal, of human perfectability.[32] The moral arguments that emerged were not mere window dressing to make the economic arguments more respectable but were part of an increasingly radical critique of society in which workers sought to redefine their relationship to their work and the nature of their autonomy.

Thus, when the women of Lowell formed the Lowell Female Labor Reform Association, they spoke of the minds given all human beings, "capable of eternal progression and improvement!" Looking around at their system of labor, and stressing the need for a shorter workday so that they might develop their intellectual attainments, they argued: "It now only remains for us to throw off the shackles which are binding us in ignorance and servitude and which prevent us from rising to that scale of being for which God designed us." The Fitchburg Workingmen's Association articulated similar sentiments in the preamble to their constitution by promising "to advocate so far as we understand them all principles of *truth* and *vitality*—so far as circumstances will allow assist the unfortunate and *elevate mankind.*"[33]

In Fall River, this inalienability was expressed by demanding time to perform the various duties required for salvation. The responsibilities were numerous, including family prayer, religious devotion, reading of the Scriptures, and attendance at church services. An anonymous writer to the *Mechanic* in Fall River spelled out the threat that his workday posed to his spiritual life. *"I cannot devote more than ten hours per day to physical labor,"* "H" wrote, *"and appropriate sufficient time to the regular, faithful and solemn discharge of the religious duties binding upon me."* How was family prayer possible when children and parents collapsed with exhaustion on returning home from work? And every day that passed without family devotion would bring each member of the household closer to backsliding. The maintenance of Christian faith required constant watchfulness. Searching the Scriptures, a fundamental responsibility of Protestant faith, required even more time. "[H]ow can the poor mechanic, and operative in the mill, search the scriptures daily and faithfully," he demanded to know, "and at the same time be compelled to labor 'fourteen hours' per day?"[34] The regular, daily demands of Protestantism meshed well with the idea of a shorter workday. It demanded constant nurturing, which could not be deferred to the leisure of a more distant future.

With these rationales for shorter working hours and increased leisure time, workers were able to adopt a tone of moral superiority to their employers. Thus, when the mechanics and operatives of Lowell held a large meeting on May 16, 1844, to fight their long hours of work, "moderation, kindness and love" were the key phrases in their strategy. To behave differently would only be to sink to the level of their employers. While those at the meeting agreed to do all they could to ameliorate the wretched condition of working people, "who have too long been oppressed by the heartlessness and avarice of combinations and individuals," they counseled that "we should not forget that we are dealing with men & brethren, whose errors we are not to imitate, but to reform."[35]

The long hours that employers required were the result of avarice, and long hours at work were viewed as a moral weakness. One speaker at a rally of workers in Lowell in 1844 pursued the "striking likeness between the rum-drinker and the capitalist" because neither was able to control his baser urges. Just as the drunkard craved ever larger amounts of alcohol, the capitalist craved ever larger profits. Working long hours was not a sign of moral virtue, but moral weakness on the part of workingmen. Editors of the *Mechanic* if Fall River, Massachusetts, urged their readers to follow the example of the Washingtonian Temperance Society when dealing with those who worked long hours. "They should be looked upon more in pitty [sic] than in anger . . . we must endeavor to raise them from their degraded state, and make them feel once more that they are MEN."[36] Echoing the concept of alcoholism in the early nineteenth century was a parallel problem: workaholism. The workaholic did not know when to stop, letting work time overwhelm and destroy the rational world of leisure.

# IV

Industry was redefined by these workers to include mental as well as physical activity. Leisure time was the appropriate sphere for mental activity, just as worktime was the appropriate sphere for physical activity. When Huldah Stone, a former operative in the Lowell mills, spoke of industry as "not only a duty binding on all men, but . . . one of the most fruitful sources of real enjoyment and peace," she also pointed out that she did not mean "mere manual labor." Broadening her description to include leisure activities, she argued, "By cultivating a love of industry whether physical or mental, we throw around our frail tenement a shield which neither despair nor vice can penetrate."[37]

For workers committed to the rational and moral use of their leisure, time was not to be equated with money. If anything, their arguments have moved away from this equation rather than toward it, as demands for overtime pay were dropped. In critiquing the idea that incessant work was somehow inherently virtuous, New England workers anticipated the criticisms that Max Weber later would make of the bourgeois work ethic, in which the need to labor continuously had lost its religious underpinnings and existed for its own sake, as "an iron cage."[38]

Describing a commitment to unremitting toil as an assault on moral and virtuous behavior, workers asserted a new work ethic, more in keeping with the requirements of nineteenth-century Protestantism. Salvation required a limit on wage work and an expansion of a distinct world of leisure with its own demands on individual time. This was not a leisure world in which time would be passed; rather, it would be improved. Instead of advocating "eight hours for what we will," as workers would do a few decades later, these workers demanded leisure to shape and discipline their wills, to improve their moral faculties, and to reform the world.

The contrast with the eight-hour movement at the end of the century is worth pursuing a bit, for it brings us back to our original question about the class implications of the struggle over time. The struggle for an eight-hour day in Worcester, as described by Roy Rosensweig, grew out of a defense of working-class leisure activities such as the culture of the saloon, which represented an "alternative culture." Drawing on the categories of Raymond Williams, Rosensweig argues that such an alternative culture rejected but did not challenge the values of the dominant culture. In large part, this particular kind of response reflected ethnic differences that not only distinguished workers from employers but divided workers among themselves.[39]

But a cultural heritage of Protestantism and moral reform did not divide New England workers from employers in a similar way during the 1830s and 1840s. A shared culture, it was a far more potent field of battle as each side sought to inflict its interpretation of morality on the other. Wage earners demanding a shorter workday were attempting to usurp what employers felt to be an important prerogative: dictating the terms of moral behavior. This was not an attempt to become middle class, but an attempt to limit middle-class domination of shared cultural concerns. Morality and religion in New England were cohesive forces for working people, complementing an ideology of republicanism. If working people did not succeed in establishing a ten-hour day for all wage earners in New England during this period, that should not surprise us too much; they confronted a unusually powerful and cohesive opposition among their employers. What is more important to recognize is the extent to which working people developed their own interpretation of work and leisure in the early years of industrialization.

## NOTES

1. *Manchester Operative* (Manchester, New Hampshire), quoted in the *Mechanic* (Fall River, Massachusetts), May 25, 1844.

2. For a discussion of where, when, and how ten-hour days were achieved in New England, see David Montgomery, *Beyond Equality: Labor and the Radical Republicans, 1862–1872* (New York, 1967), pp. 230–334; Norman Ware, *The Industrial Worker, 1840–1860* (New York, 1964), pp. 143–148, 154–162; and Charles E. Persons *et al.*, *Labor Laws and Their Enforcement, with Special Reference to Massachusetts* (New York, 1911).

3. Paul Johnson, *A Shopkeeper's Millennium: Society and Revivals in Rochester, New York, 1815–1837* (New York, 1978), pp. 137, 121; and Anthony Wallace, *Rockdale, the Growth of an American Village in the Early Industrial Revolution* (New York, 1978), pp. 388–394.

4. Bruce Laurie, *The Working People of Philadelphia, 1800–1850* (Philadelphia, 1980), p. 143; and Sean Wilentz, *Chants Democratic: New York City and the Rise of the American Working Class, 1788–1850* (New York, 1984), pp. 344–349. Since artisans in New York had already achieved a ten-hour day, wages were more important to them than hours.

5. Wilentz, *Chants Democratic*, p. 343; and Laurie, *Working People of Philadelphia*, p. 146.

6. Lengthening workdays by "lighting up" New England factories is discussed in the *Mechanic*, September 21, 1844. For a discussion of the way in which some

working people faced unemployment during winter months, see Bruce Laurie, " 'Nothing on Compulsion': Life Styles of Philadelphia Artisans, 1820–1850," *Labor History* 15 (1974): 341–343.

7. *Providence Patriot and Columbian Phenix,* October 1 and 15, 1831. For an excellent discussion of this incident, see Gary John Kornblith, "From Artisans to Businessmen: Master Mechanics in New England, 1789–1850," 2 vols., Ph.D. dissertation, Princeton University, 1983, pp. 504–505.

8. *Artisan,* May 17, 1832; Kornblith, "Artisans to Businessmen," pp. 511–513.

9. Thomas Dublin, *Women at Work: The Transformation of Work and Community in Lowell, Massachusetts, 1826–1860* (New York, 1979), p. 108.

10. Ibid., pp. 109–110; and Paul Faler, *Mechanics and Manufacturers in the Early Industrial Revolution, Lynn, Massachusetts, 1780–1860* (New York, 1981), p. 98.

11. *Mechanic,* June 8, May 18, and August 10, 1844.

12. Mary Blewett, "Work, Gender and the Artisan Tradition in New England Shoemaking, 1780–1860," *Journal of Social History* 17 (1983): 230–233; and *Mechanic,* August 3, 1844.

13. An excellent comparison of conditions in a factory town such as Lowell with those in the Philadelphia region may be found in Philip Scranton, *Proprietary Capitalism: The Textile Manufacture at Philadelphia, 1800–1885* (New York, 1983), Part I.

14. *Columbia Centinel,* April 23, 1825; *Independent Chronicle and Boston Patriot,* May 19, 1832; both reprinted in John R. Commons, ed., *A Documentary History of American Industrial Society,* 10 vols. (Cleveland, 1910), 6:79–82.

15. *Artisan* (Pawtucket, Providence, and Boston), January 5, 1832; *Mechanic,* May 4, 1844.

16. Discussions of the effects of republicanism on the ideology of antebellum workers may be found in Alan Dawley, *Class and Community: The Industrial Revolution in Lynn* (Cambridge, Mass., 1976); Howard Rock, *Artisans of the New Republic: The Tradesmen of New York City in the Age of Jefferson* (New York, 1979); as well as in the previously cited works of Faler, Laurie, Wilentz, and Dublin. The uses of republicanism in the struggle for a shorter workday, specifically, are explored by Kornblith, "Artisans to Businessmen," pp. 501–514; and David Roediger, "The Movement for a Shorter Working Day in the United States Before 1866," Ph.D. dissertation, Northwestern University, 1980.

17. Gordon Wood, *The Creation of the American Republic,, 1776–1787* (Chapel Hill, N.C., 1969); Nathan Hatch, *The Sacred Cause of Liberty: Republican Thought and the Millennium in Revolutionary New England* (New Haven, 1977); and James Turner, *Without God, Without Creed, The Origins of Unbelief in America* (Baltimore, 1985), pp. 83–84.

18. Mathias Haines, Diary, 1840–1842. Manuscript collection, New Hampshire Historical Society.

19. Charles Metcalf to Mother, June 2, 1844. Metcalf-Adams Letters, 1796–1866, Museum of American Textile History, North Andover, Massachusetts.

20. Faler, *Mechanics and Manufacturers,* pp. 102–106, 137. For arguments about

the way in which employers used religion and morality to further their own business interests, see Johnson, *A Shopkeeper's Millennium;* and Wallace, *Rockdale*. Daniel T. Rodgers provides a penetrating analysis of the contradictions emerging in "the work ethic" as a result of industrialization in *The Work Ethic in Industrial America, 1850–1920* (Chicago, 1974).

21. Cynthia Shelton, *The Mills of Manayunk, Industrialization and Social Conflict in the Philadelphia Region, 1787–1837* (Baltimore, 1986), pp. 34–35, 48–49; Robert G. Layer, *Earnings of Cotton Mill Operatives, 1825–1914* (Cambridge, Mass., 1955), p. 70; Howard M. Gitelman, *Workingmen of Waltham, Mobility in American Urban Industrial Development, 1850–1890* (Baltimore, 1974), p. 15; Dublin, *Women at Work;* and Thomas Dublin, "Rural–Urban Migrants in Industrial New England: The Case of Lynn, Massachusetts, in the Mid-Nineteenth Century," *Journal of American History* 73 (1986): 625.

22. "Resolution of Master Carpenters, from the *Columbian Centinel,* April 20, 1825," Commons, *Documentary History,* 6:70–71. Resolutions of "Gentlemen engaged in building the present season," *Columbian Centinel,* April 23, 1825, in Commons, *Documentary History,* 6:79.

23. *Mechanic,* June 15, 1844.

24. Mary Ryan, *Cradle of the Middle Class: The Family in Oneida County, New York, 1790–1865* (New York, 1981).

25. Dublin points out that this economic independence was more characteristic of the New England experience than of the European. Dublin, *Women at Work,* pp. 40–41.

26. Jonathan Prude, *The Coming of Industrial Order, Town and Factory Life in Rural Massachusetts, 1810–1860* (New York, 1983), p. 118.

27. Blewett, "Work, Gender and the Artisan Tradition," pp. 222–225.

28. Wallace, *Rockdale,* Chap. 7; and Barbara Tucker, *Samuel Slater and the Origins of the American Textile Industry, 1790–1860* (Ithaca, N.Y., 1984), Chap. 7.

29. Charles Metcalf to Mrs. Joseph A. Metcalf, June 2, 1844. Metcalf Collection, Merrimack Valley Textile Museum.

30. *Artisan,* May 18, 1832.

31. Reprinted in the *Artisan,* November 15, 1832.

32. John L. Thomas, "Romantic Reform in America, 1815–1865," *American Quarterly* 17 (Winter 1965): 656–681; and Ronald G. Walters, *American Reformers, 1815–1860* (New York, 1978), p. 28.

33. *Voice of Industry,* February 27, 1846. Records of the Workingmen's Association of Fitchburg, 1844–1845, manuscript collection, Fitchburg Historical Society.

34. *Mechanic,* May 25, 1844. For further discussion of the influence of religion on the New England labor movement during this period, see Teresa Murphy, "Labor, Religion and Moral Reform in Fall River, Massachusetts, 1800–1845," Ph.D. dissertation, Yale University, 1982; and Jama Lazerow, "A Good Time Coming: Religion and the Emergence of Labor Activism in Antebellum New England," Ph.D. dissertation, Brandeis University, 1983; Jama Lazerow, "Religion and Labor Re-

form in Antebellum America: The World of William Field Young,'' *American Quarterly* 38 (1986); and Prude, *The Coming of Industrial Order*. Much of this work has been inspired by Herbert Gutman's landmark essay on a slightly later period, ''Protestantism and the American Labor Movement: The Christian Spirit in the Gilded Age,'' *American Historical Review* 72 (1966).

35. *Mechanic*, June 1, 1984.

36. *New England Operative*, reprinted in the *Mechanic*, August 10, 1844; and *Mechanic*, May 4, 1844.

37. *Voice of Industry*, December 11, 1846; reprinted from the *Universalist Watchman*.

38. Max Weber, *The Protestant Ethic and the Spirit of Capitalism* (New York, 1976), p. 181.

39. Roy Rosenzweig, *Eight Hours for What We Will: Workers and Leisure in an Industrial City, 1870–1920* (New York, 1983).

# 5

## The Political Ideology of Short Time: England, 1820–1850

### Stewart Weaver

I

IN THE international and comparative context of this book, the early-nineteenth-century English factory movement has a simple and unique claim to our attention. Not only did it set the economic and bureaucratic precedents associated with legislative control of the working day; it also provided the first effective example of popular industrial protest. There had, of course, been movements of protest before, some of them—those joined in the 1810s by the weavers and framework knitters, for instance—specifically directed toward reform of industrial conditions. But the factory movement was the first to unite the general interests of labor behind a specific political objective: a legally defined and broadly applicable ten-hour working day. Moreover, the factory movement was the first to achieve a significant measure of success. Although officially applicable only to women and children, the Ten Hours Act of 1847 in practice affected the regulation of all textile workers.[1] Its passage, over the strenuous objections of most liberal maunfacturers and with, in spite of its technical exclusion of adult men, the unreserved approval of the workers, was the culmination of a popular struggle that began in 1818 when the Manchester Cotton Spinners Association, under the leadership of John Doherty, began to collect funds toward public agitation in support of a short-time bill.[2]

By then, a few paternally minded masters had already raised the issue. The Health and Morals of Apprentices Act of 1802,[3] sponsored through Parliament by Sir Robert Peel (father of the future prime minister), set a twelve-hour limit to the working day of children who had left their homes permanently and bound themselves to cotton masters. Together with the advent of steam power, which made it possible for masters to establish them-

77

selves in heavily populated urban areas, Peel's act put an end to industrial apprenticeship, and in 1815, he and Robert Owen, who had tried various short-time arrangements in his mills at New Lanark, started a campaign for a ten-hour day for "free" child labor generally.[4] The act they won in 1819[5] set a twelve-hour day for children, applied only to cotton mills, and was a grave disappointment to trade unionists who had joined the campaign in the hope of gaining some more palpable compensation for their recent defeat in a strike over spinners' wages. In Parliament, the cause languished (although the tepidly radical Whig Sir John Cam Hobhouse managed to win two minor improvements in 1825 and 1829); but in the north, where according to one Richard Guest the movement had turned the workers into "Political Citizens," "a fair day's work for a fair day's wage" remained a popular rallying cry throughout the 1820s.[6]

Things were thus well under way when Richard Oastler's Tory radical conscience stirred him in 1830 to launch an impassioned attack on what he called "Yorkshire Slavery."[7] Through sheer rhetorical brilliance and indefatigable demaogouery, Oastler, "the Factory King," brought the issue of short time to national public attention, and over the next few years all the essential and immediately recognizable elements of the movement fell into place. The MPs Michael Sadler, Lord Ashley, and John Fielden in turn kept the pressure on Parliament. Workers in Huddersfield, Leeds, and Bradford formed "short time committees" in their support. Across the Pennines, in the cotton districts of Lancashire, the unions threatened (and once attempted) an eight- or ten-hour strike. The government responded in 1833 with an act that set an eight-hour day for children,[8] but the radicals were not satisfied. In 1836, when a few liberal members of Parliament, led by Sir Charles Poulett Thomson, tried to rescind the existing act, "the whole of the manufacturing districts rose *en masse,* as if ignited by spontaneous combusion."[9] Thomson withdrew his motion to rescind, but not before the workers had angrily reverted to the uniform ten-hour demand.

From 1836, for reasons I discuss below, the factory movement merged indistinguishably with Chartism—the popular struggle for universal manhood suffrage. Short time reappeared as a separate issue only as Chartism waned in the aftermath of an unsuccessful general strike in 1842.[10] The government responded with a twelve-hour bill that even most MPs found inadequate; but Peel threatened to resign if Ashley's ten-hour amendment to it carried, and by nearly 140 votes, it did not. "Such is the power and such the exercise of ministerial influence!" mourned Ashley, while in the north, workers launched a new campaign against "ministerial orchestrations."[11] 'The working people [had] got it into their heads that they work too hard,'' Fielden warned the House of Commons in May 1844; to deny them the Ten Hours Bill would be to encourage insurrection.[12] After an impressive series of public demonstrations, Ashley reintroduced the Ten Hours Bill in January 1846, but by then the House had become absorbed in the repeal of the Corn Laws. Peel's government fell at the end of the year, and his successor, Lord John Russell, came in pledged to eleven hours. Fielden mounted the final agitation, defeated the ministry's eleven-hour amendment to his own Ten Hours Bill (Ashley had resigned from the House on his conversion to free trade), and won the necessary third reading on May 3, 1847. For the first time in history, Marx was later to claim, "the political economy of the middle class [had] succumbed to the political economy of the working class." [13]

Given his familiar contempt for social palliatives, Marx's evident enthusiasm for the Ten Hours Act suggests the need to reconsider its political significance. One feels quite properly hesitant to do so, for of all the subjects raised in this otherwise indispensable anthology, the English ten-hour movement is probably the least neglected. Its simple narrative history has been written more than once. [14] Each of its several leaders has found his biographer. [15] And the wealth of unusually accessible material it generated— pamphlets, newspapers, reports of royal commissions—has been put to a disconcerting array of historical and sociological uses. That the political ideology of the movement should somehow have eluded us is remarkable, but nevertheless true; for we have yet to approach it from a genuinely popular perspective. A tribute to the accommodative genius of the English government one moment, a sordid instance of bourgeois "social control" the next, short time has been wholly usurped from those whose idea it was. Even scholars whose specific concern is popular or radical movements treat it as something either granted or imposed from above. [16] And, in the end, granted or imposed from above it was. But the reasons for which something is granted can differ from the reasons for which it is demanded. My purpose here is, first, to identify in broad and schematic fashion three interpretive assumptions (one "Whig," one "Marxist," and one "Tory") that have worked to obscure a popular ideology of short time that was in its assertive rhetoric expressly and deliberately political. From the point of view of the workers, a legally defined ten-hour day was not just another social palliative. Particularly when extended to adult men (as workers insisted it be), it promised independence from the master, freedom from the mill, and, in a more abstract sense, the restoration of the lost rights of English citizenship.

## II

In its crassest form, the "Whiggish" assumption that early factory legislation marked the historical origins of the British welfare state is both the most pervasive and the easiest of the three to discredit. How was it, historians have asked, that a society steeped in the doctrines of Adam Smith and increasingly committed to *laissez-faire* liberalism should nevertheless have taken the first faltering steps toward centralized, regulatory bureaucracy? How was it that a visionary few, or, in Samuel Kydd's words, "a small band of men united together for a common purpose," managed "by force of conviction" to stem the noninterventionist tide? Such questions as these no longer fuel a full-blown academic industry, as they did in the middle decades of this century, but they continue to define the terms within which we think of factory reform. And not without reason, for the Ten Hours Act in particular did represent a momentous departure from prevailing economic orthodoxy. In effecting the uniform protection of *all* textile workers, it obliterated the distinction between "free" and "unfree" labor on which liberal market theory rested.[17] "Was it not contrary to common sense," asked Joseph Hume when, within days of repealing the tariff on corn, the House seemed ready to pass the Ten Hours Bill, "that [we] should one day be adopting a measure to relieve capital and industry from trammels, and on another, imposing them on . . . the capital of the labouring man [and] the master who employed him?" From the more approving perspective of the popular *Northern Star,* passage of the Ten Hours Act was "one of the greatest events of the century," for it had "introduced a very different principle into our legislation from that which has unhappily guided our lawmakers of late." By 1861, William Newmarch had already christened the act the turning point of the Victorian age, so I do not doubt that it was, at least, to quote Asa Briggs, "a genuine stage in the process of the conversion of values."[18]

But to see short time exclusively as a stage in the process of anything is to obscure beyond recognition its contemporary significance. The more sophisticated genealogists of the welfare state concede this. To their minds, protective legislation proceeded not from any fundamental, deliberate, or even acknowledged shift in Victorian values but from a series of erratic, *ad hoc,* even inadvertent responses to specific and exceptionally intolerable industrial circumstances. Thus *laissez-faire* remained the intellectual order of the day, while the collectivist state came in unnoticed through the back door.[19] Leaving aside the familiar and most telling criticisms of this and similar variants of bureaucratic evolutionism—that they remove ideology from history altogether, that they substitute administrative accident for historical agency—I want only to point out that, protestations to the contrary notwithstanding, their proponents share the same crippling teleology they mean to avoid. They concede, for instance, that factory reform was not, in and of itself, a conscious, measured step toward state interventionism; but they then proceed to lump it together with all sorts of other reformist initiatives that together make up the unfortunate first stirrings of a bureaucratic behemoth.[20] For the evidently more vulgar "origins of the welfare state," they have simply substituted "self-expanding administrative process" or "interior collectivist momentum"—abstractions that consign those who fought for short time to historical oblivion.[21]

Indeed, short time is particularly ill suited to any form of presentist interpretation. As Brian Harrison has pointed out, those who fought for it shared none of the faith in the future, none of the modernist administrative enthusiasms, that distinguished other social reformers.[22] Although not, as I argue shortly, the "Tory radicals" of academic imagination, hour reformers did hold the collectivist implications of their own cause in conscious if ambivalent contempt. Moreover, factory reform consistently eludes the sort of party–political analysis that teleological search for the origins of the welfare state inevitably involves.[23] "The discussions and divisions on the Factory Bill have been of the most confused and ludicrous kind," noted the *Leeds Times* in an oft-quoted but little considered passage. "Whigs, Tories and radicals are jumbled together in inextricable political disorder."[24] If we could sort out the confusion and impose some ideological order on parliamentary support for ten hours, we would have done much to further the cause of administrative genealogy. But we would again have lost sight of the thousands for whom short time was an end in itself. Only as a popular ideology will short time begin to make sense—a popular ideology well removed from our own postwar preoccupations.

## III

One might then reasonably expect Marxist or labor historians—those more concerned with popular struggles than with administrative reforms—to have come to better terms with the significance of short time. And so, on occasion, they have done. "The Factory Movement," wrote E. P. Thompson in *The Making of the English Working Class*, "represented less a growth of middle-class humanitarianism than an affirmation of human rights by the workers themselves."[25] This is the point that needs to be developed because, with few exceptions, labor historians after Thompson, even those who acknowledge his political influence, have been constrained by the second of our broadly defined assumptions: that short time, far from being in the workers' genuine interest, was in fact a bourgeois ploy to undermine proletarian militance.[26] That militance in any form, popular or proletarian, waned after 1847–1848 is indisputable, and the passage of the Ten Hours Act, which demonstrated a trend toward Liberal accommodation of industrial demands, may help explain why it did.[27] But to imagine a policy of conscious concession on the part of ruling elites is to overestimate greatly their political sophisitication. None realized, in 1847, that the effect of short time would be to assuage the sense of grievance on which collective militance depended; most, in fact, joined Peel in worrying that to concede the ten-hour day would be to encourage *more* collective radical demands.[28] Moreover, there remained, in the House of Commons and in manufacturing circles generally, a hard core of *laissez-faire* ideologues for whom factory regulation still represented an unthinkable violation of sacred principle. These yielded in 1847 neither hopefully nor purposefully, but angrily, out of a reluctant necessity imposed on them by an unparalleled agitation.

A second problem with the conspiratorial idea of "liberalization," at least as John Foster employs it, is that it consigns to the ideological wilderness of "false consciousness" workers for whom short time, as an end in itself, constituted hard-won political progress. I understand that in this post-structuralist, Foucaultean age, we are advised not to attend seriously to the things people say. "Words taken at their face value," Joan Scott warns us, "become one more datum to collect and the notion of how meaning is constructed . . . is lost."[29] Fair enough. What "meaning" those thousands of workers who marched through St. Peter's Fields in May of 1833 chanting

> We will have the Ten Hours Bill
> That we will, that we will;
> Or the land will ne'er be still
> Ne'er be still, ne'er be still;
> Parliament say what they will,
> We will have the Ten Hours Bill.

might have been (unbeknown to themselves, of course) "constructing," I gladly leave to the Parisian experts to determine.[30] But until they have done so, I see no reason to consider such a chant evidence of workers' complicity in their own oppression. Factory reform *was* arguably in the economic interest of well-established masters. By restricting the ruthless competitive practices of small firms "on the make," it may have worked to preserve the relative advantage of the capitalist elite. And, as proponents of 'social control" theory argue, it may have abetted the institution of regular work discipline.[31] But to see it as essentially oppressive requires feats of interpretive imagination no historian ought to perform. All the social-control theory in the world will not get around the fact that to work a man ten hours is more humane than to work him twelve or fifteen.

Like the Whiggish argument that factory reform represents the origins of a benevolent welfare state, the Marxist argument that it represents a liberal concession by which the middle classes preserved their social and political ascendancy harbors a teleological falacy: It judges nineteenth-century reforms from a presentist, democratic perspective and then, naturally finding them wanting, concludes that they must have been meant to serve some conservative political purpose. I accept that the *effect* of such reforms as the Ten Hours Bill may have been to preserve the status quo; but we must not, in my view, conclude therefore that preserving the status quo was their *purpose*. As far as popular radicals were concerned, a ten-hour day constituted real, even revolutionary progress. Moreover, it signified a conscious willingness on the part of middle- and working-class representatives to enter into constructive dialogue. There was nothing unnatural, conspiratorial, or covert about this radical *rapprochement*. Until the betrayal of 1832, middle- and working-class radicals had been virtually indistinguishable. They held in common a progressive critique of a society that remained, even at midcentury, staunchly aristocratic. Beneath its militant rhetoric, the popular movement had always displayed a variety of liberal tendencies, one of which was a decided preference for peaceable, gradual reform. As the hungry 1840s gave way to the relatively prosperous 1850s, popular radicalism consciously allied itself with the responsible form of liberalism even then beginning to gather around Gladstone.[32]

Consider, for instance, the political progress of William Johnson Fox, the liberal pundit from Norfolk who eventually displaced John Fielden as radical MP for Oldham. After an already distinguished career as a preacher and man of letters, Fox achieved public prominence as an orator for the Anti-Corn Law League. He was a Benthamite, but like his friend and literary colleague, John Stuart Mill, he tempered his utilitarian rationality with a romantic, almost mystical idealism. During the parliamentary reform agitation, he had joined Cobbett in addressing public meetings in Lincoln's Inn Fields. He believed in universal suffrage and was a strong supporter of the People's Charter. And although he affiliated himself with the politicians of the Manchester School, he approved of factory legislation and had long been committed to Fielden's Ten Hours Bill.[33] Fox was not, then, as Fielden after his defeat bitterly reckoned, a tool in the hands of masters eager to resist factory reform—a "stalking-horse to gull the people out of the real fruits of the Ten Hours Bill." Rather, he was a conscientious dissenting minister, whose simultaneous commitment to free trade and factory reform made him, much as Fielden had always been, a logical electoral choice for both masters and men. That there was some element of political conspiracy in this is, I suppose, possible. But to a certain extent W. J. Fox and the class of mill owners he represented had come to accept factory reform in earnest sincerity. The passage of the Ten Hours Act in 1847, and Fox's subsequent election for the radical borough of Oldham, augured a spirit of benign accommodation; they were the first manifestations of what Trgyve Tholfsen has subtly, and I think accurately, described as "the mellowing of middle-class liberalism."[34]

## IV

The suggestion that liberals had anything but inveterate hostility to short time raises immediate objection among those who revere the legend of Tory radicalism. Neither a Benthamite interventionist invention nor any form of liberal capitalist accommodation, short time, the legend has it, was the hard-won achievement of conservative humanitarians who, in the manner of William Wilberforce, brought the plight of the textile worker to public attention by force of Christian indignation. J. T. Ward, the factory movement's only modern definitive historian, still speaks of its "essential Toryism." Similarly, Patrick Joyse finds in the late Victorian period a persistent association between factory reform and what he calls "Tory populism." But this particular legend, or assumption, is not a strictly academic one. Conservative politicians from Disraeli to Macmillan proudly laid claim to short time, considering it an irrevocable part of their Tory radical inheritance. "During the last thirty or fifty years there has been a great deal of what is called social legislation," remembered Joseph Chamberlain in 1904, long after his conversion to Conservatism. "By whom has it been promoted? By the Conservative party. . . . You owe all your factory legislation to Lord Shaftesbury as its originator."[35]

The points of political contact between nostalgic, agrarian, medievally minded conservatives and stridently progressive, even socialist popular radicals are, to be sure, real, familiar, and in need of no further rehearsal. Shaftesbury, known then still as Ashley, was, until 1846, if not the originator, at least the parliamentary sponsor of the Ten Hours Act. An extremely self-righteous evangelist, he imparted to the entire short-time movement a strain of Christian paternalism. Among his more earnest supporters were Lord John Manners and Benjamin Disraeli—the two leading figures in a youthful coterie of medievalists known as "Young England."[36] The popular leader of the factory movement in Yorkshire was Richard Oastler, a church-and-king Tory passionately committed to "the altar, the throne, and the cottage." Marx and Engels did not imagine what they contemptuously described as feudal socialism; nor was Halévy wrong to suggest that, by 1830, the Tories had come to think of themselves as the party of the people.[37] As an emotional, intellectual, and rhetorical inclination, Tory radicalism was probably more pervasive than we know.

But as an explanatory construct it has long outlived its usefulness. As David Roberts argued long ago, to what should have been our satisfaction, conservative indignation seldom translated into political activism on the floor of the House of Commons.[38] Indeed, it was his own Tory party that Ashley blamed for obstructing the Ten Hours Bill. "All Peel's affinities are towards

wealth and capital,'' he mourned to his diary in 1842. ''His heart is mani-
festly towards the millowners, his lips occasionally for the operatives.''[39]
The operatives themselves, meanwhile, and their popular radical allies, deeply
distrusted Ashley, whose sense of paternal mission struck them as self-serv-
ing and insincere. ''Lord Ashley is putting himself very forward as the *children's friend,*'' wrote J. M. Cobbett (son of William) to John Fielden in
1840. ''I see nothing wrong in his acquiring the name and fame and credit
if he will do the work.''[40] But increasingly it was the operatives themselves
who did the work that counted, and when, in January 1846, Ashley resigned
from Parliament in a crisis of conscience over the repeal of the Corn Laws,
and sponsorship of the Ten Hours Bill devolved upon Fielden, once a child
laborer, popular radicals were jubilant. ''No working man feels more anxious upon the subject than [he],'' said Feargus O'Connor's *Northern Star,*
''and no one can, we believe, be possessed of more zeal upon the subject
than he is.''[41] Though himself a master, Fielden spoke in the voice of Cob-
bettite populism; that it was he and not Ashley who ultimately wrung the
Ten Hours Act out of a reluctant House of Commons is, to my mind, among
the more suggestive overlooked facts of early-Victorian social history.

For not only was Fielden a ''popular,'' as opposed to a ''Tory,'' radical;
he was also an industrialist—among the most successful in Lancashire. To
be sure, paternal myth can accommodate benevolent employers; but Fielden,
though conscientious, was no philanthropist. He was an aggressive, profit-
minded, free-trading competitor; economic as much as humanitarian considerations lay behind his commitment to short time. And judging from the
number of textile firms that supported his legislation—over 900 petitioned
Parliament for a Ten Hours Act in 1847—he was alone in none of this.[42]
The more flamboyant factory reformers were certainly Tory agriculturalists,
opposed to free trade and increasingly resentful of England's industrial progress. Correspondingly, the more vehement antireformers were strident northern industrialists who swelled the ranks of the Anti-Corn Law League. But
within the less renowned, less dogmatic ranks of both the short-time and
free-trade movements was a growing trend toward, if not cooperation, then
at least reciprocal acquiescence. ''I think it would be highly honourable to
this House,'' said the liberal Macaulay in support of the Ten Hours Bill,

to make in one week, as far as it is in our power, a reparation for two great errors
of two different kinds; for, Sir, as lawgivers, we have errors of two different kinds
to confess and repair. We have done that which we ought not to have done; we
have left undone that which we ought to have done. We have regulated that which
we ought to have left to regulate itself; we have left unregulated that which it was
our especial business to have regulated.[43]

Even thus couched in the familiar rhythms of Christian prayer, Macaulay's plea would not sway protectionist Tory radicals, whose part in the progress of short time thus remained purely rhetorical.

Outside Parliament, the rhetoric may have been less empty. Richard Oastler was a genuinely popular figure, one whose scarcely veiled revolutionary threats kept him easily abreast of workers' demands. J. R. Stephens, the apocalyptic preacher whose fiery declamations against capital and tyranny actually landed him in prison as one of the first Chartist martyrs, was devoutly conservative, the "evangel of retributive Toryism." [44] But these two and some few well-known others aside, there were in fact few factory reformers to whom the label Tory radical usefully applies. Most, after all, joined to their demand for short time a political faith in universal suffrage—the one feature of the radical program that Oastler and Stephens specifically rejected. Moreover, the ten-hour day, as an explicit political demand, arose not from Oastler's famous "White Slavery" campaign in Yorkshire in 1830 but, as we have seen, from Doherty's Cotton Spinners' Association in Manchester twelve years earlier. After Oastler had decided to throw in his lot with the reformers, Doherty, Fielden, and other popular radicals expressed reservations over his avowed Toryism; on one occasion, in halfhearted collaboration with Robert Owen, they tried to wrest control of the factory movement in Yorkshire from him. But, ultimately, they were far too practical to discourage his assistance in what was, for all their differences of motive, a common cause. Oastler was a supremely gifted speaker. His mere presence on the platform did more than anything else to inspire a ten-hour meeting. But before the meeting and after, it was the workers' organizations—the unions, the friendly societies, the workingman's associations, and the short-time committees—that sustained the movement from which Oastler drew his following. As a determining popular influence, Tory radicalism scarcely existed.

## V

To their credit, sociologists have been arguing for some time that humanitarian indignation is an insufficient explanation for collective radical action. Neil Smelser has pointed out that it could not account for the delayed emergence of the factory movement some years after the first exposure of industrial conditions. Nor could it, he said, account for the reformers' exclusive attention to textile production when human misery by almost any definition was greater in other trades. [45] At the same time, Smelser's contention that the factory movement represented an irrational response to "disturbances" in traditional family patterns is unpersuasive; Craig Calhoun has shown that collective action tended to occur in precisely those regions where

Smelser's "disturbances" obtained least.[46] The prevailing value of Smelser's work and, for that matter, the work of his equally sociologically minded critics is that it does locate the impetus for short time within the working-class communities themselves. The gist of Calhoun's argument, for example—that the ten-hour movement represented a collective defense by outworkers and artisans of traditional social relations—strikes me as a sensible, if, in his case, needlessly mystified revision of historical orthodoxies.[47] Economists and economic historians have been equally sensible. In their work, short time becomes, with varying emphases, the indirect expression of three basic workers' demands: job security, leisure, and high wages.[48] In Maxine Berg's view,it complemented a restrictive tax on power looms as "part of [a worker's] strategy for curtailing the machine and destroying factory production."[49]

To be sure, Berg overstates her case. Short timers were not Luddites, and destroying factory production was the farthest thing from their minds. John Fielden, for one, even opposed the tax on machinery, "for anything calculated . . . to facilitate and increase production," he said, "was a blessing to any people if the things were properly distributed."[50] At issue was *control* of the machinery. By demanding ten hours and a restrictive tax on motive power, workers were attempting to claim within the factory the same productive autonomy that had characterized artisanal outwork. To control the machine was to control the pace and level of production. Short time, the argument ran, would put an end to gluts and redefine the terms of the market to the worker's advantage. Thus, as Richard Price notes, "to talk about hours reductions led inevitably to talk about *power.*" Particularly when extended to adult men, short time moved out of the sphere of social reform and became what Price calls "a climacteric to that dialectic struggle between 'freedom' and 'control.' "[51] The Chartist Feargus O'Connor put it more simply: The ten-hour day would, he said, "proclaim the workingman's title to his share of the national wealth."[52]

All this is helpful, for it places the ideology of short time within the context of a working-class political economy inherited from William Thompson, Thomas Hodgskin, and John Gray.[53] Still missing, however, is the constitutional (and thus more explicitly political) dimension of short time inherited from Cobbett and Thomas Paine. To be sure, Cobbett's agrarian indifference to industrial issues is well known; indeed it was self-proclaimed. "I have never been into any manufacturing place without reluctance," he wrote in 1832, "I have no understanding of the matter, [and] the wondrous things that are performed in these places only serve, when I behold them, to withdraw my mind from things which I do understand."[54] But those things he understood, and against which he declaimed all his radical life—political patronage, Whig tyranny, working-class disenfranchisement—were more relevant to industrial issues than Cobbett imagined. In the minds of those aggrieved textile workers who fought for and secured his election to Parliament for the industrial borough of Oldham, Cobbett's assault on the fortress of political privilege translated naturally into a demand for ten hours. That the ten-hour movement should have emerged from the textile workers' unions in 1818 and 1819 was then no coincidence; these were "the heroic [years] of popular Radicalism," when redress of constitutional grievance was in full flood; when, according to Samuel Bamford, the works of Cobbett were being read on every hearth in the manufacturing districts; when the first great movement for parliamentary reform reached its bloody climax in St. Peter's Fields.[55] The demand for short time was part of all this; it was an alternative but not inapposite claim to political citizenship; it was about the freedom and liberty as much as the welfare and security of the industrial textile worker.

This will seem immediately unlikely to those who accept unreservedly Lenin's distinction between "trade union" and "class" consciousness. Short time, the Leninist will argue, is, like the minimum wage or workman's compensation, one of those petty demands of union organizers—a sadly acquisitive and materially minded obstacle to the political liberation of the working class. And so in certain contexts it may have been. But in early-nineteenth-century England, when "Old Corruption" still offended more than capitalism, these distinctions were not clearly drawn. What from our fully enfranchised perspective looks like a "social" cause may have promised to those involved in it a radical measure of political freedom. Thus, according to the Chartist Ernest Jones, short time was "a recruiting sergeant of democracy," a "staff of Chartist progression," an "aid to political organisation, for whereas other movements take your time away from politics," he told his working-class readers, "this gives it to you." Similarly, to the radical editors of the *Northern Star,* short time was "a Chartist question, a purely Chartist question," and they promised the "entire aid of the Chartist staff to agitate the manufacturing districts on the subject," if only the short time committees were "in earnest."[56] For Richard Oastler, Lord Ashley, Michael Sadler, and other Tory Radical leaders of the factory movement, the ten-hour day may have been a simple social ameliorative demanded by Christian conscience. But to the rank and file of the movement, and to those through whom they spoke, it was an indirect demand for political inclusion; it would, as its Chartist advocates often noted, literally *free* the worker to participate capably in public and civic affairs.

Here one might object that the collusion of factory reformers and Chartists does not necessarily establish the democratic bent of the former. Chartism, after all, may have been less a political than a social movement, less concerned with those "rights of man" expressed in the People's Charter than with food, welfare, and the conditions of industrial labor. This indeed was the view of many contemporary observers, including J. R. Stephens, himself a Chartist martyr. "Chartism is no political movement," he said approvingly a year before his arrest. "This question of universal suffrage is a knife and fork question . . . a bread and cheese question . . . and if any man asks me what I mean by universal suffrage, I would answer: that every working man in the land has the right to have a good coat to his back [and] a good dinner upon his table."[57] Similarly, from a less sympathetic, ministerial perspective, Lord John Russell:

Of the working classes who have declared their adherence to what is called the People's Charter, but few care for universal Suffrage, Vote by Ballot, or Annual Parliaments. The greater part feel the hardship of their social condition; they complain of their hard toil and insufficient wages, and imagine that Mr. Oastler or Mr. Fielden will lead them to a happy valley where their labour will be light and their wages high.[58]

But as the argumentative, oppositional tone in each case suggests, Russell and Stephens (and Carlyle and Engels and Gaskell and Eliot and all those middle-class worthies on whose testimony historians have relied to arrive at the meaning of Chartism) were in fact countering a more dominant view. The popular language of Chartism, as Stedman Jones argues, was expressly and sincerely political—concerned first with equal representation and then with economic restoration. The chartist movement, it follows, was neither the social expression of a new industrial proletariat (à la Engels) nor that of a declining preindustrial artisante (à la Eliot). It was not a social movement at all. It was the final and grandest collective expression of that popular constitutionalism epitomized by Paine. It was just what, under different appellations, it had been since the 1770s; "a critique of the corrupting effects of the concentration of political power and its corrosive influence upon a society deprived of proper means of political representation."[59]

Critics of Stedman Jones have argued, among other things, that the language of Chartism was untypical; that his analysis of political vocabulary "leaves open the issue of how he would interpret other movements—those more clearly aimed at redressing economic greivance by . . . an entire reorganization of relations of production."[60] Well, one such movement shared, I am arguing, Chartism's political language. Not, certainly, to the exclusion of all else; even Stedman Jones begrudgingly allows it to have directed a novel measure of proletarian hostility against employers as a *class*.[61] But even that tended to be couched in the traditional language of eighteenth-century radicalism; the individual "millocrat" or "steam lord" or "seigneur of the twist" was the enemy, not the collective abstraction of mill owners

in general. "We often speak hard of middlemen," wrote the editors of the
*Poor Man's Guardian,* the most precociously proletarian of all radical newspapers.

But give us middlemen like MR. FIELDEN—give us men who uniting good hearts to
sound heads will not despise or betray, nor trample on those,without whose labour
they would be nothing. Give us middlemen of this sort, and then—whatever we
may think abstractly of the institutions which engender middlemen—the individuals
themselves shall have our unpurchased and unpurchaseable praise.[62]

Class hostility there was in the 1830s and 1840s, but even in the context of
the factory movement, where Fielden appealed to the working class in its
lingering, literal sense of those who worked as opposed to those who did
not, where the political rights of labor remained the dominant rhetorical
theme, it could still be overcome.

How else are we to account for the national resonance of a measure that
would have shortened by two hours the daily labor of roughly 400,000 northern
textile workers? In 1857, Samuel Kydd recalled occasions on which "the
national mind," as he put it, had been concentrated on the factory question.[63] The parliamentary debates over the Ten Hours Act were the most
factious and exciting the veteran political observer Charles Greville could
remember, and that the *Northern Star* should have proclaimed the act's passage "one of the greatest events of the century" perhaps should not surprise
us.[64] But that from the relatively dispassionate and long-removed perspective of the *Illustrated London News* short time should still have seemed
"one of the great questions of the day" is odd, particularly when keeping
in mind that it would not then have seemed a first fateful step toward a
welfare state.[65] Short time was, of course, a potentially hurtful restriction of
the cotton textile industry, but that national prosperity rested on cotton has
never been proved. Early industrial historians probably exaggerated its importance, and contemporaries, who, again, were not conscious of passing
through some irreversible "Industrial Revolution," regarded it as a trade
much like any other. There were always liberal political economists, Nassau
Senior chief among them, who argued (in Cobbett's sarcastic paraphrase)
"that all our greatness and prosperity [and] superiority over other nations,
is owing to 300,000 little girls in Lancashire."[66] But the shrillness of their
rhetoric suggestions how skeptically they were heard. The undeniable economic importance of cotton cannot by itself explain the national fascination
with short time.

The national issue was that of short-time's political implication. One
master in the building trade, for instance, resisted a nine-hour strike in 1859,
not on narrow economic grounds—had the issue been simply one of wages,

he said, he would have been the first to yield—but on broad political ones. At issue, he thought, was "the republican notion of controlling the labour market."[67] Similarly, George Stringer Bull, the Tory radical preacher ordinarily well disposed toward short time, refused to lend his assistance in 1834 to an eight-hour effort organized by Fielden; Fielden's motives he thought laudable, but his plan too "republican."[68] If the purpose of the general strike, as defined by William Benbow, was "to place every human being on the same footing [of] equal rights, equal liberties, [and] equal enjoyments"; if the work-free Sunday was, as Robert Lowery said, "the 'Magna Charta' of all [our] rights and liberties," the "one day in the week when all men were equal," then to think of short time in similar terms would have taken no great imaginative leap.[69] It was essential to the survival of an artisanal radicalism under threat more from overwork and casualization than from the development of modern technologies.[70] It implied free time not merely for the various forms of social and cultural leisure but for continued involvement in preindustrial forms of popular politics. Only in this context does it makes sense that, as the *Manchester Guardian* noted, entire ministries should have once staked their existence on the defeat of the Ten Hours Bill.[71] In its insistence on the inclusion of the working poor in the protective apparatus of national government, short time was a variation on a traditional demand for political citizenship—a breach in the walls not of *laissez-faire* but of corruption, tyranny, and oligarchy.

# VI

The political impulses that lay behind the anti-Poor Law movement, from which, in terms of leadership and popular following, the English factory movement was almost indistinguishable, are even clearer.[72] "Had you any voice in the passing of this law?" asked O'Connor of his readers in 1837. "Did you send representatives to Parliament thus to betray you and rob you of your inheritance?"[73] The provisions of the new Poor Law were notoriously degrading and need no further review here. That it had been proposed at all, much less passed, constituted the affront—the political affront to popular liberties thought to be embodied as much in the traditional method of relief as in the traditional short working day. Thus the new workhouses to which, under the strict terms of the law, all indigent paupers were to be confined were, in the popular jargon, "bastilles." "No Bastilles" was the anti-Poor Law movement's rallying cry, *The Book of the Bastilles* its propagandistic anthology.[74] The law itself was known as the "English coercion law" and hence conflated in the popular mind with the recent political repression of Ireland. Its covert purpose, Cobbett thought, was to introduce under the guise of relief administration a sort of "Bourbon police" into the villages and country towns of England.[75] To John Fielden, simultaneously leader of the anti-Poor Law and short-time movements in Parliament, the new Poor Law represented "a tyranny of the worst description, surpassing the edicts of the Emperor Nicholas." Fielden's opposition to the law, thought the Chartist *Northern Liberator,* "[had] been the means of baffling one of the most dangerous stabs which was ever aimed at the liberties of Englishmen."[76]

That Fielden may have been similarly motivated in his quest for short time seems reasonable. He had long been, as his father complained, "as arrant [a] Jacobin as any in the Kingdom."[77] He was a founding member in 1818 of the relatively obscure and now extinct Methodist Unitarian church, a radical sect of mostly working men committed to popular democracy.[78] He read Thomas Paine, Henry Hunt, and William Cobbett avidly, and could quote freely from Jefferson on the floor of the House of Commons. "I am a reformer on the broad principle," he told the electors of Oldham during his first parliamentary campaign:

I have long maintained that it is the right of every man paying taxes to have a voice in the choosing of those persons who make the laws under which he has to live. . . . Should I have a seat in Parliament, I should vote for the abolition of tithes, of all sinecures, the repeal of the assessed taxes, and the total abolition of the Corn Laws. I am opposed to all injurious monopolies, a friend to Civil and Religious Liberty, and adverse to slavery in every form.[79]

He did not, in this manifesto, mention short time. But when, on his return to Parliament, short time became his cause, few among Fielden's electors would have been surprised. Along with parliamentary reform, it had long been a familiar feature of the popular political agenda.

But at parliamentary reform the Whigs meant to draw the line. In 1833, Lord Althorp sponsored on behalf of the government a factory bill designed to lessen the clamor for reform and lengthen the working day in one masterful stroke. No child under age thirteen was to be employed for more than eight hours a day in any textile industry, including, for the first time, woolens; children under eighteen were to be limited to sixty-nine hours a week, all to be worked between 5:30 A.M. and 8:30 P.M. An eight-hour day and a prohibition of night work: It seemed just what reformers demanded. In fact "Althorp's Act," as it came to be known, permitted the employment of protected children in two short-time shifts, thus consigning unprotected adults to as long as a fifteen-hour day. The schooling provisions associated with the act did represent the tentative beginnings of national education. And, in the accompanying factory inspectorate, the government had irrevocably, perhaps inadvertently, committed itself to state supervision of the economy;

it was, wrote the Hammonds, "a principle of supreme significance."[80] But Fielden opposed the establishment of the inspectorate for fear it would provide the government with one more surveillance apparatus in its continuing war against the poor (another suggestion that liberty more than welfare was the essential purpose of short time); moreover, he opposed Althorp's Act as a whole because, in failing to achieve a shorter day for laboring adults, it fell short of the explicit demands of the English working class. The working people must, he wrote to Cobbett after the passage of the act, "by unions amongst themselves . . . MAKE A SHORT TIME BILL FOR THEMSELVES."[81]

To help the workers make a short-time bill for themselves was the stated purpose of Fielden's National Regeneration Society, founded in collaboration with Robert Owen and John Doherty in November 1833. Historians have scarcely taken notice of the Regeneration Society, except perhaps to dismiss it as an "impractical" or "fatuous" aberration in the struggle for a ten-hour day.[82] Biographers of Owen dutifully add it to the list of those organizations with which Owen associated, but they take no measure of its influence or significance.[83] Cecil Driver, Oastler's biographer, considers the society to be an insignificant manifestation of ideas that were everywhere in the air. Independent of prevailing trends, he argues, "the Fielden scheme would have been an empty gesture."[84] The society did attract some furious scholarly attention when John Foster seized on it as evidence for his contention that short time was essentially a "lever for fundamental political mobilization" in the hands of fully class-conscious revolutionaries. But, not surprisingly, the society itself—its contemporary purpose and meaning— quickly got lost in the ensuing hullabaloo.[85] Even to ask whether the society was a "fundamental political organization" in the hands of a revolutionary vanguard or an apolitical agent of class collaboration is immediately to indulge the second of our distractive assumptions. It is to ask where the society tended to neglect of what the society was. For, in fact, the history of the society shows it to have been neither of these portentous things. It was, instead, the organizational expression of the first attempt by English textile workers to "*legislate* a short time bill for themselves."[86] It was a familiar and far from revolutionary claim to political independence staked nevertheless radically to the eight-hour working day.

The plan, devised by Fielden, was for all hands, regardless of age or sex, simply to leave off work after eight hours on March 1, 1834—the day the government's Factory Act was scheduled to come into effect. The role of the society would be to publicize the plan and urge all masters to cooperate toward its success. Some did, Fielden obviously among them. But more, including many heretofore inclined toward short time, were intensely skeptical. David Holt, for one, preferred "a plan that would make the masters themselves the medium through which the improved condition of the

people should come.'' This would, he said to Fielden, ''prevent that colli-
sion which the plan you propose to pursue must, I fear, inevitably produce.'' William Fitton, a radical surgeon and known supporter of the Ten
Hours Bill, expressed similar surprise that Fielden should have initiated such
a project. ''I would rather not have seen your name connected with it,'' he
wrote. The *Morning Chronicle* more hysterically concluded ''that a member
of the British Parliament [was] now engaged in promoting a revolution in
this country.''[87] So to that extent Foster is right; something more than short
time clearly was at issue—something more threatening, something more political. But it was not something particularly revolutionary to those who
sought it, for they had always thought of short time in democratic terms.
National Regeneration made disturbingly explicit the constitutional implications of an eight-hour day.

This explains why the Tory radicals on this occasion remained aloof.
''You are a rope of sand,'' wrote Parson Bull in an open letter to the Re-
generationists. ''There are many of you that would not give up one hour's
occupation, one hour's comfort, or the price of one glass of ale, to save
*your own class* from distress and ruin. . . . Now, therefore, do exercise a
little forbearance and keep your little political playthings still and quiet,
when great practical questions are under discussion.''[88] To Richard Oastler,
whose own Factory Reformation Society was threatened by public enthusiasm for National Regeneration, asking for ''eight hours work for the present
full days wages''—the slogan of the society—was tantamount to asking for
12d for 8d. ''We feel assured,'' he wrote to Owen in declining to lend his
support, ''that defeat would be our reward if we were to stand up publicly
to propound and defend a scheme, which we are obliged to confess, we
ourselves do not thoroughly understand.''[89] Cobbett understood the scheme
(as indeed did the disingenuous Oastler), and, from his more democratic
perspective, he thoroughly approved. ''The *Revolution* has begun!'' he wrote
exultantly to Fielden when in April, several weeks later than planned, the
spinners of Oldham went on strike for eight hours. ''That 'Great Change'
which you anticipated is certainly at hand.''[90]

As it happened, of course, there was no ''great change'' at hand. Though
the Regeneration Society had managed to establish forty branch committees,
some as far south as Derbyshire, nowhere outside Oldham did the strike
actually come off. And in Oldham it lasted only two weeks before being
settled on the masters' terms. Cobbett's ''Revolution'' became in the historical record an isolated ''spasm of insurrection,'' with one riot, one death,
and one sacked mill to its credit.[91] Still, the rapidity with which the society
initially displaced popular support for the established short-time committees—even those in Oastler's own West Riding—amply justified Major General Henry Bouverie's concern, as commander of the peacekeeping forces in

the north, that it had "made a very serious impression on the minds of a large portion of the workpeople."[92] The London Press was similarly concerned and denounced Fielden's scheme as one likely "to widen the breach between the employers and the employed to such an extent as to render it incapable of being healed." Fielden denied any such divisive intention, but the utilitarian radical Francis Place nevertheless attributed to his "folly of recommending a general strike all over the kingdom [much of] the mischief of these years."[93] The history of the society, however fleeting, thus may suggest much about the popular ideology of short time that exclusive attention to the ten-hour movement obscures.

For one thing, an eight-hour, not a ten-hour, day was clearly the popular choice, as Fielden who had worked in the mills himself well knew. It was the traditional standard, or so at least short timers believed, until the recent and, to their minds, pointless, productive intensification.[94] Beyond that, it was an Anglo-Saxon law, decreed, they thought, along with the naturally corresponding eight hours' sleep and eight hours' play, in the ninth century by Alfred the Great.[95] In insisting upon eight hours, then, the Regeneration Society brought short time within the familiar radical discourse of "ancient liberties." Short time was a constitutional right of freeborn Englishmen, lost, along with everything else, at some indefinably imagined time between the Norman Conquest and the Industrial Revolution. Moreover, it was a constitutional right that the workers themselves had the responsibility to restore. "The Men of Oldham have struck the first blow," announced a Regeneration Society placard distributed through the industrial districts on the occasion of the strike. "They have, to a man, ceased to work till justice be done them, and . . . they are resolved to work only eight hours a day. . . . Will you join them and be free, or reject them and be slaves?"[96]

To be sure, the eight-hour day was not merely a matter of abstract constitutional justice. In his pamphlet *National Regeneration,* published by William Cobbett in London, Fielden was particularly keen to demonstrate its economic practicality. Quite simply, he contended that the great excess of production over domestic demand was responsible for the low prices, low profits, and low wages then gripping the English textile industry. The obvious remedy—one that other "absolute overproductionists," to use current economic jargon, did not hesitate to endorse—was the abolition or restrictive taxation of machinery.[97] But Fielden was hardly in a position to abolish or tax the means of his own livelihood. Instead, he advocated the immediate reorientation of the cotton industry away from foreign trade and toward the domestic market, coupled with a 33 percent diminution in productive capacity through an eight-hour working day. Within weeks, he argued, textile earnings would be up 25 percent and "peace, concord, and mutual goodwill" would prevail between masters and men.[98]

This fantastic economic argument appealed to Robert Owen, "the benevolent mono-maniac," whose association with National Regeneration (a tag he probably chose) has led such cynics as Neil Smelser to dismiss it as "an extremely disturbed utopian movement."[99] Several things need to be said about this. First, the frequent equation of Owenism with utopianism obscures the practical basis of its contemporary appeal. Drawing upon a familiar eighteenth-century radical discourse—looking back as much as Cobbett had done to the spirit of Thomas Paine—Owen had elaborated an eminently useful critique of exploitation. Oppression and tyranny were still his themes, however much he suffered from a "fatal evasion of the realities of political power."[100] And those who could see past his messianic and openly antidemocratic rhetoric often found in Owen's theory a practical complement to traditional radical ideas. An eight-hour day, for instance, long advocated by Owen, was no more utopian than parliamentary reform. It may have ended in a redistribution of industrial resources; it would have heightened working-class control over the means of production. But it was hardly likely, and certainly not calculated, to bring in a brave new world.

Owen's role in this brief eight-hour effort has been overestimated anyway. He did launch the Regeneration Society at Prince's Tavern in Manchester; he wrote its official "catechism," complete with biblical annotations; and he promised to try to raise the support of his followers in London. But the philosophy of direct action, to which Fielden and Doherty were both ultimately committed, never sat comfortable with him, and long before the eight-hour strike in Oldham, he had become exclusively absorbed in his Grand National Consolidated Trades Union.[101] Fielden, meanwhile, had been distracted by the parliamentary struggle against the new Poor Law, leaving Doherty to preside over the society in its dotage. On May 16, 1834, the committee in Manchester rescheduled the eight-hour strike for sometime in the following September, but there is no evidence of any further preparation. The strike never took place, and by 1837, when asked what ever became of the Regeneration Society, one Mancunian worker could only recall that "somehow or other it fell to the ground."[102]

And so indeed it did; not for decades would the eight-hour day reemerge as a popular demand. But the ten-hour movement furiously revived in 1836, to win the day eleven years later. And though Oastler was again involved, though the stated provisions of the Ten Hours Act now excluded all adult males, though the paternal theme of "mercy against mammon" now dominated public debate, the strength of the movement still derived from its essentially constitutional goal. Between 1836 and 1848, to distinguish between the factory movement, the anti-Poor Law movement, and Chartism is impossible. Each was part of an autonomous working-class struggle for political freedom. "I have, all my years of manhood, been a Radical Reformer," wrote Fielden in 1836, expressing the popular ideology in its simplest terms, "because I thought Reform would give the people a power in the House of Commons that would secure to them that better condition of which they are worthy."[103] Short time was a particularly versatile part of that quest for popular power. Not only would it give "the people" time needed for domestic and moral improvement but it would, by curtailing levels of production, raise both the demand for and value of their labor. But above all else, it would do what the Reform Bill had not done: It would force their inclusion within the pale of the existing constitution; it would confirm, for those who had reason to doubt them, the political rights of man.

## NOTES

1. Of the 544,876 people employed in the textile industries in 1847, 363,796 were women and children protected by the provisions of the Ten Hours Act. To operate the mills without them would have been a practical impossibility; the act thus indirectly but deliberately established a ten-hour day for all workers in the cotton, woolen, worsted, hemp, flax, and linen industries. Passed in June 1847, the Ten Hours Act (10 & 11 Vict., c. 29) simply amended the Factory Act of 1844 (7 & 8 Vict., c. 29), which had established a twelve-hour day for women and for "young persons" between the ages of thirteen and eighteen, and either a six-and-one-half-hour day or alternate ten-hour days for "children" aged eight to twelve. For the complete provisions of all the English factory acts to 1910, see B. L. Hutchins and A. Harrison, *A History of Factory Legislation* (London, 1911).

2. British Parliament Papers, *Report of Select Committee on Combinations of Workmen,* 1837–1838, viii; evidence of John Doherty cited in J. T. Ward and W. Hamish Fraser, eds., *Workers and Employers* (London, 1980), pp. 46–47.

3. 42 Geo. III, c. 73.

4. John Fielden, *The Curse of the Factory System* (London, 1969; originally published 1834), pp. 7–12.

5. 59 Geo. III, c. 66.

6. Ward and Fraser, *Workers and Employers,* pp. 46–47; J. T. Ward, *The Factory Movement 1830–1855* (London, 1962), p. 28. For the relation between the factory movement and early Lancastrian trade unionism, see R. Sykes, "Early Chartism and Trade Unionism in South East Lancashire," in *The Chartist Experience,* ed. J. Epstein and D. Thompson (London, 1982), pp. 155–156.

7. *Leeds Mercury,* October 16, 1830.

8. 3 & 4 Will, IV, c. 103.

9. P. Grant, *The History of Factory Legislation: The Ten Hours Bill* (Manchester, 1866), p. 59.

10. For the general strike of 1842, more commonly known as the "Plug Plot" riots, see M. Jenkins, *The General Strike of 1842* (London, 1980).

11. Ashley diary, cited in Sir Edwin Hodder, *Life and Work of the Seventh Earl of Shaftesbury* (London, 1888), 2:50.

12. *Hansard Parliament Debates* (hereinafter cited as *Hansard*), 3rd series, 64 (May 3, 1844), c. 684–68. For the provisions of the act passed in 1844, see note 1.

13. Karl Marx, *Selected Works,* ed. V. Adorasky (London, 1942), 2:439. As it happened, Marx's celebration was premature. By an unimaginable oversight, the clauses of the Ten Hours Act failed to specify the time at which work should cease relative to when it commenced. Thus, to maintain a twelve- or fifteen-hour day, the masters had only to employ the workers in discontinuous shifts. Though never actually working for more than ten hours, women and "young persons" were kept tied to the mill all day; the hours of rest became, to quote Marx again, "hours of enforced idleness." *Capital* (New York, 1967; originally published 1867), 1:291. The loophole was closed in 1850 at the cost of a half hour's extra labor.

14. Alfred [S. Kydd], *The History of the Factory Movement,* 2 vols. (London, 1857); Grant, *History of Factory Legislation;* Hutchins and Harrison, *History of Factory Legislation;* Ward, *Factory Movement;* A. Robson, *On Higher Than Commercial Grounds: The Factory Controversy, 1830–1853* (New York, 1985).

15. Hodder, *Life and Work of the Seventh Earl of Shaftesbury;* C. Driver, *Tory Radical: The Life of Richard Oastler* (New York, 1946); J. C. Gill, *The Ten Hours Parson* (London, 1959); J. C. Gill, *Parson Bull of Byerley* (London, 1963); R. G. Kirby and A. E. Musson, *Voice of the People: The Life of John Doherty, 1789–1854* (Manchester, 1975); S. Weaver, *John Fielden and the Politics of Popular Radicalism, 1832–1847* (Oxford, 1987).

16. See, for example, John Foster, *Class Struggle and the Industrial Revolution* (London, 1974).

17. Alfred [S. Kydd], *Factory Movement,* 2:312. For a capable review of the voluminous literature on this theme up to 1972, see A. J. Taylor, *Laissez-Faire and State Intervention in Nineteenth-Century Britain* (London, 1972). Since then, the most significant addition has been Derek Fraser, *The Evolution of the British Welfare State* (London, 1973). See also M. A. Bienefeld, *Working Hours in British Industry: An Economic History* (London, 1972).

18. *Hansard,* 3rd series, 74 (April 28, 1846), c. 1234; *Northern Star,* May 8, 1847; *Times* (London), September 7, 1861; A. Briggs, "The Welfare State in Historical Perspective," *European Journal of Sociology* 2 (1961): 241.

19. The *locus classicus* of this "organic growth thesis" of administrative change in the nineteenth century is O. MacDonagh, "The Nineteenth Century Revolution in Government: A Reappraisal," *Historical Journal* 1 (1958). Still the best reply to MacDonagh is J. Hart, "Nineteenth-Century Social Reform: A Tory Interpretation of History," *Past and Present,* no. 31 (1965).

20. See, for example, W. C. Lubenow, *The Politics of Government Growth: Early Victorian Attitudes towards State Intervention, 1833–1848* (Newton Abbot, 1971).

21. R. Lambert, *Sir John Simon, 1816–1904, and English Social Administration* (London, 1963); O. MacDonagh, *Early Victorian Government 1830–1876* (London, 1977); W. H. Greenleaf, *The Rise of Collectivism,* The British Political Tradition, vol. 1 (London, 1983). For a recent attempt to push administrative history beyond the tired categories of "laissez-faire individualism" and "bureaucratic collectivism,"

see Peter Gowan, "The Origins of the Administrative Elite," *New Left Review* 162 (April 1987): 4–34.

22. B. Harrison, *Peaceable Kingdom* (Oxford, 1982), p. 391.

23. See, for instance, W. O. Aydelotte, "Parties and Issues in Early Victorian England," *Journal of British Studies* 5 (1966).

24. *Leeds Times,* March 30, 1844.

25. E. P. Thompson, *The Making of the English Working Class* (New York, 1963), p. 340.

26. Foster, *Class Struggle,* pp. 207ff.

27. D. Thompson, *The Chartists: Popular Politics in the Industrial Revolution* (New York, 1984), p. 333.

28. *Hansard,* 3rd series, 64 (May 3, 1844), c. 1086.

29. Joan W. Scott, "On Language, Gender, and Working Class History, *International Labor and Working Class History* 31 (Spring 1987): 1.

30. Cited in Grant, *History of Factory Legislation,* p. 47.

31. Note, for example, Clive Behagg's observation in the present volume that when workers "argued for a limitation of work time within a formalized working day they frequently did so by adopting the terms of the dominant discourse."

32. For the affinities between middle- and working-class radicalism, see T. Tholfsen, *Working Class Radicalism in Mid-Victorian England* (New York, 1977); and Hollis and B. Harrison, "Chartism, Liberalism, and the Life of Robert Lowery," *English Historical Review* 82 (1967).

33. *Dictionary of National Biography* (London, 1888).

34. Tholfsen, *Working Class Radicalism,* p. 124.

35. Ward, *Factory Movement, passim;* Patrick Joyce, *Work, Society and Politics* (London, 1980) pp. 323–327; C. W. Boyd, ed., *Mr. Chamberlain's Speeches* (London, 1914), cited in Greenleaf, *The Ideological Heritage,* The British Political Tradition, 2:229. See also J. T. Ward, "The Factory Movement," in J. T. Ward, ed., *Popular Movement c. 1830–1850* (London, 1970); and J. T. Ward, "Revolutionary Tory: The Life of Joseph Rayner Stephens," *Transactions of the Lancashire and Cheshire Antiquarian Society* 68 (1958).

36. See P. Smith, *Disraelian Conservatism and Social Reform* (London, 1967). For Shaftesbury, see, in addition to the definitive biography by Hodder, J. L. Hammond and B. Hammond, *Lord Shaftesbury* (New York, 1923).

37. K. Marx and F. Engels, *Manifesto of the Communist Party,* in *The Marx-Engels Reader,* ed. M. Tucker 2nd ed. (New York, 1978), pp. 491–492; E. Halévy, *The Liberal Awakening,* A History of the English People in the 19th Century, vol. 2, (New York, 1949), p. 283. For a recent review of the extensive literature on this theme, see Greenleaf, *British Political Tradition,* vol. 2., Chap 7, "Tory Paternalism and the Welfare State." An early study of Tory radicalism now available in reprint is R. L. Hill, *Toryism and the People 1832–46* (Philadelphia, 1975; originally published 1929).

38. D. Roberts, "Tory Paternalism and Social Reform in Early Victorian England," *American Historical Review* 63 (1957–1958). See also his *Paternalism in Early Victorian England* (New Brunswick, N.J., 1979).

39. Hodder, *Life and Work* 1:408.

40. J. M. Cobbett to John Fielden, November 12, 1840, Fielden Manuscripts, John Rylands University Library of Manchester, Deansgate, Manchester.

41. *Northern Star,* March 28, 1846.

42. Alfred [S. Kydd], *Factory Movement,* 2:255.

43. *Hansard,* 3rd series, 75 (May 22, 1846), c. 1019.

44. Driver, *Tory Radical,* p. 315.

45. N. J. Smelser, *Social Change in the Industrial Revolution* (Chicago, 1959), p. 397.

46. C. Calhoun, *The Question of Class Struggle: Social Foundations of Popular Radicalism during the Industrial Revolution* (Chicago, 1982), pp. 191–196. Smelser also evidently overestimates the disruptive effect of new industrial technology in the second quarter of the century. See W. Lazonick, "Industrial Relations and Technical Change: The Case of the Self-Acting Mule," *Cambridge Journal of Economics* 3 (1979): 231–262.

47. Calhoun, *Question, passim.*

48. Bienefeld, *Working Hours,* pp. 215–217.

49. M. Berg, *The Machinery Question and the Making of Political Economy 1815–1848* (Cambridge, 1980), p. 266.

50. *Hansard* 3rd series, 16 (March 13, 1833), c. 953.

51. "Freedom" here meaning the freedom of the employer to do whatever he deemed necessary to ensure his return on investment; "control" meaning the control by the workers of essential productive relations. See R. Price, *Masters, Unions and Men* (Cambridge, 1980), pp. 46–54.

52. *Northern Star,* December 27, 1845.

53. See N. W. Thompson, *The People's Science: The Popular Political Economy of Exploitation and Crisis, 1816–1834* (Cambridge, 1984).

54. W. Cobbett, *Tour in Scotland* (London, 1833), p. 208.

55. E. P. Thompson, *Making,* p. 603; S. Bamford, *Passages in the Life of a Radical* (London, 1967; originally published 1841), p. 7.

56. *People's Paper,* August 21, 1852; *Northern Star,* February 14, 1846.

57. Cited in G. Himmelfarb (who calls it "the most frequently cited quotation in the whole of Chartist literature"), *The Idea of Poverty* (New York, 1984), p. 264.

58. Lord John Russell, *Letter to the Electors of Stroud* (London, 1839).

59. G. Stedman Jones, "Rethinking Chartism," in *Languages of Class* (Cambridge, 1983), p. 102.

60. Scott, "Language, Gender, and Working Class History," p. 5. For other critiques of Stedman Jones, see John Foster, "The Declassing of Language," *New Left Review* 150 (March/April 1985); R. Gray, "The Deconstructing of the English Working Class," *Social History* 11 (1986); James Epstein, "Rethinking the Categories of Working Class History," *Labour/Le Travail* 18 (Fall 1986); and Neville Kirk, "In Defence of Class," *International Review of Social History* 32, no. 1 (1987).

61. Stedman Jones, "Rethinking Chartism," p. 150.

62. *Poor Man's Guardian,* December 29, 1832, cited in R. A. Sykes, "Some

Aspects of Working Class Consciousness in Oldham, 1830–1842," *Historical Journal* 23 (1980): 178.

63. Alfred [S. Kydd], *Factory Movement*, 2:223.

64. Greville diary, cited in Ward, *Factory Movement*, 289.

65. *Illustrated London News*, May 8, 1847, p. 300.

66. *Hansard*, 3rd series, 19 (July 18, 1833). Senior's actual argument was almost sillier: All industrial profit, he thought, derived from the last hours of each day's labor. To shorten the day by even one hour would destroy net profit; a Ten Hours Bill "would be utterly ruinous." N. W. Senior, *Letters on the Factory Act*, 2nd ed. (London, 1844).

67. Price, *Masters*, p. 53.

68. G. S. Bull, "To the Friends of the National Regeneration Society," *Crisis and National Co-operative Trades' Union Gazette* 26 (April 1834).

69. W. Benbow, *Grand National Holiday* (1832), cited in M. Morris, ed., *From Cobbett to the Chartists* 2nd ed. (London, 1951), p. 84; Lowery and Henry Broadhurst, cited in B. Harrison, *Peaceable Kingdom* (Oxford, 1982), p. 134. As late as the 1890s, English radicals still looked back on the Ten Hours Act as "the Magna Charta of the Factory Hand." See J. M. Davidson, *Annals of Toil* (London, 1899), p. 278.

70. G. Stedman Jones, *Outcast London*, 2nd ed. (New York, 1984).

71. *Manchester Guardian*, March 6, 1847.

72. Cf. N. Edsall, *The Anti-Poor Law Movement 1834–1844* (Manchester, 1971). See also J. Knott, *Popular Opposition to the 1834 Poor Law* (New York, 1985).

73. Cited in M. Hovell, *The Chartist Movement* (Manchester, 1918), p. 82.

74. G. R. Wythen Baxter, ed., *The Book of the Bastilles; or, the History of the Working of the New Poor Law* (London, 1841).

75. *Cobbett's Weekly Political Register*, April 6, 1833.

76. *Manchester and Salford Advertiser*, January 18, 1837; *Northern Liberator*, January 14, 1835.

77. Alfred [S. Kydd], *Factory Movement*, 1:325.

78. For the close involvement of Methodist Unitarians in successive political reform movements, see H. McLachlan, *The Methodist Unitarian Movement* (Manchester, 1919).

79. John Fielden, "To the Electors of Oldham," n.d. (1832?), Fielden Manuscripts, John Rylands University Library of Manchester.

80. Hammond and Hammond, *Lord Shaftesbury*, p. 35.

81. *Cobbett's Weekly Political Register*, December 14, 1833.

82. Kirby and Musson, *Voice of the People*, p. 301; Ward, *Factory Movement*, p. 106.

83. G. D. H. Cole, *The Life of Robert Owen* (London, 1930), p. 270; J. F. C. Harrison, *Quest for the New Moral World* (New York, 1969), p. 210; J. T. Ward, "Owen as Factory Reformer," in *Robert Owen: Prince of Cotton Spinners*, ed. J. Butt (Newton Abbott, 1971), pp. 122–130.

84. Driver, *Tory Radical*, p. 262.

85. Foster, *Class Struggle*, pp. 109–111. Those who took exception were

G. Stedman Jones, "Class Struggle and the Industrial Revolution," *New Left Review* 90 (March–April 1975); A. E. Musson, "Class Struggle and the Labour Aristocracy, 1830–1860," *Social History* 3 (1976); D. S. Gadian, "Class Consciousness in Oldham and Other North West Industrial Towns, 1830–1850," *Historical Journal* 21 (1978). For a deft arbitration see Sykes, "Some Aspects of Working-Class Consciousness in Oldham, 1830–1842." See also my *Fielden,* Chap. 3, "Towards National Regeneration."

86. *Herald of the Rights of Industry,* February 8, 1834; italics added.

87. J. Fielden and W. Fitton, *National Regeneration* (London, 1969; originally published 1834), Appendix 1 (Holt to Fielden), p. 1; *Morning Chronicle,* December 11, 1833.

88. *Crisis,* April 26, 1834.

89. Richard Oastler to Robert Owen, November 11 and 22, 1833, nos. 664, 668, Co-operative Union Ltd. Collection of Robert Owen Documents, Holyoake House, Manchester.

90. William Cobbett to John Fielden, April 24, 1834, from a transcript generously provided to me by John Foster.

91. S. Webb and B. Webb, *The History of Trade Unionism* rev. ed. (London, 1920), p. 152.

92. H. Bouverie to J. M. Phillips, February 25, 1834, Public Record Office, Kew, H(ome) O(ffice) 40/32(1) folio 36. For the progress of the society in the West Riding, see Joshua Hobson's *Voice of the West Riding,* November 1833–April 1834.

93. *Morning Chronicle,* December 11, 1833; Francis Place to [?], August 2, 1839, British Library Add. Mss. 27835.

94. The customary nature of the eight-hour day would remain a stock argument of short timers right into the twentieth century. See John Rae, *Eight Hours for Work* (London, 1894).

95. See, for instance, William Cobbett, *Legacy to Labourers* (London, 1834).

96. Colonel Foster to Melbourne, n.d. (April 1834?) HO 40/32(3), folio 192.

97. N. Thompson, *People's Science,* p. 206.

98. Fielden, *National Regeneration,* pp. 20 et *passim.*

99. Smelser, *Social Change,* p. 243. For a contemporary critique of Fielden's economic views—the "Oldham School of Political Economy"—see R. Torrens, *On Wages and Combinations* (London, 1834).

100. E. P. Thompson, *Making,* p. 805.

101. From time to time, Owen is identified as the founder of the Regeneration Society, but as Owen himself said, "John Fielden has a better right to the title . . . for in deliberating together upon what was best to be done towards obtaining the rights of industry for the producers of wealth, the idea of eight hours labour for the present day's wages first occurred to him; and he it was who, at the same time, proposed to carry the measure into practice by means of a parent society." *Crisis,* February 1, 1834.

102. *Parliamentary Papers,* 1837–1838, viii (646), 276.

103. Fielden, *Curse,* p. 1.

# 6

# "The Greater Part of the Petitioners are Female": The Reduction of Women's Working Hours in the Paid Labor Force, 1840–1917

## *Kathryn Kish Sklar*

## I

SINCE WOMEN were among the nation's earliest industrial workers, they were also among the first to protest against employers' insistence on workdays of twelve or more hours. Such a lengthy workday might have been appropriate in a preindustrial setting where work was diverse and task oriented, with many long breaks, but working women felt it was inappropriate in factories where machines demanded constant attention, work was repetitive, and employees' productivity was vastly increased.

Yet, in spite of women's early entrance into the struggle to reduce the length of the working day in American manufacturing, women were among the last to benefit from shorter hours. The story of their struggle is a long one, reaching from the 1840s to the first decades of the twentieth century. And it is a complex story involving three dimensions: the history of the struggle to reduce women's hours, the history of efforts to reduce men's hours, and the relationship between these endeavors. Like other topics in women's history, it embraces men, work, and children, requiring us to expand the scope of our inquiry, but rewarding us with new insights into the process of historical change.[1]

Historians of women have generally taken a negative view of the process by which workingwomen's hours were reduced in the United States. Three salient features of that process seem to have contributed to the oppression of working women. First, the chief means of reducing women's hours was through legislation by state governments; this legislation usually emphasized the need to protect women from deleterious effects of long hours on their health, especially on their reproductive capacities, and thereby stereotyped women as weaker than men and dependent on them. Second, although it was limited to women, this legislation was understood by all involved in its passage and enforcement to affect men workers as well. Men seemed to derive unfair advantages from the statutes, benefiting indirectly when their own hours were reduced along with those of their female co-workers, and benefiting directly when, as a result of gender-specific statutes, women were excluded from certain jobs. Third, middle-class women reformers were central to the process by which hours laws were passed after 1890, and historians have suspected their motivations, sometimes viewing them as maternalistic meddlers in working-class affairs.[2] Alice Kessler-Harris, in the most comprehensive study of American working women, *Out to Work: A History of Wage-Earning Women in America,* expressed this negative view when she concluded that the gender stereotypes involved in labor legislation for women released "some women from some of the misery of toil, but simultaneously confirm[ed] their places in those jobs most conducive to exploitation."[3]

Yet this perspective ignores the very substantial support that wage-earning women gave to the statutory reduction of working hours. Viewing that support, another side of the story has begun to emerge. Diane E. Kirkby, focusing on the legislative strategies of the Women's Trade Union League, has found much to praise in the process by which the working hours of the great majority of wage-earning women were reduced in the first decade of the twentieth century.[4] Kirkby argued that trade union and statutory strategies were compatible and that protective legislation did not always "rest squarely on the assumption that all women were homemakers." Instead, she concluded, it "rested on the assumption that women's right to work at the occupation of their choice was severely curtailed by the existing operation of the labor market over which they, as the least powerful group, had least control."[5] The attitude of the Women's Trade Union League, Kirkby maintains, "had nothing to do with genteel notions about femininity but were prompted by the League's awareness of the realities of factory work and the League's objective of legitimating women's permanent participation in the labor force."[6] Defenders of protective legislation for women around 1900 argued that it did women no favor to permit them to work in exploitative circumstances, for this merely confirmed their second-class status in the labor force at the same time that it eroded their health. They also argued that state and municipal governments should provide support for families in which poverty forced mothers of young children to work. And to solve the hardship that such legislation brought to some skilled or professional women workers whose working conditions did not warrant protection, such as printers, they pointed to the common practice by which state legislatures exempted such occupations from the law.[7]

This chapter focuses on the support that wage-earning and middle-class women brought to the statutory regulation of women's working hours. That support confronted challenging obstacles and required the dedicated efforts of middle-class and working-class men and women over more than six decades in order to succeed. In particular, this chapter focuses on four critical junctures that channeled that effort. Each built on what had gone before in such a way as to preclude other options. The outcome was not determined from the start, but the process by which the outcome was accomplished was an incremental one in which available options were shaped by what had gone before. Thus the conclusion of the process in 1907 was rooted in its origins in the 1840s.

The four critical junctures were as follows:

1. In the 1840s, patterns of action established by early industrial women workers, acting autonomously and separately as women, sought legislative remedies for long hours, viewing their appeal as a complement to labor organizing, and justifying their actions on health grounds.
2. In the 1860s, men and women industrial workers decided to imitate the English example of legislation for women only, which would also serve to limit men's working hours.
3. During the heightened struggle between capital and labor in the 1890s, this strategy gathered new advocates among middle-class women and new opponents in state judicial opinions.
4. A new form of jurisprudence finally resolved this struggle in 1908.

## II

Women marched in the forefront of the nation's first campaigns for shorter hours because they constituted the majority of the nation's most mechanized occupation, the textile operatives. The mechanization of spinning and weaving vastly increased workers' productivity, so women felt justified in demanding shorter days than their preindustrial work habits had required. But the competitive basis of textile production, the low level of skill required for most textile work, and the *laissez-faire* ideology of legislators and employers meant that managers resisted workers' demands. The result was more than two decades of industrial struggle with only minimal gains by workers.

In Lowell, Massachusetts, an important center of the ten-hour movement, the opportunity to attend public lectures, to read or write for the *Lowell Offering,* and to pursue peer companionship made early textile workers sharply aware of the uses to which they could put their leisure time. Opportunities for self-improvement were much greater at Lowell than in the farming communities from which the young women came.[8] These early workers were also keenly aware of the speed-up in productivity that made their work more fatiguing than it had been earlier.[9]

Given the freedom of returning home to family farms, and the solidarity that had developed in their collective living patterns in boardinghouses, it is not surprising that women's protest in the 1840s coalesced into an insurgent movement to limit their working day to ten hours. Setting a pattern that would be followed later, this movement petitioned state legislators to pass statutes limiting women's working day. The peak of the campaign occurred in 1846 when 10,000 signers, most of them women workers or those recruited by women workers, urged the Massachusetts legislature to act.[10] Since textile corporations were licensed by the state, it was logical for workers to appeal to the state to regulate their hours of labor. Such appeals had been initiated by craft journeymen in Philadelphia in the 1820s and 1830s. Another group of male workers had succeeded in using political pressure to obtain shorter hours in 1840 when President Martin Van Buren granted an eight-hour day to all manual laborers employed by the federal government.[11]

As in England, the ten-hour-day campaign attracted skilled male mechanics as well as relatively unskilled women operatives, but the goal of the American movement in the 1840s was more radical than that of the English, for the Americans called for legislation to limit the hours of "all persons" who worked in textile factories. In England, that goal was supplanted by the Factory Act of 1847, which limited the hours of women industrial workers, but was knowingly enacted as a means of limiting the hours of all industrial workers.[12]

Differences in the leadership of the English and American campaigns for shorter hours in textile mills in the 1840s help explain this and other important differences in the process by which hours legislation was achieved in the United States. Women workers were more critical to the process in the United States. In England, rural Tories, skeptical about the benefits of industrialization and the competitive marketplace, lent critical political support to the movement, beginning with a limitation on the working hours of children by statute in the 1830s. Conservative opponents of industrialization were not nearly so powerful in the United States. The closest equivalents to conservative advocates of hours legislation in England, such as Lord Ashley, were educators like Horace Mann, who supported early hours laws for children, and abolitionists like William Lloyd Garrison, who supported the eight-hour day for free labor.[13] But unlike Ashley, Mann and Garrison did not figure in the struggle over women's hours. In England, partly as a result of Tory support, the struggle to limit factory hours gained a widespread consensus in the nation's polity during the 1850s—a consensus that supported limiting women's working hours as a means of limiting the hours of all industrial workers. In the United States, partly because the effect of such legislation would be to limit the hours of men as well as women, no such consensus was ever reached, and the struggle to defend legislation for women remained embattled until 1907, drawing more emphatically on the talents of women workers before 1860, and after 1890, on their middle-class allies as well.[14] Thus the failure of paternalism led ultimately to what might be called "maternalism" in the United States.

The greater autonomy of women's efforts in the United States was vividly demonstrated in the response of the Massachusetts legislature to the predominantly female petition campaign of 1845. The legislature appointed William Schouler, editor of a pro-corporation Lowell newspaper and a prominent opponent of the workers' demands, to head an investigating committee. Emphasizing women's need to speak for themselves at the same time that he tried to discourage them from confronting the legislature, Schouler wrote Sarah Bagley, a leader of the petition campaign: "I would inform you that as the greater part of the petitioners are female; it will be necessary for them to make the defense, or we shall be under the necessity of laying it aside." Even though women had not heretofore addressed a state legislature and only recently (in the antislavery movement) had begun to speak before assemblies that included men, Bagley, undaunted, replied: "We hold ourselves in readiness to defend the petitions referred to at any time when you will grant us a hearing."[15] This was the first chapter in a long process in which women workers carried their own banners into the political domain, where no conservative champions awaited them with support.

In another pattern that remained true into the late nineteenth century, women workers in the 1840s viewed legislative strategies as complementary to trade union activity. One of the first women's labor organizations, the Lowell Female Labor Reform Association, arose within the petition campaign. This separate organization for women empowered women workers in multiple ways. For example, it facilitated the interaction of women with male groups, such as the New England Workingmen's Association and the New England Labor Reform League. As individuals, women would have had great difficulty overcoming the discrimination against their participation in men's organizations, but as a group with their own power base, they gained ready access.[16]

Another lasting feature of the struggle for shorter hours for women in the United States was the emphasis that early industrial women workers placed on the ill effects of long hours on their health. In their first petition to the Massachusetts legislature, operatives had protested against work schedules that confined them "from thirteen to fourteen hours per day in unhealthy apartments," thereby "hastening [them] through pain, disease, and privation down to a premature grave." In 1845, witnesses upheld that claim at legislative hearings in Massachusetts, where women workers cited health reasons as the single most important basis for their call for state intervention.[17] One woman attributed her ill health "to the long hours of labor, the shortness of time for meals, and the bad air of the mills."[18] Sarah Bagley, an eight-year veteran of millwork, testified that "the health of the operatives is not so good as the health of females who do house-work or millinery business." Although some "girls" tried to make more wages by working longer hours, Bagley thought most would prefer to work but ten hours. "In a pecuniary point of view, it would be better, as their health would be improved," she said.[19]

Finally, in both the 1840s and the 1890s, *laissez-faire* values about state action obstructed reform goals. The Massachusetts legislature gave three reasons why it was not recommending regulation of mill hours. First, any law limiting hours should apply to all workshops, the legislators said, not solely to textile corporations, Second, the factory system was "not more injurious to health than other kinds of indoor labor"; to conclude otherwise would mean that Massachusetts "could not compete with our sister States, much less with foreign countries." Third, since "labor is on an equality with capital, and indeed controls it," changes in working conditions are better left to labor than to the legislature to impose. The legislators also maintained that improvements in the present system should come from the "progressive improvement in art and science," not the legislature.[20] Leaders of the Lowell Female Labor Reform Association fought back. They publicly deplored "the lack of independence, honesty, and humanity in the committee" and contributed substantially to Schouler's defeat in the next election.[21]

Closely aligned with male workers, members of the Lowell Female Labor Reform Association went on to purchase the press and type of New England's leading labor newspaper, the *Voice of Industry,* to which they contributed a "Female Department." Sarah Bagley, editor of the column, emphasized the need for women to defend their own interests, both physical and cultural.

Other department devoted to woman's thought will also defend woman's rights, and while it contends for physical improvement, it will not forget that she is a social, moral and religious being. It will not be neutral because it is female, but it will claim to be heard on all subjects that affect her intelligence, social or religious condition.[22]

With these words, Bagley set the stage for women's autonomous influence on the history of hours reductions later in the nineteenth century. Later organizations of women devoted to shortening women's hours also would pursue women's interests as they defined them, paying particular attention to exploitation that deprived women of their health or the ability to meet the needs of their personal lives and maintaining a close relationship with male labor organizations.[23]

## III

The first shortening of women's working hours occurred in 1853 in circumstances that differed significantly from those that preceded and followed. Trade union activity waned among both men and women in the textile industry. Skilled (male) workers in other industries moved ahead to the goal of eight hours, leaving textile and other relatively unskilled workers to fend for themselves. The latter, including women, still retained political influence, however, and this eventually brought them shorter hours.

Universal white male suffrage brought unskilled men much more political power in the United States than their equivalents enjoyed in England, where suffrage was achieved in three gradual steps in 1867, 1884, and 1918.[24] Even though they did not vote, women were members of families where men *did* vote, and in this way women shared in the power of the popular suffrage. For example, in 1852, some Massachusetts corporations responded to political pressure and reduced factory hours for male machinists to eleven hours. Women's hours remained unaltered, but in 1853, when Boston capitalists wanted to influence a critical popular vote on a new state constitution, women's hours were also reduced to eleven.[25] Thus women participated in the larger political economy by which power was exercised and social resources were distributed.

This larger political economy shaped the next stage of the struggle for women's shorter hours. After the Civil War, Short Time Committees, unaffiliated with organized labor, sprang up in factory towns.[26] Such committees emphasized political power, conducting their crusade with mass meetings and huge petitions on behalf of the ten-hour day. Although at Lowell women formed their own Short Time Committee, most of the leadership of the movement was male. Nevertheless, women populated the movement's grass roots.[27]

There was a decline in women's labor organizations and the ability of women millworkers to strike in the 1850s and 1860s. This was caused primarily by the replacement of unmarried, native-born workers with immigrant families, many of which were headed by women. Without a farm to which they could retreat, with immediate family obligations, and without the collective living of the boardinghouse, women millworkers after 1850 were increasingly deprived of those factors that had promoted their mobilization earlier. But their need and desire for shorter hours probably increased, since speed-ups in the work process continued to extract greater productivity from each worker, and as more workers lived in family groups, their need to contribute to household labor increased.[28]

At first, the Short Time Committees made little headway. In 1867, the Massachusetts legislature, following the advice of a governor's commission, passed legislation that regulated child labor only, apparently agreeing with the commission's conclusion that the law "may not interfere with the personal liberty of those who are of an adult age." A minority report, however, recommended a legal limit of ten hours for factory workers and eight for mechanical trades.[29] Since factory workers were mostly women and those in the mechanical trades were mostly men, this minority report highlighted a major problem confronting those trying to reduce women's hours: Women were assumed to work longer hours than men.

Efforts to limit women's hours were incorporated with those made to limit men's until around 1866 when Short Time Committees began to imitate the example of England's Factory Act of 1847, which had established a ten-hour day for women and children employed in manufacturing. Petitions requesting a bill that would apply only to women and children began to circulate among the committees in 1866; as in England, advocates of shorter hours hoped to ease the bill's passage by excluding male operatives. Men, concentrated in the ranks of the most skilled textile workers, would thereby increase their ability to negotiate shorter hours, and in any event would not be expected to work longer than the less skilled women. Elizabeth Brandies in 1935, and others thereafter, have pointed out that this strategy meant that men had decided to "fight the battle behind the women's petticoats."[30] Yet the claim could also be made that women workers benefited from the ability of unskilled men to press for shorter hours for women. In any case, men's and women's work under the same roof was so closely related that even though they did not work at the same task, shorter hours for one group brought shorter hours to the other.

One interesting assumption that accompanied the debate over the regulation of adult working hours between 1867 and 1874 was that women had become a permanent part of the paid labor force. The more women became the focus of state regulation, the more they were assumed by prolabor and procapital politicians alike to be permanent, not transient, features of the labor market. The debate did not consider the pros and cons of their employment, but only whether their presence could justify the intervention of the state to protect *all* workers, since that would be the effect of protecting women.[31]

Precisely because it was understood to serve as a surrogate for all millworkers, legislation for women was passed only after years of industrial struggle and experimentation had demonstrated the necessity and feasibility of the ten-hour day for all unskilled and semiskilled workers. During the Massachusetts legislative debate of 1867, the number of petitioners was placed at between 7000 and 8000, many of them women. The Lowell Ladies Short Hours Committee joined the petitioners by expressing a nearly unanimous desire for a law limiting the hours of women and children.[32] The *Lowell*

*Evening Voice,* which supported an eight-hour law applying to all workers, in 1867 gave its grudging endorsement of the more moderate ten-hour bill for women and children by declaring that "half a loaf is better than no bread."[33]

In public rallies, Short Time Committees did not mention gender. Instead, their arguments focused on workers' rights to increased leisure based on their greater productivity. This view was eloquently stated in an 1867 speech:

You know that you are not intended to be beast of burden; you are not intended to spend all your lives in toil as tributaries for the wealth of others; but you are designed to have the advantage of all the discoveries and improvements which this age of progress is constantly producing. . . . Give us ten hours a day instead of eleven and it will give us an opportunity to some extent of making ourselves answer-the ends of our being more perfectly than we can possibly under the present system.[34]

Employers and other adversaries of the movement countered with republican notions that each individual was at liberty to labor under whatever conditions he or she chose. (Such notions continued to justify opposition to legislative remedies until the Fair Labor Standards Act was ruled constitutional in 1941.) One opponent in the 1860s declared:

A compulsory ten-hour law for adults . . . would take from them the right to dispose freely of the only thing they have to sell, that is to say, *their time.* If the petitioners, being of mature age, will declare themselves incompetent to manage their own concerns, and will ask to be put under guardianship, their prayer would be entitled to some attention.[35]

Knowing that proponents of the legislation were advocating its limitation to women and children, this same opponent insisted that such laws violated women's rights:

A ten-hour law to be applied only to women and children would imply a legal restriction upon women which would work great injustice, and would be a serious infringement of woman's rights.[36]

This disingenuous defense of women's rights as a cover for hostility to workers' desires for shorter hours remained a staple of the opposition's rhetoric until 1917.

Arguments based on workers' rights to leisure were not able to overcome opposition founded on workers' rights to contract for any terms of employment; thus arguments based on workers' health became more important within the proponents' arsenal. As was true in 1845, in 1867 women presented most of the evidence. One female operative testified that "about three years was the average time women were able to stand the work" and "that it was generally the case that females employed in the mills have their constitutions broken down after a few years."[37] Furthermore, it was argued, the 1867 ten-hour law for children was impossible to enforce without legislation restricting the working hours of adults, since when inspectors visited factories, they could not tell whether or not children were working shorter hours than adults.[38]

When the Massachusetts House finally passed the first ten-hour law for American women workers in 1871, it justified its actions on the grounds that "it was for the protection of the health of a large class of the women of the State, and for the advancement of education among the children of our manufacturing communities."[39] This explanation was not untrue, but it was only part of the truth. The governor approved the bill and noted that since three-fourths of the workers in the state already enjoyed a ten-hour day, he did not see why the other fourth should not, and he added: "I know of no reason why it should not apply as well to male as to female operatives."[40]

Highlighting the near impossibility of obtaining a more extensive bill to include men, however, Senate opposition delayed the bill's passage until 1874. When the Supreme Judicial Court of Massachusetts sustained the law in 1876, its offhanded manner revealed the infancy of the debate over such statutes: "There can be no doubt that such legislation may be maintained either as a health or police regulation. . . . This principle has been so frequently recognized in this commonwealth that reference to the decisions is unnecessary."[41]

Practical as the law may seem, its path-breaking dimensions are revealed by the determination of the opposition to it. Not until 1879, thirty-five years after the first petition of 1842, were the last attempts to repeal the 1874 law defeated.[42]

## IV

After 1880, the struggle to reduce women's hours moved from the mechanized textile mills in company towns to low-capitalized industries in the diverse economies of urban centers—from making textiles in Lowell to making garments, shoes, and paper boxes in Chicago. Essentially, this entailed a shift from the factory to the sweatshop. Deprived of the organizing advantages that accompanied their large numbers in factories, sweatshop workers were also deprived of a common language, since massive immigration from southern and eastern Europe after 1880 brought together people from a wide variety of cultural and linguistic backgrounds. These changes intensified the problems of organizing against long hours and shifted much of the burden of protest to the shoulders of the English-speaking "labor aristocracy" and middle-class reformers. It also gave special prominence to some immigrant groups, particularly Russian Jews, who dominated industries, such as garment making.

A basic tenet of the short-hour movement was that workers' daily wages would not diminish with reduced worktime. In this respect, the hours movement was merely the most visible manifestation of a pervasive effort to improve wage-earners' standard of living along with the quality of their working conditions. By the 1890s, it had become clear that the statutory reduction of hours in textile mills, like the reduced working day achieved through strikes by skilled workers, did not lead to reduced wages. Although wages might dip temporarily, they were restored through more efficient use of workers' time.[43] The extension of the hours struggle to sweatshops was therefore an effort to bring these marginalized workers into the mainstream of improvements experienced by more elite groups of American wage earners.

As Chicago's garment-making sweatshops demonstrated, competition within low-capitalized industries exacerbated the problem of women's longer hours. The tremendous expansion of garment making in the city was fueled by the introduction of the sewing machine, the arrival of millions of immigrants seeking work, and the emergence of a vast market for garments in the western states. Wages fell and sweatshops abounded as the work shifted from factories to subcontractors. Subcontractors, too, were often immigrants, their only assets being rented sewing machines and the family's living quarters. Since workers and subcontractors alike were paid very little for each piece of work, profits derived primarily from the long hours that workers labored; even with long hours, workers often earned less than it cost to keep themselves alive.

At the same time that sweatshop labor was increasing, relations between capital and labor rose to an unprecedented level of conflict in heavy industries such as railroad transportation and steel. Class war had never before been so real in American history as it became in those industries after 1870, when armed violence was a regular feature of industrial conflict. This context increased the need for enlightened public policy on labor questions; at the same time, it brought a new rigidity to the opponents of state intervention in labor–capital relations.

Thus, what was fluid and exploratory in the question of women's hours before 1870 became embattled and unbending by 1890. In these circumstances, it was less likely that legislation could be passed for men as well as women, and even more likely that gender-specific strategies, which had worked in the past, would be relied on in the present. Meanwhile, ongoing practice in the textile industry in some states demonstrated to both proponents and opponents of state intervention that legislation for women was *de facto* legislation for all workers.

The most notable struggle over women's hours after 1880 took place in Chicago in the mid-1890s after the passage of a path-breaking eight-hour-day law for women and children employed in Illinois manufacturing. Supporters and opponents of the law generated strategies that endured until hours legislation for women was approved by the U.S. Supreme Court in 1907. Among supporters, strategies included the mobilization of middle-class opinion to join that of labor. Among opponents, strategies included the formation of employers' associations.

After 1880, middle-class women in Chicago and elsewhere, responded in various ways to support shorter hours for working-class women. Cross-class organizations of women created greater autonomy for women than ever before. The campaign for shorter hours, once a movement closely tied to workingmen, became a movement controlled by middle-class and working-class women, who, depending on their circumstances, might or might not work closely with male allies. Especially important in this regard were the National Consumers' League (founded in 1898) and its many local leagues, along with the Women's Trade Union League (founded in 1903).

Before these organizations were founded, the need for them was amply demonstrated in Chicago. In 1893, Chicago was ripe for the radical legislative proposal of an eight-hour day for women. The eight-hour movement of the mid-1880s had peaked in the city on May 1, 1886, when more than 20,000 men and women marched in an eight-hour-day demonstration. The movement was dramatically deprived of its momentum three days later, however, when at a rally by immigrants in Haymarket Square, protesting raised drawbridges that prevented them from joining mass meetings in the city center, a bomb exploded, killing one policeman. In the ensuing melee, a host of demonstrators and policemen were wounded. The event created an atmosphere of hysteria among the middle class throughout the country, discredited the eight-hour movement with the taint of foreign radicalism, and terminated the alliance between skilled and unskilled workers that the movement had forged.[44]

The bargaining strength of many skilled craftsmen had already established an eight-hour day in Chicago's construction trades, but they did not necessarily endorse the passage of legislation mandating shorter hours for less skilled workers. Shortening hours inevitably raised wages, they believed, and since the "iron law of wages" held that only a limited amount of capital was available for wages, increases in the earnings of unskilled workers threatened to reduce the earnings of skilled workers. Moreover, after 1886, the official policy of the skilled workers, who made up the membership of the American Federation of Labor (AFL), was to avoid legislative solutions to labor problems. Samuel Gompers, president of the AFL, thought that "the power of the courts to pass upon constitutionality of law so complicates reform by legislation as to seriously restrict the effectiveness of that method."[45] What legislatures could make, courts could unmake.

Moreover, the ability of unskilled workers, men and women, to improve their working conditions through labor unions and strikes was diminished by the economic depression of 1893. Chicago was hit especially hard by the international depression of 1891–1896, as unemployed men throughout the Midwest migrated there to find work. Throughout the winter of 1893, the halls and stairways inside municipal buildings provided shelter to a fortunate few hundred of the thousands of homeless unemployed men who camped along the lakefront. Under these desperate conditions, the grass-roots character of the eight-hour movement of the mid-1880s did not continue into the 1890s. Nevertheless, prolabor legislators who might otherwise have scorned legal solutions now were more likely to support them, and a groundswell of support for such candidates brought a reform governor and legislature into office in 1893.[46]

These were auspicious circumstances for the emergence of a new stage of the struggle to limit women's hours by statute. Two women's organizations, the Illinois Woman's Alliance, formed in 1889 in response to a crusading woman journalist's depiction of "slave girls" in the city's garment industry, and Hull House, one of the nation's first social settlements, combined their efforts in 1892 in a successful campaign against sweatshop conditions in the city. Elizabeth Morgan, founded of the Woman's Alliance, and Florence Kelley, a resident at Hull House, issued separate reports on sweatshop conditions. Morgan's was commissioned by the Chicago Trade and Labor Assembly, an organization consisting primarily of skilled male workers, Kelley's by the Illinois and federal Bureaus of Labor Statistics. Morgan's report treated sweatshops as a foreign importation that could be solved through child-labor legislation, better enforcement of health ordinances requiring air and light in manufacturing locations, and pamphlets printed in languages other than English to inform immigrant workers of their rights.[47] Kelley's report urged better opportunities for women workers because the wages of a large proportion of them were critical to their own and their family's support. Her analysis of the problem required her to seek legislative remedies beyond those proposed by Morgan.[48] When a state investigating committee held hearings in Chicago in 1893, she proposed an eight-hour day for women. The shorter day would put sweatshops out of business because it would eliminate the long hours on which their profit was based.

Kelley's efforts were greatly enhanced by her alliance with Abraham Bisno, the leading organizer of skilled and unskilled workers in Chicago's garment industry and a co-drafter of the eight-hour legislation. Bisno, a frequent participant in Hull House discussion groups, readily affiliated himself with Kelley's perspective on the sweatshop problem. As a relatively unskilled Jewish immigrant, he found Hull House more congenial than the Chicago Trade and Labor Assembly. His testimony before a state investigating committee established important links between the sweatshop problem and the legislative solution.

In his testimony, Bisno identified long hours as the crux of the problem. "The sweating system exists because the sweaters are able to employ people longer hours than they could possible employ them in the factories themselves," he declared at the outset of his testimony. Through long hours, the sweater forces workers to pay for the rental costs of machines. "He doesn't invest anything," Bisno said. Improvements such as electricity and steam power meant that the work of factory workers was quite different from that of sweatshop employees, who labored with foot-powered machines. Bisno's characterization of the sweatshop contractor was moral as well as economic:

The man that has the fox faculty, the man who is the shrewdest, the man that is without any moral scruples whatever, who has got the ability to grind women and children up to their utmost, and can hunt them out and find them—find the greenhorns that don't know anything. That is the man that survives in the sweating business and is the successful sweater. Others can't be.[49]

Bisno described the process by which clothing manufacturers fostered the growth of the sweating system by contracting out stages of garment making that previously had been done in factories, naming the firm of Joseph Beifield as the worst offender.

Long hours spent operating foot-powered sewing machines were debilitating, Bisno insisted. Defending the "eight-hour plan for women," he said that under the sweating system, women who drive sewing machines by foot power "in Chicago by the thousands are being murdered by superior powers to that of their own, working for twelve, thirteen or fourteen hours a day."[50] Bisno and Kelley also condemned the effects on men's health. In her testimony before the same committee, Florence Kelley mentioned one man who

had been operating a machine in the ordinary sweaters' shops since he was 14 years old, and was entirely incapacitated by exhaustion from further work . . . and at 33 he was superanuated and wholly dependent upon charity for supporting himself and his five children. I found a large number of cases in which the children were supporting fathers who ranged in age from 38 to 45 years, and were incapacitated purely by reason of having speeded the machine from fifteen to twenty years.[51]

In garment factories, by contrast, where machines were driven by steam, the demands on employees' physical stamina were reduced, employees were more productive, they worked shorter hours, and they had greater access to union representation.

In his testimony, Bisno emphasized the setbacks in unions among garment makers since 1886:

An attempt to organize those people is being made and has been made continually every year since the last seven years. In 1886 we have had an organization of sweat shop employees in Chicago that numbered more than ten thousand people, under the Knights of Labor. It was during the eight-hour movement in Chicago. That organization died.

Current conditions made organizing impossible:

It is impossible under the sweating system to keep up an organization. An organization has got to have some ability to have control over its members. In the sweat shop system the members are so distributed that one is in a basement and the second is on the fourth floor, one is in an alley and one is in a stable.

Nevertheless, he said that an organization of sweatshop employees in custom-made tailoring in Chicago, "numbering about six hundred people," had been formed. But when they sought "to abolish the sweat shops by single petitions to the manufacturers' organizations asking them to establish big shops," they were ignored. The Cloak Makers' Union had only 230 members, but there were thousands of men working in the trade, many of them in sweatshops or threatened by the prospect. Meanwhile, the numbers of women in the trade were increasing. Bisno estimated that about 4000 engaged in cloak making in Chicago, but the Women's Cloak Makers' Union, partly because of sweatshop conditions, had only 30 to 50 members.[52]

Separately and together, Florence Kelley and Elizabeth Morgan conducted tours of sweatshops for investigating state legislators, and each submitted proposed legislation to the investigating committee. But because of skilled labor's reluctance to pursue legislative solutions to the hours problem, Morgan's proposal dealt only with children and lacked any effective enforcement mechanism. Kelley's proposal for an eight-hour day for women and children was passed by the legislature, along with a clause that prohibited garment making in tenements, and provisions for the law's enforcement in the creation of a State Office of Factory Inspection with a chief inspector and twelve deputies.[53]

Florence Kelley's association with a community of women reformers at Hull House, one of the earliest social settlements in the United States, was a key means by which she formulated this legislation and, later, as chief factory inspector for Illinois, enforced it. The Hull House community brought her together with Abraham Bisno and others with whom she might not otherwise have collaborated. As Kelley described the settlement to her mentor, Friedrich Engels,

We have a colony of efficient and intelligent women living in a working-men's quarter with the house used for all sorts of purposes by about a thousand persons a week. The last form of its activity is the formation of unions of which we have three, the cloak-makers, the shirt-makers, and the book-binders. Next week we are to take the initiative in the systematic endeavor to clean out the sweating dens. . . . I am . . . learning more in a week, of the actual conditions of proletarian life in America than [in] any previous year.[54]

Bisno, who often attended Hull House events, said that Kelley's proposal was written "with the advice of myself, Henry Lloyd, and a number of prominent attorneys in Chicago."[55] The settlement was also critical to the bill's passage by organizing support among the members of the Chicago Women's Club, many of whom traveled to Springfield to lobby for the bill.[56]

Signifying the importance of Hull House to Kelley's enforcement efforts after the reform governor, John Peter Altgeld, appointed her the law's chief enforcer, Kelley located the inspector's office just across the street from the settlement. The merging of that office and the settlement was further strengthened by the residence in Hull House of her chief assistant, Alzina Stevens, and one of her most effective deputies, Mary Kenny, both of working-class origins and both experienced union organizers. Stevens also served as president of the Women's Council, a consortium of women's trade unions. After Bisno's appointment as deputy inspector, he spent even more time at the settlement.[57]

Bisno described enforcement efforts as "radical" and "fanatical."[58] They affected men and women workers, not only in the garment industry but throughout Illinois industries where women were employed. Summing up their success, Kelley wrote Engels on New Year's Eve, 1894:

We have at last won a victory for our 8 hours law. The Supreme Court has handed down no decision sustaining it, but the Stockyards magnates having been arrested until they are tired of it, have instituted the 8 hours day for 10,000 employees, men, women and children. We have 18 suits pending to enforce the 8 hours law and we think we shall establish it permanently before Easter. It has been a painful struggle of eighteen months and the Supreme Court may annul the law. But I have great hopes that the popular interest may prove too strong.[59]

In her annual report that year, Kelley said that the muscle power behind the 1893 law's passage came from labor unions. But her own experience demonstrated that a more immediate cause for the law's effective enforcement sprang from her own actions and that of her dedicated staff.

Did working women benefit from such enforcement? Did they want shorter hours? Although some women workers, particularly those who headed households with small children, must have opposed the law's enforcement, others, especially single women and mothers able to arrange for child care, stood to gain from the benefits of factory employment. The factory setting was more likely to be equipped with labor-saving devices, such as steam-powered sewing machines; more likely to abide by state hours legislation and therefore to provide wage-earning women with a shorter working day; more likely to comply with state sanitary laws that upgraded toilet facilities; and, perhaps most importantly, more likely to nurture the growth of unions among women workers. In Chicago in 1893, the Women's Shoemakers Union was especially vigorous in its support for the legislation's enforcement. Far from retaining women in the most exploitative jobs, the law eliminated those jobs and channeled women into improved conditions in factories.[60]

Some of the best evidence of women's needs and desires for shorter hours can be found in data collected by an investigation of the Pennsylvania Bureau of Industrial Statistics in 1894.[61] The study asked more than two hundred women sales and clerical workers to state complaints about their jobs. The women objected to many features of their working conditions, including low wages, the lack of provision of seats, and poorly ventilated toilet rooms, but the largest number of complaints were lodged against the length of the working day and the need for Saturday hours.[62] In an article analyzing this material, Gary Cross and Peter Shergold concluded that the problem of the long day was more acute for women because their family and home responsibilities pressed more urgently on their non-wage-earning hours than was the case with men. They speculate that women's labor militancy arose in part from their desire to reduce the length of their working day.

Women's enjoyment of the eight-hour day in Chicago ended in 1895 when the Illinois Supreme Court found that portion of the law unconstitutional. In this period of accelerated struggle between capital and labor, greater mobilization on behalf of hours legislation was matched by greater mobilization against it. *Laissez-faire* views may not have been stronger in the United States than elsewhere, but since American federal and state constitutions gave courts a more powerful position in the polity, courts could employ *laissez-faire* ideas with more destructive effect. Two months after the eight-hour law was passed, a group calling itself the Illinois Manufacturers Protective Association met with the explicit purpose of "cooperating to test the constitutionality of a recent act of the Legislature of this State limiting the hours of Female Labor."[63] For public relations reasons, at its next meeting the group changed its name to the Illinois Manufacturers' Association (IMA).

Early members of the IMA included manufacturers of shoes and paper boxes, but clothing manufacturers dominated. Joseph Beifield served on the group's board of directors. By April 1894, the group had spent $1525 "in suits brought to test the Constitutionality of the Eight hour labor law" and expected "additional expenditures of at least $2,000." The IMA employed a full-time secretary and assistant (paid $25 a week) to supervise fund-raising efforts and expenditures.[64]

At first, the IMA covered the court expenses of manufacturers accused by Kelley's office of violating the law. Given the active prosecution by the inspector's office, however, this policy ceased in April 1894. A memorandum that month noted: "As a great many suits were being brought for infraction of the Eight hour law," the IMA would pay for the

"defense of members arrested for infraction of the Eight hour female labor law up to and including Sat. the 21st of April . . . but that any expense incurred by reason of arrests for violation of the law after said date shall be borne by person or firm violating the same."[65]

By that time, the organization was sponsoring enough cases to achieve their goal of challenging the law's constitutionality.

After the Illinois Supreme Court unanimously declared the eight-hour portion of the 1893 law unconstitutional, the logic of the IMA argument was partially revealed by its attorney, Levy Mayer, who in an interview with the *Chicago Tribune* welcomed women to the doctrine of rugged individualism:[66]

[The eight-hour law] sprang from the needs of paternalism and socialism, neither of which has any place in this country. . . . I am therefore doubly glad the Supreme Court has applied and enforced in a way so rugged and decisive the doctrine that woman is equal to man before the law and that her right to her labor, which constitutes her property, is as sacred and impregnable as is the similar right of man.[66]

A *Tribune* editorial took special care to discredit health as a justification for the eight-hour legislation:

The mere fact of her being a woman does not justify the Legislature in limiting her right to contract unless it can be shown that the health, comfort, and welfare of the people require it. The court confesses its inability to see any reasonable ground for fixing upon eight hours in one day as the limit at which a woman can labor without injury to her physique.

The *Tribune* also noted that laws for women could serve as a precedent for laws for men:

This decision will be intensely distasteful to some of the labor demagogues for two reasons. They hoped if they could make a breach in the principle of free contract by securing a division to the effect that the Legislature could fix compulsorily the length of the working day of female citizens they could get a similar decision regarding male citizens.[67]

The *Tribune* concluded: "In far reaching results the decision is most important. It is the first division in the United States against the eight-hour law and presents a new obstacle in the path of the movement for shorter hours." After this defeat, Florence Kelley and her deputies fought back by proposing a new eight-hour law for all minors under the age of eighteen. The IMA mobilized fierce opposition to that proposal and was probably responsible for the bill's defeat.[68]

Thus, in the 1890s, the struggle over hours legislation for women grew in intensity. More than ever, it was closely linked with men's hours; but more than ever, it was carried forward by women.

## V

The impasse between opponents and proponents of hours legislation for women was broken in 1907 by a path-breaking argument before the U.S. Supreme Court in *Muller* v. *Oregon*. The argument focused on a theme that had been endemic to the struggle for shorter hours: the ill effects of long hours on women's health. Thereafter called "the Brandeis Brief," after Louis D. Brandeis, who presented it to the Court, the argument marked a major turning point in American jurisprudence; thereafter, sociological evidence, based on people's actual experience, gained admission to the legal process, and court decisions were not rendered on the basis of legal precedent or theory alone.[69]

Between 1895, when the Illinois law was found unconstitutional, and 1908, only eight states passed new hours laws for women—a paucity reflecting the legal cloud cast by the Illinois ruling.[70] That cloud was disbursed in 1908 by the *Muller* decision. Thus, sixty-six years after women workers first petitioned for ten-hour labor in Massachusetts, the legality of such statutes was finally settled. The importance of *Muller* was visible in the twenty-four states that passed or expanded similar laws in the legislative sessions of 1911 and 1913.[71]

Just before this dawn of a new day, the night was darkest for proponents of hours legislation for women. A U.S. Supreme Court decision (*Lockner*

v. *New York)* in 1905 voided a 1895 New York law that had limited bakers' hours to ten per day on the grounds that excessive labor was injurious to health in that trade. Bakers often worked in cellars, beginning their day in the middle of the night; tuberculosis could be the result. In a 5–4 decision, the majority found

that the trade of a baker in and of itself, is not an unhealthy one to that degree which would authorize the Legislature to interfere with the right to labor and with the right of free contract on the part of the individual either as employer or employee.[72]

This decision rendered more difficult the strategy with which reformers and labor advocates had gained judicial support for statutory limitation of working hours since 1898, when the Supreme Court approved a Utah hours law for miners on the grounds of health.[73] That decision confirmed health or bodily injury as the sole means by which advocates of statutory hours restrictions could bypass the claim that restricting hours violated workers' rights. Now that route seemed to be blocked. Added to this reversal was the 1906 decision by the New York Supreme Court, in *People* v. *Williams and O'Rourke,* which nullified a 1899 law that had prohibited women from working after 9:00 P.M.[74] There, too, the court ruled that the law infringed upon the liberty of workers to contract for employment under whatever terms they chose.

These setbacks demonstrated the power of the courts to determine public policy about working hours in the United States. Although many areas of American life had abandoned the *laissez-faire* attitudes embodied in these decisions, the courts seemingly ignored such change. Matching their determination was that of women reformers, who allied with women workers, had one last opportunity to salvage the statutory restriction of hours on health grounds. For the Supreme Court had not yet ruled on women's health as grounds for the limitation of daytime hours.

What later became known as the Brandeis Brief was actually written by Josephine Goldmark, sister-in-law of the distinguished Boston attorney. In 1898, Florence Kelley had moved to New York to assume the position she retained until her death in 1932 as secretary general of the National Consumers' League (NCL). Building a powerful network of local leagues throughout the country, Kelley headed the single most powerful lobbying agency for labor legislation for women and children. As the NCL's director of research, Goldmark was Kelley's chief assistant. After the *Lockner* and *Williams* decisions, Goldmark gathered evidence about the health effects of long hours from reports made to the British Parliament, from American reports of industrial commissions and state bureaus of labor statistics, from medical books, and from state boards of health. These conclusions were eventually published in *Fatigue and Efficiency: A Study in Industry* (1912), a landmark document of the hours movement in the United States.[75]

Almost immediately after the *Lockner* and *Williams* decisions, a likely case presented itself to the National Consumer's League to test the validity of women's hours laws. Representatives of one of the most active leagues in one of the most progressive states, Oregon, where the legislation was well written and likely to withstand judicial scrutiny, informed Florence Kelley that the state's ten-hour law for women was being challenged by a laundry owner named Muller. When the state supreme court upheld the law, and Muller appealed, the stage was set for a showdown on the constitutionality of hours legislation for women, which in turn would determine the acceptability of hours legislation for men.

Louis Brandeis, acting on behalf of the National Consumers' League, signed two briefs in *Muller* v. *Oregon*. One, written by the Oregon attorney general, focused on questions of legal precedent and theory. The other, written by Josephine Goldmark, presented sociological evidence about the effects of long hours on women's health. The fundamental argument in Goldmark's commentary was articulated by the Massachusetts Bureau of Statistics of Labor in 1881:

The flesh and blood of the operatives have only so much work in them, and it was all got out in ten hours, and no more could be got out in twelve; and what was got extra . . . was taken right out of the life of the operatives.[76]

As Beatrice Webb put it, in another source quoted by Goldmark:

If employers in a particular trade are able to take such advantage of the necessities of their workpeople as to . . . work them for hours so long as to deprive them of adequate rest and recreation . . . that trade is clearly using up and destroying a part of the nation's working capital.[77]

Such industries "are therefore not really self-supporting" but are "parasitic" upon the society. These quotes were typical of most of the sources Goldmark included, since most did not refer to women specifically but spoke of the need for the regulation of industry for the general welfare.

That emphasis did not persist in the Court's decision. The decision, written by Justice Brewer, noted that Curt Muller argued that the principles upheld in *Lockner* should apply in this case, but Brewer replied that "this assumes that the difference between the sexes does not justify a different rule respecting a restriction of the hours of labor."[78] Because Justice Brewer wanted to avoid the conclusion that the Court's decision in *Muller* overturned the *Lockner* decision, he emphasized the gender-specific aspects of the case, stating that "legislation designed for her protection may be sustained, even when like legislation is not necessary for men and could not be sustained." Brewer therefore provided the most complete list of gender-based differences imaginable:

The two sexes differ in structure of body, in the functions to be performed by each, in the amount of physical strength, in the capacity for long-continued labor, particularly when done standing, the influence of vigorous health upon the future well-being of the race, the self-reliance which enables one to assert full rights, and in the capacity to maintain the struggle for subsistence. This difference justifies a difference in legislation.[79]

Essentially the Court in 1908 ruled that differences between men and women meant that women's exercise of the right to work should be protected by the state, even though men's right should not be so protected.

Ten years later, the Court's arguments in *Muller* were rendered obsolete in *Oregon* v. *Bunting*. In that decision, the Supreme Court acknowledged the constitutionality of hours legislation for men. The National Consumers' League was just as critical in shaping that decision as it had been in *Muller*, cooperating with the Oregon league and obtaining the services of the attorney Felix Frankfurter.[80] In that case, the court finally laid *Lockner* to rest. Ironically, the decision was justified partly on the gender-specific grounds that emphasized the need to protect men from exploitation that would render them unable to fight for their country as soldiers. (The decision was rendered in 1917 in the midst of World War I, after surveys had shown that a large proportion of those who volunteered for military service were physically unfit.[81])

The National Consumers' League was not alone in orchestrating the Supreme Court's decision in *Muller* v. *Oregon*. While the league mobilized middle-class opinion and resources, the Women's Trade Union League (WTUL), founded in 1903 by women trade unionists and residents in the social settlement movement, mobilized important support within the labor movement. Founded to promote unions among women workers and to affiliate those unions with the American Federation of Labor, the WTUL had the same autonomous characteristics as the Lowell Female Labor Reform Association, but, like the Lowell association, was institutionally linked to a larger male labor movement.[82]

Asserting a strong legislative agenda from the time of its founding, the WTUL passed three resolutions at one of its early New York meetings. The first read: "That the Committee declare itself in favor of an eight hour day and demands a law that no woman shall be allowed to work more than fifty-eight hours a week, not after 9 P.M.''[83] Another instructed three members to consult with an expert "about securing a law to prevent hiring of workers under false pretenses," and a third recommended the creation of employment bureaus at each local. Of these three resolutions, the first was clearly the most important to the league.

Although much of the league's activities revolved around union organizing and strikes during the insurgent years of 1907–1910 in the garment industry, the league's first agenda item at their annual meeting in 1907 was the *Muller* case. The agenda stated that although the Oregon Supreme Court had "decided the law limiting the hours of work for women to ten a day was constitutional," the Laundrymen's Association was appealing the case to the U.S. Supreme Court.[84] Supplying "legal aid, money and backing" to the Laundry and Shirt Waist Workers who were fighting to retain Oregon's ten-hour law, the WTUL clearly believed that statutory strategies were an ongoing part of union activities. While those legislative goals became and even more salient part of the WTUL's agenda after 1920, when organizing became more difficult, they were crucial to the WTUL from its beginning and recruited labor support for the *Muller* case in 1907.

# VI

Between 1840 and 1910, conditions fostered by rapid, unregulated industrialization and ideological commitments expressed through the powerful medium of state courts meant that hours legislation for women became a radical cause. Nevertheless, it also remained an eminently practical solution to the problems workers faced, especially women workers. Far from confirming women's place in the most exploitative jobs, statutes limiting women's working hours were often the means of eliminating those jobs and opening improved employment opportunities to women. Furthermore, hours limitation by statute historically went hand in hand with trade union organizing, as complementary rather than competing strategies. Such laws emphasized the physical limitations of women's ability to work long hours, but so too did women workers, who demanded shorter hours. Moreover, hours laws for men, when they were finally upheld as constitutional in 1917, emphasized the physical limitations of men's ability to work longer hours. In the United States, the structure of, and beliefs about, government meant that legislative limitations on working hours were justified on the basis of sociological and physiological necessity, not on the basis of workers' rights to leisure.

From the origin of the need for state protection in the 1840s to the recognition of that need for both men and women by the highest legal authority in 1917, four themes interacted to blaze a historical path of change. The close relationship between men and women workers, the mobilization of women workers and their middle-class allies, the power of courts in American life, and the appeal of *laissez-faire* ideas combined in such a way as to limit the development of new options after the earliest resolution of the issue was reached in 1874. As time passed, mobilization increased on both sides, women in support of hours legislation and employers against it. During critical junctures of that process, gender did the work of class by promoting the protection of all workers. In the United States, more than in other political economies, the protection of all workers rested on the mobilization of women.

## NOTES

1. The historic struggle to reduce the length of the working day for wage-earning women had many gender-specific components, including the fact that until 1880 it was limited to a minority of women workers, those employed in manufacturing occupations. After 1880, the increasing number of women employed as sales-clerks joined this struggle, demanding earlier closing of stores during the week and only half a day's work on Saturday. Nevertheless, it should be remembered that, until 1900, a majority of American wage-earning women labored as servants or in agriculture; for them, it was even more difficult to achieve their goals through unions and strikes. They remained largely unaffected by the struggle to shorten women's hours in manufacturing and commerce establishments before 1910, but their long hours exerted a drag on the efforts of other women to gain shorter hours.

Also gender specific was the fact that this struggle was waged by and on behalf of a working population that, on the average, was much younger than that of men. Two-thirds of working women before 1920 were between the ages of sixteen and twenty-five. Women left the paid workforce after marriage because their contributions to the family economy as housewives were more valuable than the meager wages they could earn outside the home. The female labor force was disproportionately young compared to the female population as a whole and the male labor force. It manifested a higher degree of turnover, as young women in their twenties were constantly replaced by younger women in their teens. Married women who reentered or remained in the paid labor force usually came from economically desperate families, particularly those lacking a male wage earner.

2. This negative view started as early as 1925 with Elizabeth Faulkner Baker, *Protective Labor Legislation: With Special Reference to Women in the State of New York* (New York, 1925). Baker concluded that "in occupations where women predominate, protective laws for women are found to be likely to protect both men and women" (pp. 425–426), but in occupations where men dominate, such as printing or street-railway employees, protective laws jeopardized women's jobs. Clara M.

Beyer took a more positive view in *History of Labor Legislation for Women in Three States* (Washington, D.C., 1932), as did Elizabeth Brandeis, in "Labor Legislation," in *A History of Labor in the United States, 1896–1932*, ed. John R. Commons (New York, 1935), 3: 399–539. Historians have tended to follow Baker's example rather than that of Beyer or Brandeis, exhibiting more concern over the laws' effects on occupations in which few women worked than those where women dominated. See Alice Kessler-Harris, *Out to Work: A History of Wage-Earning Women in the United States* (New York, 1982), pp. 180–214; Susan Lehrer, *Origins of Protective Labor Legislation for Women, 1900–1925* (Albany, 1987); Jacob Andrew Lieberman, " 'Their Sisters' Keepers': The Women's Hours and Wages Movement in the United States, 1890–1925," Ph.D. dissertation, Columbia University, 1971. More sympathetic to protective legislation is Nancy Schrom Dye, *As Equals and as Sisters: Feminism, Unionism, and the Women's Trade Union League of New York* (Columbia, Mo., 1980), pp. 140–166. Judith A. Baer, *The Chains of Protection: The Judicial Response to Women's Labor Legislation* (Westport, Conn., 1978), summarizes secondary sources from the perspective of a political scientist.

3. Kessler-Harris, *Out to Work*, pp. 213–214.

4. Diane Kirkby, " 'The Wage Earning Woman and the State': The National Women's Trade Union League and Protective Labor Legislation, 1903–1923," *Labor History* 28, no. 1 (Winter 1987): 54–74; and Diane Elizabeth Kirkby, "Alice Henry: The National Women's Trade Union League of America and Progressive Labor Reform, 1906–1925," Ph.D. dissertation, University of California, Santa Barbara, 1982.

5. Kirkby, "Wage-Earning Woman," p. 55.

6. Ibid., p. 56.

7. See Beyer, *History of Labor Legislation*, p. 109, for a summary of successful efforts to obtain the exemption of printers and journalists.

8. Thomas Dublin, *Women at Work: The Transformation of Work and Community in Lowell, Massachusetts, 1826–1860* (New York, 1979), pp. 58–86.

9. Preindustrial work hours, included lengthy breaks for meals and other diversions. With machine production, task-oriented work habits gave way to the time-oriented demands of the machine. Mill operatives worked for an average of 12 hours a day, 6 days a week, 309 days a year. The length of working days varied by the season, with the longest days (13.5 hours) occurring in April, and the shortest (11.5 hours) in January. In the 1820s, factories usually assigned two looms to each operative; in the 1840s, at least three and usually four looms per person were typical. Breaks were possible only if a neighboring worker tended one's looms. Paid by the piece rather than by the hour, workers recognized that they were not benefiting fairly from their increased productivity. In 1846 they resolved that "we will not tend a fourth loom (except to oblige each other) unless we receive the same pay per piece as on three, and that we will use our influence to prevent others from pursuing a course which has always had a tendency to reduce our wages." *Voice of Industry*, May 15, 1846, quoted in John R. Commons *et al.*, *Documentary History of American Industrial Society* (New York, 1958), 8:231.

10. Dublin, *Women at Work*, p. 113.

11. David Montgomery, *Beyond Equality: Labor and the Radical Republicans, 1862–1872* (Urbana, Ill., 1981), p. 243.

12. Beyer, *History of Labor Legislation,* p. 16; and Eric J. Evans, *The Forging of the Modern State: Early Industrial Britain, 1783–1870* (London, 1983), pp. 228–236.

13. For Lord Ashley's role in early factor legislation, see William C. Lubenow, *The Politics of Government Growth: Early Victorian Attitudes toward State Intervention, 1833–1848* (Hamden, Conn.: 1971).

14. The British context has been extensively explored in Lubenow, *The Politics of Government Growth* pp. 137–179; Neville Kirk, *The Growth of Working Class Reformism in Mid-Victorian England* (Urbana, 1985); Oliver MacDonagh, *Early Victorian Government, 1830–1870* (London, 1977), pp. 22–77; Peter March, "The Conservative Conscience," in *The Conscience of the Victorian State,* ed. Peter Marsh (Syracuse, 1979), pp. 215–242; Theodore Rothstein, *From Chartism to Labourism* (New York, 1984); and Keith Burgess, *The Origins of British Industrial Relations: The Nineteenth Century Experience* (London, 1975), pp. 231–302. For the American side, see Susan M. Kingsbury, *Labor Laws and Their Enforcement with Special Reference to Massachusetts* (New York, 1911), pp. 3–54.

15. *Voice of Industry,* September 18, 1846, quoted in Dublin, *Women at Work,* p. 114.

16. For a theoretical analysis of the significance of women's separate organizations, see Estelle Freedman, "Separatism as Strategy: Female Institution Building and American Feminism, 1870–1930," *Feminist Studies* 5, 3 (Fall 1979): 512–529.

17. Massachusetts House Document, No. 50, March 1845, in Commons *et al., Documentary History,* 8:133. (p. 143).

18. Commons, *et al., Documentary History,* 8:137.

19. Massachusetts House Document, No. 50, March 1845, in Commons, *et al. Documentary History,* 8:136; and Dublin, *Women at Work,* pp. 109–111.
The use of artificial lighting for night work came in for special criticism as a health hazard through the fumes generated by oil and gas lamps, and through increased risk of fire. One woman said that as many as 61 large and small lamps burned to illuminate a workroom containing 150 employees. Massachusetts House Document, No. 50, March 1845, quoted in Commons *et al., Documentary History,* 8:135.

20. Ibid., 8:148–150.

21. *Voice of Industry,* September 18, 1846, and November 28, 1845, quoted in Dublin, *Women at Work,* pp. 114–115.

22. *Voice of Industry,* 1846, quoted in Dublin, *Women at Work,* p. 119.

23. Elsewhere, early industrial workers also protested against long hours. At Manayunk, on the outskirts of Philadelphia, the predominantly female labor force walked off the job in 1833–1834, demanding a ten-hour day. In 1845, 4000 Pittsburgh textile operatives maintained a month-long unsuccessful strike for a ten-hour day. One of the more dramatic confrontations occurred in Nashua, New Hampshire, in 1846. When women mill workers left their looms and refused to work after dark, overseers locked the factory gates, forcing the women to remain in the mill yard

until the evening bell. Meanwhile, nearly 1000 persons outside the gates cheered the protesters, including male machinists whose signs read *No Lighting Up*. However, the Lowell Female Labor Reform Association had soon devolved into a mutual aid society; the heyday of women's trade union activity did not extend into the 1850s. See Cynthia J. Shelton, *The Mills of Manayunk: Industrialization and Social Conflict in the Philadelphia Region, 1787–1837* (Baltimore, 1986), pp. 163–164; Hannah Josephson, *The Golden Threads: New England's Mill Girls and Magnates* (New York, 1949), pp. 267, 276; and David Randall Roediger, "Movement for a Shorter Working Day in the United States Before 1866," Ph.D. dissertation, Northwestern University, 1980, p. 163.

24. Evans, *Forging the Modern State*, p. 352.

25. Josephson, *Golden Threads*, pp. 284–285.

26. Kingsbury, *Labor Law*, pp. 106–07.

27. Montgomery, *Beyond Equality*, p. 286.

28. Dublin, *Women at Work*, pp. 198–207.

29. Montgomery, *Beyond Equality*, p. 292.

30. Brandeis, "Labor Legislation," in Commons, *History of Labor*, 3:462.

31. For example, the assumption of the permanent presence of women workers pervades the sources cited by Montgomery in *Beyond Equality* as well as his own analysis.

32. Montgomery, *Beyond Equality*, p. 286.

33. After the passage in 1847 of a ten-hour-day law for women and children in English textile mills, American corporations added fifteen minutes to the workers' lunch break. Josephson, *Golden Threads*, pp. 281–282. Culturally accustomed to better, not worse, working conditions than women, and possessing greater bargaining power—based on their greater degree of skilled labor—men could assume their *de facto* inclusion in any legislation that applied to women. One example of the grounds for this expectation was visible in Lowell in 1867 when employers restored wage cuts they had levied on male employees, while retaining cuts for women. See Montgomery, *Beyond Equality*, p. 286; and Kingsbury, *Labor Laws*, pp. 106–109. The traditional trade union strategy of the strike persisted alongside these legislative maneuverings. A two-week walkout led by the Fall River Short Time Amalgamated Association prompted the political intervention of a state senator who obtained the owners' agreement to adopt a ten-hour schedule with no loss in wages. Industrial peace prevailed in that very class-conscious city until 1871 when, failing to obtain legislation that would force other mills to adopt the shorter hours, Fall River's mill owners precipitated a violent strike and three years of industrial struggle by reinstating longer hours. At the Atlantic Mills in Lawrence, however, where enlightened management had instituted the ten-hour day in 1868, the experiment was deemed a success after 1871 when the labor cost per pound of textiles proved to be less than it had been with longer hours. Thus, by 1871, when the Massachusetts legislature again considered legislative solutions to capital–labor relations, the economic viability of shorter hours had been demonstrated. See Montgomery, *Beyond Equality*, p. 278; and Kingsbury, *Labor Laws*, pp. 110–113.

34. Kingsbury, *Labor Laws*, p. 104.

35. Ibid., p. 116.

36. Ibid.

37. Reported in the *Daily Evening Voice,* February 27, 1867, and quoted in Kingsbury, *Labor Laws,* p. 117.

38. Kingsbury, *Labor Laws,* pp. 97–98.

39. Ibid., p. 123.

40. Ibid., p. 124.

41. George Gorham Groat, *Attitude of American Courts in Labor Cases: A Study in Social Legislation* (New York, 1911), p. 293.

42. Kingsbury, *Labor Laws,* p. 125. Although in 1847 New Hampshire became the first state to pass a ten-hour law, that statute was unenforceable, since it permitted individual agreements between employers and employees, and provided no penalties for violation. "The First Ten-Hour Law, New Hampshire, 1847," in Commons, *et al., Documentary History,* 8:188–199.

43. The best compilation of sources available in the 1890s on the question of the relationship between women's hours and wages is Josephine Goldmark, *Fatigue and Efficiency: A Study in Industry* (New York, 1912), pp. 395–406.

44. Henry David, *The History of the Haymarket Affair: A Study in the American Social-Revolutionary and Labor Movements* (New York, 1936), pp. 188, 198–219.

45. Samuel Gompers, *Seventy Years of Life and Labour: An Autobiography,* 2 vols. (New York, 1925), 1:194.

46. *Chicago Tribune,* November 7, 1892 and November 15, 1893.

47. Chicago Trade and Labor Assembly [Elizabeth Morgan], *The New Slavery: Investigation into the Sweating System as Applied to the Manufacture of Wearing Apparel* (Chicago, 1891), Elizabeth Morgan Papers, Folder 16. For an analysis of Morgan's reform career, see Ralph Scharnau, "Elizabeth Morgan, Crusader for Labor Reform," *Labor History* 14, no. 3 (Summer 1973): 340–351.

48. *Seventh Biennial Report of the Bureau of Labor Statistics of Illinois* (Springfield, Ill., 1893), pp. 355–443. "The sweating system seems to be a direct outgrowth of the factory system," Kelley wrote. It resulted from "the modern demand for ready-made clothing in great quantities," and the "subdivision of the labor on garments" (pp. 357, 358).

49. *Report and Findings of the Joint Committee to Investigate the "Sweat Shop" System, Together with a Transcript of the Testimony Taken by the Committee* (Springfield, Ill., 1893), pp. 236–238.

50. Ibid., p. 241.

51. Ibid., p. 137.

52. Ibid., p. 242.

53. Ibid., pp. 138–139, 148–149. See also Kathryn Kish Sklar, "Hull House in the 1890's: A Community of Women Reformers," *Signs: Journal of Women in Culture and Society* 10, no. 4 (Summer 1985): 658–677.

54. Florence Kelley to Friedrich Engels, Hull House, Chicago, April 7, 1892, Archive Institute of Marxism–Leninism, No. 8490 a, b, c. See also Dorothy Rose Blumberg, " 'Dear Mr. Engels': Unpublished Letters, 1884–1894, of Florence Kel-

ley (-Wischnewetzky) to Friedrich Engels," *Labor History* 5, no. 2 (Spring 1964): 103–133. Kelley's relationship with Engels began in 1884 when she decided to translate his *Condition of the English Working Class in 1844* (New York, 1887). Until 1958, hers was the only English translation of this classic work and remains today the version preferred by scholars.

55. *Report and Findings,* pp. 235–244.

56. Sklar, "Hull House in the 1890's," p. 668.

57. Abraham Bisno, *Abraham Bisno, Union Pioneer: An Autobiographical Account of Bisno's Life and the Beginnings of Unionism in the Women's Garment Industry* (Madison, Wisc., 1967), pp. 148–149.

58. Ibid., p. 148.

59. Florence Kelley to Friedrich Engels, Hull House, December 31, 1894.

60. For further analysis of the benefits women derived from the law, see Sklar, "Hull House in the 1890's."

61. Gary Cross and Peter Shergold, " 'We Think We Are of the Oppressed': Gender, White Collar Work, and Grievances of Late Nineteenth-Century Women," *Labor History* 28, no. 1 (Winter, 1987): 23–53.

62. Ibid., pp. 34–36.

63. Memorandum, August 24, 1893, Illinois Manufacturers' Association (IMA) Papers, Box 1.

64. Memorandum, April 19, 1894, IMA Papers, Box 1, folder 1.

65. Memorandum, April 19, 1894, IMA Papers.

66. *Chicago Tribune,* March 16, 1895. The same story said that "eight other cases which came up from Cook County at the same time and upon the same points are disposed of by this opinion."

A variety of factors combined to render government even less likely to mediate conflicts between capital and labor in the last quarter of the nineteenth century than it had been before. Chief among these was the ideology of *laissez-faire,* inherited from social Darwinist thought, which viewed human survival, not as a social right, but as a test of individual fitness. Highlighting the centrality of the judiciary in American governmental structures, this ideology dominated American jurisprudence after 1880, providing courts with intellectual justification for overturning legislative acts designed to support labor. In the name of preserving individual liberty and the right of workers to contract with employers on any terms they wished, state and federal courts made it extremely difficult for government tó redress injustices generated in the workplace. The first such rulings occurred in 1886 with the Supreme Court of Pennsylvania, which declared unconstitutional a law prohibiting the payment of wages in scrip redeemable at the company store. For a discussion of the emergence of "freedom of contract" in American jurisprudence, see Lehrer, *Origins of Protective Labor Legislation for Women,* p. 50.

One telling example of judicial attitudes was an 1884 decision by the New York Supreme Court, which ruled unconstitutional a law prohibiting the production of cigars in tenements. Samuel Gompers, president of the Cigarmakers Union, and beginning his long career as president of the AFL, drew an important moral from the court's action. After a long and unsuccessful effort to defend the constitutionality of the tenement legislation, Gompers concluded that "the power of the courts to pass upon the constitutionality of the law so complicates reform by legislation as to seriously restrict the effectiveness of that method." Thus began the policy of "voluntarism" within the nation's chief labor organization, a policy that rarely sought political solutions for labor's problems. See Gompers, *Seventy Years,* p. 194. See also Claire Brandler Walker, "A History of Factory Legislation and Inspection in New York State, 1886–1911," Ph.D. Dissertation, Columbia University, 1969, pp. 93, 224; and Michael A. Gordon, "The Labor Boycott in New York City," in *American Workingclass Culture: Explorations in American Labor and Social History,* ed. Milton Cantor (Westport, Conn., 1979), pp. 319–320.

For exceptions of this rule, see Gary M. Fink, "The Rejection of Voluntarism," *Industrial and Labor Relations Review* 26 (1972–1973): 805–819; Stephen J. Scheinberg, "Theodore Roosevelt and the A.F. of L.'s. Entry into Politics, 1906–1908," *Labor History* 3, no. 2 (Spring 1962): 131–148; and Keith L. Bryant, Jr., "Labor in Politics: The Oklahoma State Federation of Labor during the Age of Reform," *Labor History* 11, no. 3 (Summer 1970): 259–276. An important exception to this rule was labor's continued interest in opposing antilabor strategies by the state, particularly the antistrike injunction. In 1890, before the injunction was widely used, the AFL national convention voted against a proposal to establish a lobby in Washington, but after the use of injunctions to repress strikes in 1893–1894, the AFL began to lobby Congress for the passage of an anti-injunction bill, and it established a permanent lobbying committee in 1896. See Commons, *et al., History of Labor,* 2:501–503. See also M. Karson, *American Labor Unions and Politics, 1900–1918* (Carbondale, Ill., 1958), pp. 29–30; and Irving Yellowitz, *Labor and the Progressive Movement in New York State, 1897–1916* (Ithaca, N.Y., 1965).

The literature on Gompers's voluntarism is extensive. See, for example, Vivian Vale, *Labour in American Politics* (New York, 1971), pp. 25–50; and P. Taft, *The A.F. of L. in the Time of Gompers* (New York, 1957).

67. *Chicago Tribune,* March 16, 1895; clipping in IMA Papers.

68. See, for example, newspaper clipping in IMA Papers, April 8, 1895.

69. Writings on the Brandeis Brief are voluminous. One example is Philippa Strum, *Louis D. Brandeis: Justice for the People* (Cambridge, Mass., 1984), pp. 114–131. Sociological jurisprudence became the norm in the mid-twentieth century, influencing such landmark decisions as *Brown* v. *Topeka Board of Education* in 1954.

70. E. Brandeis, "Labor Legislation," p. 466. Although several states had passed such legislation, the law was enforced almost nowhere outside Massachusetts, where a tradition of strong government often made it the exception to the American rule of weak or nonexistent governmental regulation.

71. Ibid., p. 474. The states were Arizona, California, Colorado, Connecticut, Delaware, Idaho, Illinois, Massachusetts, Montana, Nebraska, New Hampshire, New York, Ohio, Oregon, Pennsylvania, Rhode Island, South Carolina, South Dakota, Tennessee, Texas, Utah, Virginia, Washington, Wisconsin.

72. *Lockner* v. *New York,* 198 U.S. 45 (1905). See also Groat, *Attitude of American Courts in Labor Cases,* pp. 319–322; Marion Cotter Cahill, *Shorter Hours: A*

*Study of the Movement Since the Civil War* (New York, 1932), pp. 124–126; and Michael Les Benedict, "Laissez-Faire and Liberty: A Re-Evaluation of the Meaning and Origins of Laissez-Faire Constitutionalism," *Law and History Review,* 3, no. 2 (Fall 1985): 293–331.

73. See Cahill, *Shorter Hours,* pp. 119–123.

74. *People* v. *Williams and O'Rourke,* 189 N.Y. 131 (1907).

75. For Goldmark citation, note 43 above.

76. *Report of the Massachusetts Bureau of Statistics of Labor,* 1881, quoted in Louis D. Brandeis and Josephine Goldmark, *Women in Industry: Decision of the United States Supreme Court in Curt Muller vs. State of Oregon Upholding the Constitutionality of the Oregon Ten Hour Law for Women and Brief for the State of Oregon* (New York, n.d.), pp. 67–68.

77. Brandeis and Goldmark, *Women in Industry,* pp. 53–54.

78. Ibid., p. 4.

79. *Muller* decision reprinted in ibid., p. 7.

80. Cahill, *Shorter Hours,* p. 131.

81. See Chapter 7, Notes 28 and 31 in this volume.

82. The two basic sources on the WTUL are Dye, *As Equals and as Sisters* on the New York WTUL, and Kirkby, "Alice Henry," on the national WTUL.

83. National WTUL Papers, Box 1, "Headquarters Records, 1903–04," Library of Congress.

84. The results of the WTUL meeting were later reported in the *Union Labor Advocate.*

Legal aid, money and backing was needed by the laundry workers to carry on the trial. Miss Mary Dreier and Miss Agnes Nestor were appointed a committee to lay the matter before the convention of the A.F. of L. then in session. After consulting Mr. Manning of the Laundry and Shirt Waist Workers and President Gompers, though late, a resolution was introduced by unanimous consent of the house urging that Executive Board of A.F. of L. take some action in the case.

National WTUL Papers, Box 19, "Historical Data, 1903–1911."

# 7

# The Limits of Corporate Reform: Fordism, Taylorism, and the Working Week in the United States, 1914–1929

## David R. Roediger

### I

IN A 1916 article praising Henry Ford, the socialist Kate Richards O'Hare imagined that "Schmidt," the worker celebrated by Frederick W. Taylor as the archetypal "high-priced man" produced by Taylor's system of scientific management, had moved on to work in a Ford plant. Oppressed, overworked, and manipulated under Taylor's regime, Schmidt gained, according to O'Hare, dignity, meaningful leisure, and a more just wage in Highland Park, Michigan.[1] Such radical homage to Ford was far from unique. As Upton Sinclair wrote, the result of Ford's January 1914 labor reforms was that

a furious controversy arose—on the one side labor and the social uplifters, on the other side manufacturers, business men and the newspaper editors. . . . The former said that Henry Ford was a great thinker, a statesman of industry; the latter said he was a self-advertiser, a man of unsound mind, a menace to the public welfare.[2]

Among Ford's adulators were William Z. Foster, the Michigan Socialist party, John Reed, and, later and more reservedly, Antonio Gramsci. Those expressing horror included the *Wall Street Journal,* the *New York Times,* and the Detroit Employers' Association.[3] The scenario is fascinating in view of Ford's later and deserved reputation as an open-shop extremist. The friends' and enemies' lists must appear somewhat odd to contemporary scholars accustomed to reading that the trajectory of the leading actors in American, if not world, capitalism in the twentieth century has been toward "Fordism."[4]

Of course, Ford's pacifist activities early in World War I and his insti-

135

tution of the famous "five-dollar day" in 1914 partly underlay his appeal to radicals. But his attitudes on the working day also firmly set him apart from, and above, Taylor. As John Reed put it, Ford "smashed the doctrine that the more hours you work a man, the more work you get out of him; he voluntarily reduced his workmen's hours from 10 to 8 a day."[5] At a time when other employers, especially in the Taylorized industries, fought bitterly before conceding labor's long-cherished goal of the eight-hour day, Ford gave the concession away, along with raises in pay (and, it must be added, along with tremendous speed-ups in production).[6] Although, as Harry Braverman has observed, Fordism shared much with scientific management, the two ideas differed sharply where the working day was concerned.[7]

This chapter explores the shorter-hour position developed by Ford, a stance that briefly made him a hero of the Left. It traces how, during and after World War I, Taylorist management moved in directions more compatible with what Reed had called the "Ford idea" and developed limited rationales for cutting the working day, especially during the campaign against very long hours in the steel industry. It finally considers how limited those rationales proved when, after the steel campaign, Ford and the American Federation of Labor (AFL) leadership attempted to initiate the five-day week. Despite changes *toward* Fordist ideas, based on profit and efficiency and now embraced by labor, few managerial reformers and very few employers supported Ford's five-day schedule. Corporate liberalism proved ultimately illiberal where the working week was concerned. Fordism, far from describing a whole period of capitalist development, won only small support, at least with regard to its concern with the hours of labor. The hopeful radicals of the World War I era had long since ceased to see Ford as a hero. The increasingly conservative AFL leaders, who attempted to appropriate the logic of Fordism to appeal to employers for a voluntary transition to the five-day week, found few takers.

## II

Before World War I, reform arguments regarding the physiological and psychological benefits of the shorter working day—benefits said to be productive of a happier, healthier, and richer industry and nation—suffered from a failure to mesh well with scientific management. Although Taylor and other scientific managers held out the possibility of reducing hours to provide an incentive to workers, in practice they more often used pay differentials to win workers to higher productivity. Taylor's ideal of a "high-priced man," set apart from his fellows by the desire for premium pay, translated easily into managerial practice regarding wages. Cuts in hours, in contrast, would have had to influence whole departments, producing the kind of group feeling that was anathema to Taylor. As historians and his contemporary rivals in management theory have pointed out, Taylor had little concern with physiology, basing his studies most often on mechanics.[8] Finally, the premises of scientific management denied that the psychology of individual workers played a very complex role in determining how hard they labored. Instead, it was held that, deskilled and weaned from group loyalties, the individual would more or less automatically respond to wage incentives by working at the prescribed pace. Thus Taylorism undercut the older rationales for securing cooperation from a healthy workforce through reduction in hours. The standard guidebook of the Taylorists, published in 1911, featured a daily time clock, calibrated to the hundredth of an hour. It was a ten-hour clock.[9]

Reformers wishing to draw on Taylorism to argue for shorter hours therefore had to make a largely negative case. Louis Brandeis, Josephine Goldmark, and Felix Frankfurter, in their impressive legal documentation for statutes regulating the hours of women's labor, did hold that Taylorism lay the groundwork for shorter hours, but they stressed not so much the leisure-creating possibilities of scientifically managed productivity as the alienating aspects of many newly designed jobs. Embracing both scientific management and reduced hours, they portrayed the latter as an antidote for the former.[10] Moreover, with labor unions firmly arrayed against scientific management, the reformers could hardly point to shorter hours, in combination with Taylorism, as keys to harmony at the workplace.

Henry Ford, in contrast to Taylor, developed a strong case for the shorter working day as a managerial reform. Although little given to theorizing, Ford (along with his staff) raised an array of arguments for more leisure. As early as 1912, in response to poor production in Ford's drop-hammer unit, the company linked production and leisure in a way that Taylorists, whose mentor professed not to "care a hoot what became of the worker after work" as long as he "was able to show up the next morning in fit condition," would not.[11] Perceiving that "sickness, indebtedness, and fear and worry over things entirely related to the home had crept in and put a satisfactory human unit . . . out of harmony with things . . . necessary for production," Ford management cut daily working hours from ten to nine.[12] Similar logic applied two years later when the eight-hour, five-dollar day came generally to Ford factories. In instituting the eight-hour day, Henry Ford termed it a matter of "proven" efficiency, arguing that eight hours "happens [to be] the length of time [which] gives the best service from men, day in and day out."[13] Ford saw shorter hours as part of a cure for the astronomical turnover and absence rates (and, to an extent, the labor militancy) plaguing his fast-paced assembly line at the new Highland Park plant. He found reform an effective strategy to secure workers' cooperation, soon pronouncing the 1914 changes "one of the finest cost-cutting moves ever made." Ford also implied that shorter hours forced industries to be more innovative, maintaining that "the harder we crowd business for time, the more efficient it becomes."[14]

By adopting a formula that Stuart Ewen has termed "shorter hours, higher wages," Ford created visionary possibilities that went beyond, but were never unrelated to, higher productivity and profits.[15] For a time, through the Sociology Department in his company, Ford tried to create leisured, Americanized, temperate families of workers in which the male heads of households made enough money to obviate the need for females working or taking in boarders.[16] The Fordist argument for free time could be ringingly utopian: "Man needs leisure to think and the world needs thinkers."[17] More often, it stressed the value of leisure to industry.[18] Workers with more leisure, Henry Ford wrote, "have time to see more, do more—and, incidentally they buy more." Shorter hours and higher wages, he added, mean that "wives are released from work, little children are no longer exploited and, given more time, they both become free to go out and find new products." Not coincidentally, Ford was engaged in the mass marketing of cars. He held that "people who have more leisure time have more clothes." They also, he concluded, "must have more transportation facilities."[19]

But with Taylorism the ascendant managerial reform strategy and with few employers matching either Ford's vision or his specific material interest in mass marketing a product that required leisure for its use, few voluntary Fordist reductions in hours took place. Marion Cahill, who conducted a close study of voluntary reductions of hours during this period, concluded that "not only did employers fail voluntarily to reduce hours but . . . they did not give the matter serious consideration." His survey of the welfare capitalist journal *Human Engineering*'s four 1911 issues, for example, yields but one example of an employer-initiated reduction. Cahill mentions five other examples of voluntary reductions between 1907 and World War I, the most important being among employers belonging to the National Association of Lithographers who, in 1910, introduced the eight-hour day in an effort to keep the open shop. So slow was the pace of voluntary reform that in 1916, Henry Ford proposed to Woodrow Wilson that the latter include a national eight-hour law in his presidential platform. That Ford would make such a proposal speaks to the lack of private corporate initiative in cutting hours. That Wilson declined reflects a continued ambivalence, even among progressives, toward legislative action regarding the working day.[20]

## III

After 1915, and especially during and immediately after World War I, many of the impediments to the development of an efficiency-based, profit-oriented reform argument for a shorter working day dropped away. With Taylor's 1915 death, the work-reform movement, building on his basic framework of deskilled labor, began to devote more attention to the problem of motivation through psychological incentives.[21] Taylor's heirs turned to the encouragement of supervised leisure in a broad management style that is in some ways better termed Fordist than Taylorist. The post-1915 management experts also emphasized physiology far more than Taylor had and, especially through the efforts of Robert Valentine, made efforts toward *détente* with conservative trade unionists. Finally, and crucially, the new breed of efficiency experts resembled Ford in seeing not only loafing but also turnover and absenteeism as central management problems and in believing that these problems required a broad welfare-capitalist strategy that did not hinge preponderantly on wage incentives.[22]

The coming of the war and the institution of Prohibition after the war helped solidify the trend toward a welfare-capitalist management style that could coherently attack very long working days. War production elevated the attack on waste, including waste of human resources, into a national duty. The War Labor Board encouraged labor–management cooperation, often by granting shorter days to unions and scientific-management-based work-rule concessions to employers. Such actions cemented the AFL's making of peace with a wing of the scientific management movement led by Valentine and Morris Cooke, and culminated in Gompers cooperating with Cooke on the 1920 treatise "Labor, Management and Productivity," a systematic statement of AFL cooperation with reformed Taylorism.[23] The tremendous mass strikes of 1919, especially in coal and steel, were struggles in which, as Selig Perlman and Philip Taft have written, "shorter hour's demand made for greater fellow feeling between trades and industries."[24] Their occurrence led to a greater reform emphasis on ending very long shifts to forestall class conflict. Their defeat propelled the AFL further toward *détente* with Taylorism. The formula of granting work-rule adjustments in exchange for shorter hours also enshrined the idea, earlier described by various students of experiments with the use of works councils or company unions, that in exchange for fewer hours, workers might submit freely to aspects of scientific management. Indeed, in some instances employee representative bodies initiated such management changes in exchange for very modest decreases in hours.[25] Prohibition, considered by many executives a tremendous boon to productivity, helped disarm the nineteenth-century employer objection that shorter hours led to debauchery.[26]

By 1920, John R. Commons and John B. Andrews could write: "Of the many lessons which the world war taught industry, none is more clear-cut than that long hours do not pay," [27] and could be certain that management experts and reformers would understand their point on several different levels. All could point to a number of wartime studies of specific industries that showed shorter hours compatible with maintained production levels in at least some of the factories surveyed. In some instances, such as a study of the boots and shoes industry undertaken by the National Industrial Conference Board (NICB), nearly half of the workers affected by a reduction in the workweek (ranging from 57 to 60 hours to a 54-hour schedule) maintained the same output.[28] Moreover, studies emphasized that, for much of the day, workers were resting or waiting for work and that therefore increased actual working time was possible within the context of shorter shifts.[29] Finally, the celebrated postwar *Waste in Industry* report, prepared under the direction of Herbert Hoover, so overwhelmingly identified inefficiency among managers and owners as its culprit that small changes in production based on reductions in hours paled by comparison.[30]

Other reform arguments for reduced hours reflected the reality of a war in which a third of the 2.5 million men examined for army service were rejected as physically unfit by pointing out that a long day did "not pay" in terms of national health. With both "social well-being and productive efficiency" at stake, experts considered whether long hours contributed to disease, particularly occupational disease. Although some early studies held out little prospect that adjusting hours much fostered health or decreased accidents, by 1924 a growing body of literature linking shorter hours with decreased absenteeism due to illness or disability enabled the economist P. Sargant Florence to argue that "about one-quarter" of the eight-hour difference between a fifty-two-hour and a sixty-hour workweek was simply given back in decreased lost time due to sickness.[31]

Other efficiency-minded reformers developed similarly sophisticated positions, much like Henry Ford's, on behalf of a shorter working day. For Sumner Slichter, then a young expert on labor turnover, a reduced workweek promised a more stable workforce.[32] Some stressed that disputes at work, flare-ups inimical to productivity, resulted from tiredness. Indeed, one management expert who worked in steel mills in order to observe them held that "if it is true, as a member of the War Labor Board reports, that 98 percent of the disputes they were asked to solve simmered down finally to some petty dispute between a foreman and a man, then I am willing to wager that the majority of these 98 percent [came] when both the foreman and worker were just plain tired."[33] U.S. Public Health Service research suggested that the adoption of an eight-hour day might significantly decrease tardiness among workers.[34] Shorter weeks also were seen as capable of leading to harder, more efficient work by removing the bitterness that caused loafing on the job and easing the psychophysiological tension that sometimes led to inefficient work near to lunch and closing time. Long hours were inefficient, Whiting Williams succinctly wrote, because "men are paid for energies which they simply are not able to deliver." [35] It remained for a crusading department store owner, Edward Filene, to add, after the fashion of Ford, that management ought not apologize for alienating jobs but should hold out increased consumption and the eventual possibility of a five-hour day as compensation for "monotony." "Increasing freedom," Filene added, "will lie at the end of [the working] day." [36]

The campaign to rid the steel industry of the twelve-hour day, ultimately successful in 1923, marked the climax of a "Fordist" style of managerial reform being applied to the working day. Paul Kellogg, the reform editor who in 1920 persuaded his fellow Cabot Fund trustees to reopen the hours issue in steel, opted for an efficiency engineering approach. The fund commissioned Morris Cooke, the Taylor follower instrumental in bringing the AFL into cooperation with scientific management, to study the economic feasibility of a transition to eight hours. Cooke, working with Horace Drury of the American Engineering Council, studied a score of U.S. steel plants working under a three-shift system, and found "no outstanding obstacle" to the adoption of that system. The Cooke–Drury study, published by the Taylor Society, predicted that as little as a 3 percent rise in costs would accompany the transition. A Cooke report even found a dairy farm more profitably run under the eight-hour system and concluded, "If the cow seems able to adapt herself, it ought not be hard for some others to make the change." Reformers, emphasizing that the three-shift system was one that "practically every steel production center in the world, excepting the United States, has universally introduced," also drew on studies from abroad to show that managerial improvements "could enable employees to earn more in eight hours than they previously had in twelve." [37]

Kellogg moved to commit the Cabot Fund to further action, but he met resistance from other trustees. Only after giving assurances that fund contributions would not be used to undertake a publicity campaign against the steel industry but only to mobilize internal pressure did Kellogg's designated leader for the new campaign, Columbia University professor Samuel McCune Lindsay, secure necessary funding. Lindsay, a prominent Republican with ties to Secretary of Commerce Herbert Hoover and President Warren Harding, found in the former an especially strong ally. As president of the Federated American Engineering Societies, Hoover had initiated studies that he thought showed the long day to be "barbaric" and "uneconomic." By early 1922, cooperating with Lindsay, he initiated a Commerce Department investigation as well. Hoover wanted quick progress because he thought that high stakes were involved. Reform would forestall the spread of radical unionism, he maintained, and would give "the steel industry credit for some kind of initiative instead of waiting until they are smashed into it by some kind of legislation."[38]

## IV

Trade unions were greatly weakened in the 1920s, and, as Irving Bernstein has observed, AFL President William Green's relationship with (Fordized) Taylorist managerial reformers was "blossoming into a love affair."[39] It is not surprising, therefore, that in 1926, when the five-day week became an important national issue, it did so both from Ford's initiative and from the AFL's, and that the latter's rationales for the five-day week differed little from the former's. More surprising is the fact that the initiative of Ford and the unions sparked so little support from managerial reformers, and especially from corporations themselves, even in the prosperous 1920s. If the 1923 campaign against long hours in the steel industry marked a high tide in managerial and corporate reform activities on behalf of more leisure, the ebb tide was so swift as to suggest that only a very special and heinous case like steel could call forth a broad liberal capitalist initiative for reductions in hours. Only the efficiency aspects of Ford's critique of long hours had been internalized, and those only incompletely. Aside from the conservative trade union leadership, Fordism would prove to have few followers.

Henry Ford, eyeing increased consumption and more production from man and machine, towered over all other corporate officials in systematizing the rationale for a five-day week and actually providing workers with the new schedule. The 270 companies identified by the National Industrial Conference Board as having the five-day week in 1928 employed just over 218,000 workers; 80 percent of them worked for just one firm: Ford. Fuller figures estimated that 400,000 wage earners had a five-day week. More than two in five of that total were Ford employees.[40] Ford, who had begun five-day experimentation in 1922, announced general elimination of Saturday work, with the exception of a few jobs, throughout his factories in October 1926. In public statements on the change, he reasoned as he had twelve years previously when he had granted the eight-hour day.[41]

The context of Ford's reforms made it easy for other employers to reject and even ridicule them, and made it hard for unions to use them to launch broad discussions of the working week. The five-day week at Ford came amid a serious slump in demand for the company's products. Critics rightly observed that Ford, after an initial noncommital comment about whether wages would stay the same on the five-day system, cut weekly pay. Some workers complained of receiving as little as three days of work per week.

Given such considerations, Ford's reforms could be dismissed as a mere cover for a slowing down of production. Of the eighteen corporate officials commenting directly on Ford in a 1926 National Association of Manufacturers' (NAM) publication on the working week, eleven explicitly said that he was using the five-day system to hide a decline in demand for Ford products. One dubbed Ford "Alibi Henry" for his alleged duplicity. Other corporate leaders observed that though the system might benefit auto manufacturers, it could not apply to other industries.[42]

The very proximity of Ford's October announcement and the AFL's five-day resolution during the same month ensured that Ford's and William Green's arguments would be mentioned together frequently. Some AFL leaders welcomed the comparison. Indeed, Green mounted an ill-starred campaign to organize the Ford plants, a campaign based on the premise that Ford would voluntarily assent to unionization. But militant unionists and such prounion reformers as the young minister Reinhold Niebuhr had to balance Ford's open-shop position, speed-ups, and institution of pay cuts, estimated by the *Christian Century* at $4 to $6 per week, against his five-day-week position. Some pointed out that since Ford boasted that output in five days could equal that of the longer week, the reform was in effect a speed-up paid for by lost wages among the workers. Although the labor press sometimes reported on Ford sympathetically, he was far from a perfect ally. Indeed, the five-day week received scathing indictment as "bunk" (a favorite Ford word) in several labor papers.[43]

The AFL convention of October 1926, meanwhile, made a case for the five-day week by subsuming older and more class-conscious arguments within an essentially Fordist logic. For example, James Lynch of the International Typographical Union urged fewer hours as an "alleviation for depression cycles." Indeed, the AFL made some sophisticated use of statistics on mechanization and productivity designed to show that the shorter week addressed not only periodic depressions but also a serious tendency toward technological displacement of jobs. Andrew Furuseth, of the Seamen, connected leisure with the uplift and self-culture of the working population.[44] Another delegate saw the five-day demand as a way "to create human happiness" and recommended that parts of the Declaration of Independence might be inserted into the resolution. Others stressed the long-term health benefits of shorter hours.[45] Virtually all emphasized that leisure bred new wants among workers and led to economic growth. But these familiar shorter-hour refrains all had a different ring—more the sound of Ford or Filene than of earlier shorter-hour radicals like Ira Steward or Seth Luther—because they came alongside a fundamental and open revision of labor thought concerning the working day.[46] Free time no longer was seen as part of a package of demands associated with greater working-class happiness, control, and power on and off the job, but as compensation for work that was, inevitably, dehumanizing.[47]

Green had in 1925 led the AFL in proposing a "social wage" tied to productivity and given in exchange for union cooperation on work rules.[48] The five-day week was, as *Labor* pointed out at the time, an extension of the same logic.[49] In the 1926 debate on the workweek, Green made it clear that labor must accept not only machinery (as the unions long had) but also increasingly alienating relations of production:

We would not go back to the old times if we could, but we are adjusting ourselves to the new, and as we look upon a modern factory with its mass production, with its specialization and with its standardization, we realize that we . . . must point the way by which we can adjust ourselves to this new industrial order.

That adjustment, he added, hinged on increased wages and increased leisure for "recuperation" and "readjustment."[50]

Other delegates echoed this point. John Frey held that the new educational campaign was not a "continuation" of old AFL work on the issue but a new departure based on "increased per capita production." Lynch specifically added that he did not "believe that Henry Ford himself could eliminate these processes that have grown up . . . [especially] the continuous performance by the individual of the same task." But, he continued, "the committee has indicated the remedy for the fatigue and atrophy that follows the repetitive processes in industry" by proposing a shorter week.[51]

But even with arguments developed before and during the shorter-hour campaign in steel and with management offered an opportunity to lead and coopt further a compliant labor movement, the AFL–Fordist initiative regarding a five-day week was a failure in the 1920s. Only a relative handful of managerial experts, and still fewer employers, embraced either the five-day week or working days of fewer than eight hours. Indeed, once the steel reform had been partially implemented, the urgency of attacking even very long hours diminished. Hoover, who later contended his actions in the steel campaign rid all American workers of the twelve-hour and even the ten-hour day, joined most other corporate reformers in ignoring the continued existence of such long days, sometimes combined with seven-day weeks, through the 1920s. The oil industry, railroad telegraphy, and rubber manufacturing were especially notorious on these scores. Some occupations seem to have witnessed attempts to lengthen the week to seven days during the decade.[52] In the climate of reform through voluntary business–government association, even legislation providing one day's rest in seven made only slow headway.[53] The very success of the steel drive, with its plethora of specific productivity-oriented research reports in its later stages, may have led to later inaction, both by producing an example that suggested legislation was superfluous and by making reformers hesitant to act in industries in which comparable studies had not been prepared. Few reformers advocated that employers lower hours *below* the long-sought ideal of forty-eight per week. Sober perusal of the NICB studies, for example, would have revealed that, for all their considerable animus against very long hours, they consistently opposed even reductions in hours to forty-eight weekly, finding efficiency best served at just above that standard.[54]

Large corporations almost universally opposed the five-day week during the 1920s. Through 1927, according to NICB statistics, only three corporations, employing over 2000 people, had followed Henry Ford's lead in establishing the shorter schedule. Elbert Gary, representing U.S. Steel, found the five-day system deplorable on every count and repeated as evidence against it the biblical injunction his company had until so recently defied by requiring Sunday work: "Six days shalt thou labor and do all thy work." Westinghouse's president censured Ford in strong terms, which he thought "express[ed] the view of practically every manufacturer and employer in this country."[55]

Smaller manufacturers and employer associations also decried concessions on the workweek. John Edgerton, head of the National Association of Manufacturers (NAM) and president of a Tennessee woolen mill, proclaimed it "time for America to awake from its dream of an eternal holiday" and linked extra leisure with dissipation. Particularly feared was union imposition of the shorter week. One Buffalo bronze-casting manufacturer found the AFL idea that production could be maintained during a five-day week to be "unadulterated bunk," predicting that no "union man" would exert himself "one iota more per hour." The 1926 article "The Five Day Workweek: Can It Become Universal?" answered its title's question with a resounding "It will not!"[56] *Iron Age, Bulletin of the National Association of Building Trades Employers, Commerce and Finance, Commercial West, Manufacturer's News, Real Estate Board and Builders' Guide,* and the Philadelphia Chamber of Commerce all viewed the five-day plan negatively, as did the U.S. Chamber of Commerce.[57]

In contrast to the situation prevailing during the campaign against the long day in steel, even companies that had adopted the five-day week did not speak enthusiastically on its behalf. The *New York World*'s mid-decade study of the five-day week in stores in fourteen large cities where Saturday closings had been adopted revealed wide divisions of opinion as to the efficiency of the system. Some mercantile leaders objected that the closings kept workers from shopping, but no sentiment for extending the system to industry found expression.[58]

Similar early studies of five-day industrial concerns found almost an even split between employers satisfied and those upset by the results. Those factories keeping hours of greater than forty per week, but spreading them over five days, were happiest with the system. An ambitious NICB study, published in 1929, found greater approval for the five-day week among the 270 plants it surveyed, but over half those plants worked greater than forty-hour schedules. Of those plants reducing hours, 6.4 percent reported "substantially less" production, and 25.4 percent saw no increase in per hour output under the five-day format.[59]

Nor did many efficiency, management, economics, or engineering experts embrace the five-day week in the 1920s. The AFL, although anxious to show the reform as part of a strategy to increase production and consumption, could cite only a handful of experts in direct support of its theories.[60] The AFL president, William Green, so cast about for corporate reform supporters that he strained in 1926 to claim that Secretary of the Treasury Andrew Mellon supported the five-day week, when Mellon did so only to the extent that he commented, "If a man can accomplish his work in five days, there is no reason why he should work six days."[61] *Labor Age* and other magazines of the socialist labor movement often published articles by efficiency engineers, most of whom only generally criticized the waste associated with long days and others of whom eschewed specifics concerning what schedule should apply, while asking "Is a Shorter Work-Day Enough?" The *American Labor Legislation Review* greeted the call for a five-day week with lukewarm interest, using it as an occasion to call for abolition of the seven-day week. The Society of Industrial Engineers published criticisms of the reform.[62]

The rare employers who supported the five-day week usually engaged in the production or sale of consumer goods or services. Richard Feiss, whose 1920 article recounted the positive impact of a five-day system, pointed to increased productivity, less turnover (especially among women workers, whom his firm more easily attracted), and a "speeding up" of "the slower workers." Feiss, a Clevelander, manufactured clothing in a nonunion shop. Edward Filene, who lauded the shorter week as part of a plan to "Fordize America," was among the nation's largest department store owners.[63] W. Burke Harmon, a leading New York realtor, welcomed the five-day week as likely to spur homeownership. The National Amusement Parks Association listened to descriptions of the reform with lively interest.[64]

## V

Just as few employers followed Ford to voluntary concessions regarding the five-day week, few unions secured that goal through bargaining. At its 1928 convention, the AFL boasted of about 165,000 members working five-day, forty-hour weeks. Although this represented an increase of about 75,000 since 1926, about 70 percent of the total came from five extremely well organized building trades' unions. The painters' union alone furnished 38 percent of the total, with the bricklayers, carpenters, electrical workers, and plasterers accounting together for about one unionized five-day worker in three. At least a fifth of those unionists benefiting from the reform, and perhaps nearly 25 percent, came from communist-influenced unions in the fur and clothing industries.[65] Conservative AFL leaders could hardly take much comfort from these figures, nor from the fact that more manufacturing establishments adopted the new system in the year before AFL agitation began than in the year after.[66] Nonetheless, the AFL leadership maintained that "steady progress" was being made and held out hope that "public demand" would bring the five-day week.[67]

Even in the building trades, the adoption of the five-day system, outside of the painters' union, came slowly before 1929. During that year, the number of five-day building tradesmen more than doubled in a single stroke when the Building Trades' Employers Association of New York granted the reform to between 125,000 and 150,000 workers.[68] The action came despite the fact that most of the unions involved had earlier agreed not to bargain over the working week until 1930. But the reform leadership of the Brotherhood of Electrical Workers won the five-day week and a 10 percent pay hike effective February 1, 1929. Other building trades responded by seeking the same schedule, citing language in their contracts "stipulating that basic improvements won by any other trade in the industry" would apply.[69] The New York Building Trades Council won the new system on May 4 and defended it from an employer attempt in late May to break up craft solidarity by locking out unionists who refused to work with nonunion electricians. The reform quickly spread to Chicago, Saint Louis, and other cities.[70] But the brief contagion of five-day fever in the building trades in 1929 did not signal a further spread until the Great Depression made more easily justified "share-the-work" plans lively issues.

The shorter-week initiative of the AFL leadership and Ford in the 1920s failed. Its greatest shortcoming was that it relied on corporate reform support, which simply did not exist. Its weaknesses included a continuing AFL commitment to voluntarism, which made the organization disdain legislation on the working week even as its leaders spoke of the power of "public demand." Throughout the decade, labor lobbying for federal hours legislation remained confined to laws extending a forty-four-hour week to more government employees and remained unsuccessful.[71] The fact that many workers, including some unionists, had not approached even the forty-eight-hour week, and that some still worked seven days, also complicated the agitation. This forced the AFL to defend the six-day week at eight hours daily, instead of the forty-hour week.[72] Many unions ignored the five-day-week call. Even the Machinists, considered prominent in five-day agitation, continued through all of 1928 to print preambles in their journal calling for a forty-four-hour week with a Saturday *half*-holiday.[73] At least one union leader, George L. Berry of the Pressmen, openly opposed the five-day week in the name of "promoting the spirit of cooperation" with employers.[74]

In the period from 1906 to 1919, strikes and labor protests, along with legislation and War Labor Board decisions partly responsive to such militancy, carried forward the movement for shorter hours, and the demand came in tandem with attacks on Taylorism. The workweek in nonagricultural industries fell by an average of 7 hours. In the decade thereafter, with Fordist ideas in full flower in an ideal setting of prosperity and with little labor opposition to a partially Fordized Taylorism, the workweek fell by just 1.3 hours, a figure buoyed mainly by Ford's 1926 reforms, the attack on the twelve-hour day in steel, left-wing union campaigns, and some 1919 settlements borne of militant organizing and strikes.[75] The Fordist initiative for a five-day week was virtually stillborn. During the Great Depression to follow, corporate sentiment was overwhelmingly arrayed against the Black bill's provision for a thirty-hour week and against the Fair Labor Standard Act's forty-hour provision. Nor have shorter workweek initiatives emerged from the corporate sector in the decades since the depression. Indeed, the stark truth is that the "Fordist" period of America's political economy has been productive of less growth in leisure than any other in U.S. industrial history.[76] On the important issue of the working week, corporations and corporate reformers were not typically Fordists. The 1920s and the whole twentieth century to date have doubtless evidenced corporate initiatives to secure cooperation of workers through reforms and through efforts that encourage workers to view themselves as consumers. But if such efforts have ushered in a period of consumer capitalism, they have done so largely without employers bowing to Ford's advice regarding the utility of increasing leisure in order to raise productivity and consumer demand, except when pressured hard by labor to do so.

NOTES

1. *National Rip Saw,* January and February 1916; Frederick W. Taylor, *The Principles of Scientific Management* (New York, 1967; originally published 1911), pp. 42–47. Parts of the research for this chapter were done under grants from the American Council for Learned Societies. George Rawick had nothing to do with my writing of this particular chapter, but without his encouragement, advice, and example over the years, I doubt that it would have been written.

2. Upton Sinclair, *The Flivver King* (Detroit and Pasadena, 1937), p. 28.

3. John Reed, "Why They Hate Ford," *Masses,* October 1916, pp. 11–12; John Reed, "Industry's Miracle Maker," *Metropolitan* 65 (October 1916): 10–12, 64–68; Antonio Gramsci, *Selections from the Prison Notebooks* (New York, 1971), pp. 278–322; Keith Sward, *The Legend of Henry Ford* (New York, 1948), p. 54; *Butcher Workman,* September 1916; Sinclair, *Flivver King,* 28–29; and Allan Nevins with Frank Ernest Hill, *Ford: The Times, The Man, The Company* (New York, 1954), pp. 536–550.

4. See, e.g., Michel Aglietta, *A Theory of Capitalist Regulation* (New York, 1979); Mike Davis, "Fordism in Crisis," *Review* (Fernand Braudel Institute) 2 (Fall 1978); Mike Davis, "Late Imperial America," *New Left Review* 143 (January–February 1984); Aldous Huxley, *Brave New World* (London, 1932); Charles Sabel, *Work and Politics: The Division of Labor in Industry* (Cambridge, Mass., 1982), pp. 32–34 *et passim;* and, more tentatively, Gramsci, *Prison Notebooks,* pp. 278–322; and Michael Buraway, *The Politics of Production: Factory Regimes under Capitalism and Socialism* (London, 1985). The literature using "Fordism" as a construct has generated substantial insights. My own view is that the term has stuck as much because of its vagaries as its precision, but this chapter attempts no general critique. Instead, it observes that, with exceptions such as Gramsci, various authors have seen Fordism as centering on mass production and mass consumption, and have missed the specific role of leisure in Ford's ideas.

5. Reed, "Why They Hate Ford," p. 11.

6. For a fuller treatment of the period, see David Roediger and Philip S. Foner, *Our Own Time; American Labor and the Working Day* (Westport, Conn., 1988).

7. Harry Braverman, *Labor and Monopoly Capital: The Degradation of Work in the Twentieth Century* (New York, 1974), pp. 146–150.

8. Ibid., pp. 106–108; Frederick S. Lee, *The Human Machine and Industrial Efficiency* (Easton, 1974; originally published 1918), pp. 10–23, 90–99; and P. S. Florence, *Economics of Fatigue and Unrest* (New York, 1924), pp. 87–95.

9. Bryan Palmer, "Class, Conception and Conflict: The Thrust for Efficiency, Managerial Views of Labor and Working Class Rebellion, 1903–1922," *Review of Radical Political Economics* 7 (Summer 1975): 38–39; and H. L. Gantt *et al., How Scientific Management Is Applied* (Easton, 1974; originally published 1911), p. 73.

10. See, especially, Felix Frankfurter, *The Case for the Shorter Work Day,* 2 vols. (New York, 1916), 1:193–226.

11. Frank B. Copley, "Frederick W. Taylor—Revolutionist," *Outlook* 3 (September 1915): 42.

12. John R. Lee, "The So-Called Profit-Sharing System in the Ford Plant," *Annals of the American Academy of Political and Social Science* 65 (May 1916): 299–308.

13. Henry Ford, *Today and Tomorrow* (Garden City, N.Y., 1926), p. 158. The other key texts describing Ford's ideas on shorter hours are "The Five-Day Week in Ford Plants," *Monthly Labor Review* 23 (December 1926): 1162–1166; Lee, "Profit-Sharing System," pp. 299–308; Henry Ford, *My Life and Work* (Garden City, N.Y., 1923), pp. 103, 120; and Henry Ford, *My Philosophy of Industry* (New York, 1929), pp. 50–51.

14. Ford, *Life and Work,* p. 147; Samuel Crowther, "Henry Ford: Why I Favor Five Days' Work with Six Days' Pay," *World's Work* 52 (October 1926): 613–616; Roediger and Foner, *Our Own Time,* Chap. 9; and Jack Russell, "The Coming of the Line: The Ford Highland Park Plant, 1910–1914," *Radical America* 12 (May–June 1978): 39–42.

15. Stuart Ewen, *Captains of Consciousness: Advertising and the Social Roots of Consumer Culture* (New York, 1976), pp. 23–30. Ewen finds Ford rather narrow in his social outlook and sees the formula as being developed by others who, as Edward Filene put it, wished to "Fordize American business and industry" (p. 24). *Captains of Consciousness,* an intriguing, uneven book, suggests far wider acceptance of shorter hours and higher wages than in fact existed in the business and industrial world.

16. Gramsci, *Prison Notebooks,* pp. 278–322; and Stephen Meyer, *The Five-Dollar Day: Labor Management and Social Control in the Ford Motor Company, 1908–1921* (Albany, 1981), especially pp. 123–168.

17. Ford, *Today and Tomorrow,* p. 159; Ford, *My Philosophy of Industry,* pp. 50–51; Ford, *Life and Work,* p. 103; and Nevins, *Ford,* pp. 549–560.

18. See, e.g., Crowther, "Henry Ford," pp. 613–616; and Ford as told to William A. McGarry, "Prosperity—What Is It?" *Saturday Evening Post* 198 (April 10, 1926): 205.

19. Ford, *Philosophy of Industry,* pp. 17–18; "Five-Day Week in Ford Plants," p. 1166.

20. Marion Cotter Cahill, *Shorter Hours: A Study of the Movement Since the Civil War* (New York, 1932), pp. 236–248.

21. Palmer, "Class, Conception and Conflict," pp. 34–40; and Braverman, *Labor and Monopoly Capital,* pp. 139–151.

22. Braverman, *Labor and Monopoly Capital,* pp. 146–150; Palmer, "Class, Conception and Confict," pp. 38 ff.; Foster, "Capitalist Efficiency 'Socialism,' " pp. 94–95; and Sumner H. Slichter, *The Turnover of Factory Labor* (New York), pp. 257–258.

23. Milton Nadworny, *Scientific Management and the Unions* (Cambridge, Mass., 1955), pp. 122–141; Morris Cooke, Samuel Gompers, and Fred J. Miller, eds., "Labor, Management and Productivity," *Annals of the American Academy of Political and Social Science* 91 (September 1920): *passim;* and Samuel Gompers, "Organized Labor and Industrial Engineers," *American Federationist* 28 (January 1921).

24. Selig Perlman and Philip Taft, in John R. Commons *et al., History of Labour in the United States,* (New York, 1918–1935), 4:460; and Roediger and Foner, *Our Own Time,* Chap. 10.

25. Ben M. Selekman, *Sharing Management with the Workers* (New York, 1924), pp. 64–65; James Myers, *Representative Government in Industry* (New York, 1924), pp. 142–143; and John Leitch, *Man to Man: The Story of Industrial Democracy* (New York, 1919), pp. 183 ff.

26. Herman Feldman, *Prohibition: Its Economic and Industrial Aspects* (New York, 1927), pp. 242–250.

27. John R. Commons and John B. Andrews, *Principles of American Labor Legislation* (New York, 1920), p. 221.

28. National Industrial Conference Board (NICB), *Hours of Work as Related to Output and Health of Workers: Boot and Shoe Industry,* Research Report No. 7 (Boston, 1918), pp. 42, 50–52; NICB, *Hours of Work as Related to Output and Health of Workers: Wool Manufacturing,* Research Report No. 2 (Boston, 1918), pp. 18, 28–29; NICB, *Analysis of British Wartime Reports on Hours of Work,* Research Report No. 2 (Boston, 1917), *passim;* Josephine Goldmark and Mary D. Hopkins, "Comparison of an Eight-Hour Plant and a Ten-Hour Plant," *Public Health Bulletin,* No. 106 (Washington, D.C., 1920); and Slichter, *Turnover,* pp. 261–264.

29. See, e.g., NICB, *Wartime Employment of Women in the Metal Trades,* Research Report No. 8 (Boston, 1918), pp. 63–64; and William L. Chenery, "Waste in Industry," *Survey* 44 (August 1, 1920): 545.

30. Federated American Engineering Societies *Waste in Industry* (New York, 1921), *passim;* and Herbert Hoover, *The Memoirs of Herbert Hoover,* 3 vols. (New York, 1952), 2:31.

31. See the NICB reports cited in note 28. See also Florence, *Economics of Fatigue,* pp. 188, 302–346, especially pp. 328–311; and Charles Rumford Walker, *Steel: The Diary of a Furnace Worker* (Boston, 1922), pp. 151–152.

32. Slichter, *Turnover,* pp. 226, 234, 239, 258–263; and Florence, *Economics of Fatigue,* pp. 137–178.

33. Whiting Williams, *What's on the Worker's Mind* (New York, 1920), p. 287.

34. Florence, *Economics of Fatigue,* p. 189.

35. Ibid., pp. 212–273, especially pp. 226–228, 236–237, 266–270; Williams, *Mind,* p. 287; and Walker, *Steel,* p. 151.

36. Edward Filene, *The Way Out* (Garden City, N.Y., 1925), pp. 218–223.

37. H. Drury, "The Three-Shift System in the Steel Industry," *Bulletin of the Taylor Society,* February 1921; Cahill, *Shorter Hours,* pp. 213–214; "Engineers on Hours," *Survey* 45 (October 30, 1920): 151; "Three Shifts in Steel," *Survey* 45 (December 11, 1920): 387; "Shorter Work Day Increases Output," *Labor,* October 20, 1920; "Three Shifts in Foreign Countries," *Survey* 45 (March 5, 1921): 810; Thomas Blaisdell, Jr., "Fatigue and the Steel Worker," *Survey* 46 (June 4, 1921): 312.

38. Hoover, *Memoirs,* 2:103; Gary Dean Best, *The Politics of American Individualism: Herbert Hoover in Transition, 1918–1921* (Westport, Conn., 1975), p. 45; Robert Zeiger, *Republicans and Labor, 1919–1929* (Lexington, Ky. 1969), p. 100; Kirby Page, *Industrial Facts* (New York, 1921), pp. 11–12; and Roediger and Foner, *Our Own Time,* Chap. 10.

39. Irving Bernstein, *The Lean Years: A History of American Workers, 1920–1933* (Baltimore, 1970), pp. 102–103.

40. John B. Andrews, "One-Day-of-Rest-in-Seven Legislation," *American Labor Legislation Review* 13 (September 1923): 175–176; NICB, *The Five-Day Week in Manufacturing Industries* (New York, 1929), p. 11. See also Benjamin Kline Hunnicutt, "The End of Shorter Hours," *Labor History* 25 (Summer 1984): 377.

41. *Labor,* April 1, 1922; Crowther, "Henry Ford," pp. 613–616; and Samuel Crowther, "What Is Henry Ford Going to Do?" *Review of Reviews* 75 (February 1927): 147–153.

42. Reinhold Niebuhr, "Ford's Five Day Week Shrinks," *Christian Century* 44 (1926): 713–714; National Association of Manufacturers (NAM), "Five Day Week," *Bulletin,* 1926, pp. 2–12; *New York Times,* October 5, 1926; *Cleveland Employer,* June 1, 1927; and Sward, *Legend of Henry Ford,* pp. 201–204.

43. Craig Phelan, "William Green and the Ideal of Christian Cooperation," in *Labor Leaders in America,* ed. Melvyn Dubofsky and Warren Van Tine (Urbana and Chicago, 1987), pp. 147–149; Niebuhr, "Five Day Week Shrinks," pp. 713–717; editorial, *Christian Century* 43 (November 4, 1926): 1354; Irving Weinzweig, "Ford's Five-Day Work Week," *Advance,* October 22, 1926 p. 10; "Debunking Ford's Five Day Week," *Advance,* November 19, 1926; *Union Reporter* (Canton, Ohio) 25 (October 1926); *Labor,* January 1–3, 1927; "Labor Now Out for Five-Day Week," *Literary Digest* 91 (October 16, 1926): 9–11; American Federation of Labor (AFL), *Proceedings, 1926,* p. 201.

44. James Lynch, "Shorter Working Day Urged as Alleviation for Depression Cycles," *American Labor World,* November 1926, pp. 28–29; AFL, *Proceedings, 1926,* pp. 206–207, 199–202; AFL, *Proceedings, 1927,* p. 400. See also James Lynch, "The Shorter Workday: The Complete Argument," *American Federationist* 33 (March 1926).

45. AFL, *Proceedings, 1926,* pp. 204–207. Cf. *New York Times,* October 17, 1926; AFL, *Proceedings, 1927,* p. 198.

46. AFL, *Proceedings, 1926,* pp. 200–206; Lynch, "Depression Cycles," p. 29. On the older arguments, see David Roediger, "Ira Steward and the Antislavery Origins of American Eight-Hour Theory," *Labor History* 27 (Summer 1986): 410–426.

47. Of course, adverse working conditions, standardized tasks, and speed-ups had long been associated with the desire for shorter hours. But never before had the struggle over one set of issues (time) been so explicitly posed as a *substitute* for struggle over another (control over work).

48. Bernstein, *Lean Years,* pp. 102–103; Nadworny, *Scientific Management and the Unions,* Chaps. 7–8.

49. *Labor,* October 16, 1926; Sister J. M. Viau, *Hours and Wages in American Organized Labor* (New York, 1939), pp. 81–85.

50. AFL, *Proceedings, 1926,* p. 206.

51. Ibid., pp. 200–201.

52. *Labor,* October 14, 1929; "Legislative Notes," *American Labor Legislation Review* 13 (September 1923); Robert S. Lynd, "Done in Oil," *Survey* 48 (November 1, 1922); Harvey O'Connor, *History of the Oil Workers International Union—CIO* (Denver, 1950), pp. 27–29; Leon Platt, "The World Struggle for Rubber," *Communist* 6 (May 1927): 176; "Launching the Five-Day Week," *American Labor Legislation Review* 16 (December 1926): 290.

53. Andrews, "Day-of-Rest," pp. 175–176.

54. See Cahill, *Shorter Hours,* pp. 236–248. See especially William L. Che-

nery, "48 Hours or Less," *Survey* 46 (April 23, 1921): 118–119; and "Eight- and Ten-Hour Work Day," *Survey* 45 (October 9, 1920).

55. NICB, *Five-Day Week,* p. 22; *New York Times,* October 5–6, 1926; "Attitude of Certain Employers to 5-Day Week," *Monthly Labor Review* 23 (December 1926): 16–17; NAM, "The Five-Day Week: Can It Become Universal?" *Pocket Bulletin* 27 (October 1926): 2–12; "Labor Now Out for Five-Day Week," p. 11. See also W. H. Grimes, "Curse of Leisure," *Atlantic Monthly* 142 (April 1928): 355–360; and Hunnicutt, "End of Shorter Hours," p. 386.

56. NAM, "Five-Day Week," pp. 2–12; "Attitude of Certain Employers," p. 17; J. Charles Laue, "The Five-Day Week Is Now a Vivid Issue," *New York Times,* October 17 and 25, 1926.

57. William Boyd Craig, "Business Views in Review," *Nation's Business* 14 (December 1926): 72–75; "Business Attitudes Toward the Five-Day Workweek," *Nation's Business* 15 (April 1927): 32; Lamar T. Beman, comp., *Five Day Week, The Reference Shelf* (New York, 1928), 5:38–41; *Coal Age,* October 28, 1926, p. 592; and Bernstein, *Lean Years,* pp. 180–181.

58. "How the Five-Day Work Week Works," *Literary Digest* 86 (August 15, 1925): 10–11.

59. "Industry Tries the Five-Day Week," *Michigan Manufacturer and Financial Record,* June 30, 1923, pp. 1–2; NICB, *Five-Day Week,* pp. 25–39, 41–42, 64–66; and "The Five-Day Week in Industry," *Monthly Labor Review* 17 (September 1923): 652–653.

60. See, e.g., William Green, "The Five Day Week," *North American Review* 223 (December 1926): 566–574; John Frey, "Labor's Movement for a Five-Day Week," *Current History* 25 (December 1926): 369–372; Lynch, "Depression Cycles," pp. 28–29; and especially Beman, comp., *Five-Day Week,* p. 86.

61. Cf. *Trade Union News* (Philadelphia), October 14, 1926, and *Labor,* August 8, 1928. The latter was able to report that C. W. Barron of the *Wall Street Journal* did favor a five-day week.

62. See Rex B. Hersey, "Is Shorter Work-Day Enough?" *Labor Age,* October 1925; "Launching the Five-Day Week," pp. 228–289; and Beman, comp., *Five-Day Week,* p. 41. For a different reading stressing evidence of reformers' support for shorter hours in the late 1920s, and the view that such support was significant, see Hunnicutt, "End of Shorter Hours," *passim.* Many of the consumption-oriented reform proposals were extremely vague, but Hunnicutt is persuasive in arguing that labor's claims to leisure, at least in the abstract, had strong support in recreational reform publications. See, e.g., Matthew Woll, "Leisure and Labor," *Playground* 19 (1925): 322–323.

63. "A Five-Day Week That Pays Both Employer and Employees," *Literary Digest* 67 (October 2, 1920): 80–82; Feiss, "Why It Paid," *Factory* 25, (August 15, 1920): 523–525; Amalgamated Clothing Workers of America, *Seventh Annual Report of the GEB* (Montreal, 1926), p. 122; Filene, *The Way Out,* pp. 218–223; *New York Times,* October 17, 1926; and *Labor,* November 29, 1926.

64. Ethelbert Stewart, "Five-Day Week Used in Several Industries," *United States Daily,* December 2, 1926; NICB, *Five-Day Week,* pp. 22–54; Beman, comp.,

*Five-Day Week,* p. 19; *New York Times,* December 13, 1926; "Launching the Five-Day Week," p. 289; and Frey, "Labor's Movement," p. 370. See also the comments in note 62.

65. NICB, *Five-Day Week,* pp. 15–16, The lower figure assumes the AFL figure of 15,800 ILGWU members on the new schedule is correct. But see "Progress of the Five-Day Week," *Labor,* May 18, 1928, for much higher figures. On the painters, *Labor,* June 12, 1925; George F. Hedrick, "The Five-Day Week," *Painter and Decorator* 40 (November 1926); Brotherhood of Painters, Decorators and Paperhangers of America, *Reports of the General Offices to the Twelfth General Assembly* (Lafayette, Ind. 1921), p. 39.

66. NICB, *Five-Day Week,* p. 18.

67. *Labor,* August 18 and September 22, 1928; AFL, *Proceedings, 1929,* p. 388. See also Cahill, *Shorter Hours,* p. 168.

68. NICB, *Five-Day Week,* p. 16.

69. *Labor,* January 19, 1929.

70. *Labor,* May 25, July 27, and September 14, 1929.

71. AFL, *Proceedings, 1926,* pp. 196–197; AFL, *Proceedings, 1929,* p. 388; *Labor,* March 31 and September 22, 1928.

72. *Labor,* October 14, 1929; "Why the Six-Day Week?" *American Federationist,* September 1929; "Forty-Eight Hour Week," *American Federationist,* March 1927.

73. See, e.g., *Machinists' Monthly Journal* 40, no. 12 (December 1928): cover; and *Labor,* August 18, 1928.

74. "Labor and the Five-Day Week," *New York Times,* February 6, 1927; George L. Berry, "The Five Day Week," *American Pressman,* February 1927.

75. William McGaughey, Jr., *A Shorter Workweek in the 1980's* (White Bear Lake, Minn., 1982), p. 200.

76. Roediger and Foner, *Our Own Time.*

# 8

# Worktime in International Discontinuity, 1886–1940

## Gary Cross

### I

MOVEMENTS FOR shorter working hours express the essentially discontinuous character of labor history. The quest for reduced worktime has been most pronounced during peak years of labor organizing. These movements also cap periods of political or classwide mobilization following wars and depressions. Not only did the post–Civil War era and the years following World Wars I and II produce hours movements, but so did the depressions of the 1840s, 1880s, and 1930s.

The demand for fewer hours also increasingly became an international phenomenon. Agitation for a shorter workweek was pronounced during the following periods: 1844–1850 in Britain, France, the United States, and (slightly later) Australia; 1867–1873 in the United States and Britain; 1886–1891 in the United States and virtually all of industrializing Western Europe; and, more narrowly, 1897–1907 in Britain, France, and the United States. These efforts culminated in 1915–1922 when not only American, Australian, and European movements for shorter hours were widespread but even Latin America shared in a worldwide drive to reduce worktime. Although this international quest for short hours became fragmented in the 1920s, the call for the forty-hour week (or less) and the paid holiday animated European and American labor movements in the Popular Front period.[1]

With some exaggeration, one could argue that short-hour drives were synonymous with international working-class movements. The American Federation of Labor's (AFL) call for national eight-hour demonstrations on

*Portions of an earlier version of this chapter appeared in "Worktime between Haymarket and The Popular Front." *International Labor and Working Class History*, 30 (Fall 1986): 79–93. By permission of University of Illinois Press.

May 1, 1890, encouraged admiring European labor at the first meeting of the Second International to join the Americans in an international strike for eight hours. Given these oft-noted facts, it is ironic that the subsequent history of the hours issue has been largely neglected by both American and European labor historians.

Partially, this blind spot to worktime is a result of the common presumption that short-hour demands were "reformist." Not only were the eight-hour and Sunday-rest movements coopted by a variety of middle-class and religious groups, but they were frequently transposed from the rank and file to the political and legal arena where the hours issue was stripped of its radical intent, diluted in law, and bureaucratized in practice.

There is a good deal of truth in this assessment. Of course, the United States had its corporatist economists and jurists in George Gunton and Felix Frankfurter, who took up the short-hour cause in order to promote social peace; so also the British had their Fabians and Whitley Committees and the French their reformist law professors like Raoul Jay and right-wing socialists like Albert Thomas, who played leading roles in legitimizing and winning legal hours reductions. Yet, as recent labor historians have noted, we must reassess the relationship between politics—even the "reformist" variety—and labor movements. Clearly, the militancy of labor and the reformism of politicians interacted more positively than historians of "corporate capitalism" have assumed. Especially in Europe, the eight-hour day required a political or classwide mobilization in addition to a trade union or shop-floor movement for success.[2]

The focus of labor historians on the struggle of skilled workers for shop-floor control has also inadvertently obscured the hours problem. Although some students of workers' control have stressed the concomitant demands for shorter hours, others have interpreted short-time goals as primarily popular façades for workers' real intentions of shop-floor control, or as a means of effecting labor hegemony on the job. To be sure, hours reductions were effective means of controlling workloads, decreasing outputs, and thus linking production to pay. These tactics may reflect workers' learning the "rules of the game," as Hobsbawm puts it. Further, short-hour demands sometimes were designed to force employers to introduce more efficient methods in order to reduce wasted time at work (e.g., in the mines of Britain in the 1890s).[3] In all these ways, hours goals reflected the quest for control of labor time.

Yet this focus on work, as valuable as it is to understanding the motivation of labor, tends to deny an equally important desire: time for leisure and family. Increasingly, social historians have attempted to correct this by exploring the linkages between work and community/family—without, however, paying significant attention to the fundamental problem of the allocation of time between work, family, and leisure.[4] Hours movements expressed a growing popular desire for time liberated from work and available for new leisure opportunities and emerging family-centered values.

Finally, the local or national focus of almost all contemporary labor and social history neglects the broader, often international context in which most significant changes in the labor standard occurred. Short-hour movements generally emerged in the apogee of general strike waves and political mobilizations, were not confined to either arena of action, and were won only in periods of relative employer impotence. They also succeeded in the context of international and simultaneous working-class action. Although waged and won with economistic, legalistic, and paternalistic appeals, hours struggles were often rooted in militant action and class mobilization.

In particular, only in the world crisis of war was the resistance to the eight-hour day overcome. This required the context of both an international insurgency and a political "reformist" network. The combination was essentially discontinuous: It existed in 1919 but not in 1891 or 1936. In large part, this explains the fates of these differing hours movements. My objective here is to suggest a framework for reassessing the role of the workday, especially, but not exclusively, in Britain and France, roughly between the founding of the Second International and the Popular Front.

## II

Between 1886 and 1891, a wave of agitation for the eight-hour day swept Western European and American labor. The economic and social causes of this upsurge are complex. Despite diminutions of worktime at midcentury, continuing industrialization had not produced a corresponding decline of the workday. Although Britain had led Europe in hours legislation (e.g., the 1847 Ten Hour Law for the cotton textile industry), no appreciable reduction in hours occurred in the 1880s despite the nine-hour gains in some skilled trades and the extension of the ten-hour system to other female-dominated industries between 1867 and 1874. In France, only 40 percent worked as few as eleven hours a day in 1885. The only statutory regulation of adult worktime was a twelve-hour limit on manufacturing employees.[5]

Yet, unlike wage- and work-control issues, the eight-hour day was a demand that unified workers across skill and trade lines. The eight-hour day became the leading issue of radicals in the British Trades Union Congress (TUC) after 1886 and the theme of the New Unionists in their efforts to organize unskilled "general labourers." It played a similar role in the somewhat less developed French movement of the same period in an early effort to span the difficult gap between craft–localist unions and a more effective industrial–national confederation.[6] Despite gains in real daily wages, sharp trade slumps produced jobless rates of 10 to 12 percent in skilled British trades in the mid-1880s, which led organized trades to seek hours reductions in order to reduce excess inventory, share work, and thus assure job security. Yet the movement became widespread only in 1890–1891 during a minor boom that encouraged unionization.[7]

The power of the eight-hour message lay not only in its promise of economic security but in the dream of increased leisure. The development of recreational opportunities in the 1870s and 1880s suggest the attraction of this reallocation of time from work. And the testimony of British workers before the Royal Commission on Labour (1892–1894) confirms the conscious desire for additional time for family and individual pursuits.[8]

In Europe, the call for a universal eight-hour day was necessarily posed in terms of legislation; only legal means could overcome the impotence of seasonal, low-wage, or other weak trades. Legislation alone could obviate the threat of competition that prevented stronger trades or regions from imposing the eight-hour day on their employers without undermining their own economic interests. The failure of even strong unions to win hours reductions and the recourse of employers to "systematic overtime" led skilled workers in Britain to seek a legal solution.[9]

The idea of a uniform hours maximum, regardless of age or sex or even the intensity or danger of work, was essentially an economic extension of the rights of citizenship. Still, whether that goal could be best achieved through industrial action or legislation split workers in both countries. In France, the question of legislated worktime divided the anarchosyndicalists from the socialists. The struggle between the "parliamentarians" and the advocates of direct action continued until the gradual eclipse of the syndicalists in the General Confederation of Labor (CGT) after 1906.[10]

Although British workers before 1848 had favored maximum-hour laws, the TUC, throughout the 1880s, had rejected the parliamentary path to reduced worktime for adult males, labeling such bills as "grandmotherly legislation" and a threat to union autonomy.[11] More pragmatic British unions increasingly advocated the political path to shorter hours. Supporters of the parliamentary approach included small, weak unions unable to reduce hours through collective bargaining and the strike threat; but stronger trades such as the engineers joined the legalist group when they realized that hours reductions won in negotiations could be lost in the next round of bargaining. "New unionists" such as Keir Hardie, Tom Mann, and John Burns believed that shorter hours for all workers, especially the unorganized, required legislation. And only an hours law would guarantee that if a district or firm granted the eight hours, it would not be undermined by others who continued the longer workday.[12]

Most important, the logic of national legislation pushed workers toward international tactics. Both the First and Second Internationals rested on two related assumptions: (1) that there existed a world economy composed at least of core industrial nations at relatively parallel levels of technological and social development; and (2) that labor was capable of taking concerted action against the divisive and competitive economic order promoted by the national business elites. While the British and American labor movements might have been roughly in unison in the 1866–1873 period, the potential for international coordination was obviously premature for the France of the Second Empire and in the reactionary generation following the Commune. It was also impossible during the period of antisocialist agitation in Bismarck's Germany. The opportunity for a coordinated assault on long hours and other fruits of competitive capitalism improved in the late 1880s when the franchise expanded to unskilled males in Britain, unions and socialists began to recover in France and Germany, an intercolonial trade union organization was emerging in Australia, and the labor movement in the United States was on the move. The labor intelligentsia in Europe looked to American (and Australian) workers as trailblazers in the quest for a higher labor standard.

Western Europeans had special reasons for seeking international solutions. Britain's position on the world market was threatened by a reduction of worktime. The French worried about the twelve-hour days common in Belgium and the threat of German economic growth. Sidney Webb and Tom Mann in England argued that a shorter workday would allow Britain to jettison marginal industries, which relied on sweated labor; still, the British faced increased costs in textiles, mining, and engineering if they alone reduced worktime. The practical solution was an international eight-hour day— a kind of economic disarmament treaty. By 1889, British, French, and most other European and American labor movements advocated a simultaneous reduction of hours.[13] This ideal challenged the prevailing economic nationalism that made the "market" the measure of the labor standard.

Yet, despite some trade union growth in this period, the eight-hour movements were not successful. Eight-hour bills died in committee in Britain and France, and May Day demonstrations declined after 1891; in the United States, the national short-hour movement became fragmented and localized. There are several possible explanations for these failures. The British TUC allowed divisions between the skilled trades and New Unionists, and splits within the miners' unions, to prevent a legal eight-hour day in the 1890s. If anything, the French were even more divided between the political and syndicalist camps. In the United States, the AFL after 1891 abandoned the legal route and the annual struggle for eight hours in strong trades.[14] In all countries, the demand for classwide reductions was narrowed to hours reforms for the legally incompetent (women and children) and workers in especially dangerous trades (especially miners). Religious and philanthropic reformists played decisive roles in promoting the weekly rest law in France, early-shop-closing legislation in Britain, and protective hours legislation for minors and women in America.[15]

Still, it would be an exaggeration to claim that labor movements ceded the hours issue to middle- or upper-class reformists or that there was a decline of an autonomous working-class hours ideology. Unions independently sought early shop closings, weekly rest days, and the Saturday half-holiday. Note the role of American women reformers and trade unionists discussed in Chapter 6. French retail clerks displayed an impressive struggle to enforce a weekly rest law in 1906–1907 without significant involvement of reformists. Of course, after the 1880s, hours agitators placed less value on expanding leisure time as a means of empowering workers with political, cultural, and vocational education. Yet unionists on both sides of the Atlantic expressed disquiet when they perceived workers "wasting" hard-fought shorter hours. The problem of adequate physical culture, the need to reduce alcoholism, and the value of family life were not merely the concerns of a paternalistic bourgeoisie; they were issues that radical trade unionists addressed in Germany, France, and elsewhere. It is difficult to label as conservative or radical changes in the appeals of shorter hours after the early 1890s. In fact, all the rationales for the eight-hour day or other worktime reductions (wage increases, additional jobs, improved productivity, enhanced family life, and "rational" wholesome leisure) played important roles in both the late 1880s and 1890s in Europe and the United States. Shifting emphases may simply reflect economic and political conditions.[16]

To blame the failure of the eight-hour-day movement on these ideological and institutional factors is perhaps to confuse an effect for a cause. The real culprit was more likely the international recession of 1891–1896, which certainly stalled the advance of labor organization. The political efficacy of labor everywhere was in its infancy. This impotence explains the conservative tactics of union leaders. Clearly, the internationalism of the 1886–1891 period proved to be ephemeral. Not only was the Second International incapable of exercising any influence on national affairs, but it could not discipline national labor movements (e.g., in Britain or the United States). The move for shorter hours did not have a chance anywhere in this period.

Of course, the eight-hour cause reappeared at the peaks in the major strike in British engineering in 1897–1898 and, more generally, in France in 1905–1906. Agitation for a Sunday or weekly rest day and the Saturday half-holiday also expanded from 1906 to 1914. French agitation, orchestrated by syndicalist elements in the CGT, perhaps influenced the International Workers of the World and western U.S. unions in strikes over hours in 1907 and especially 1912. Yet none of these efforts achieved measurable success. With few exceptions, including the experiments of maverick employers such as Henry Ford and state-operated armories and shipyards in the United States and Western Europe, the eight-hour day was virtually unknown in 1914.[17]

What is perhaps most instructive about the post-1891 period is not the failure of the short-hour movement but the hostility of employers toward any breach in the hours standard. Roediger and Foner stress the persistent opposition of employer associations to any hours reductions in the United States. A similar mobilization of employers against shorter worktime was evident in the long parliamentary struggles for the ten-hour day in France, involving not only a ten-year legislative battle but also a struggle to make it effective as loopholes were opened in the law through court challenges. A similar lengthy battle over an eight-hour law for British miners resulted in 1908 in a compromised law that did not credit workers with all the time spent in the mines. Such powerful employer associations as the Engineering Employers of Britain organized to defeat eight-hour drives of relatively well organized unions in 1897.[18]

The breakthrough for the shortening of worktime came only in the war years. Both the American War Labor Board and the British and French ministries of munitions concluded that production did not rise with the length of the workday. In Britain, work efficiency experts gained significant influence over working hours through the Health of Munitions Workers Committee. They successfully promoted not only the idea of the efficiency of a compressed workday but also that the one-break system, shift work, and the regular holiday were superior to unstinted overtime.[19] In any case, experiments in shorter hours in Europe and the United States in the 1890s had proven the efficiency engineer's case.[20]

More significant than the profitability of shorter working hours was the winning over of a reforming and governmental elite to reduced workdays. Roediger and Foner stress the role of the Consumers' League, the Women's Trade Union League, and Progressivist jurists in promoting shorter hours, especially for women and children. These groups had their analogues in Europe, especially in the influential International Association for the Legal Protection of Labor (founded in 1900). This network of jurists, labor ministry officials, and class-mediating politicians (which became the core of the International Labor Office in 1919) played an important role in legitimizing increased leisure. They stressed the advantage of hours reductions on women and family life, the feasibility of shorter days without undermining the political or economic status quo, and the inevitability of technological progress, which alone could compensate for reduced labor time. As important were the efforts of these groups in promoting international protective labor legislation. They had few successes before 1914, but they did set the international reformist agenda in 1919.[21]

## III

The discontinuity of the war itself created the opportunity for international reductions of worktime. War markets and mobilization assured labor shortages, improved bargaining positions, and increased state intervention in labor relations—all factors that encouraged hours diminutions. In the United States, the Wilson administration's desire for labor peace led to the "basic" eight-hour day for railroad workers and children, and later the eight-hour standard for employment under defense contracts. Government action encouraged union initiatives as the eight-hour day became a perceived right of citizenship; this resulted in a million new eight-hour workers between 1915–1918. Quite likely, these advances stimulated European and Latin American interest in the eight-hour standard when Wilson became identified in 1917 and 1918 not only with a democratic peace but with the eight-hour day. While the labor discipline imposed on battlefront nations of Europe frustrated similar victories, some concessions were made. For example, in French war industries in 1917, militant women won a fifty-four-hour week with a Saturday half-holiday.[22]

The "three-eights," the equal division of the day between work, rest, and leisure, had symbolized the aspirations of labor and reformers for a generation before World War I. Suddenly and with unprecedented universality, the eight-hour day became the norm in the aftermath of the war. While Lenin's dream of world revolution failed, the eight-hour day swept across Europe as governments and employers conceded this major reform to exhausted and often militant people.

An insurgency, which spread across Europe between 1917 and 1920, issued as its first and most permanent fruit an eight-hour day. Although there was no international coordination of these hours struggles, a wave of eight-hour movements spontaneously emerged. Beginning with an eight-hour day proclaimed by the Bolshevik government in November 1917, eight-hour decrees spread in early 1918 to Finland, Norway, and Germany in the wake of its revolution in November. The eight-hour day passed then to the new states of Poland, Czechoslovakia, and Austria by mid-December. From the revolutionary regimes of Eastern and Central Europe, hours agitation spread to Switzerland, where up to 400,000 struck for eight hours in December. Militant strikes for the eight-hour day in British mining and railways, also in December, culminated in a general strike in Glasgow for the forty-four-hour week in January 1919. This was followed by successful strikes in most major British industries. The movement spread to Italy in February 1919 in the metal goods industries and led to a wave of shutdowns in March and April in textiles, chemicals, and even agriculture.[23]

With the peace came an explosion of trade union bargaining for increased leisure. While in Britain, railway workers, iron workers and steelworkers, and engineering unions successfully negotiated at the national level for an immediate six-day/eight-hour week, by March 1919, miners had won a seven-hour day. Meanwhile, radical shop stewards, especially in the munitions works, agitated for forty-four-, forty-, and even thirty-six-hour workweeks, although without success. Fears of postwar layoffs in war industries stimulated the more radical worktime demands. But so did the general insistence on a "real change" in life.[24] Robert Horne, a stern Tory minister of labour, recognized that "the question of working hours" had become "acute and pressing" and that workers were unwilling to submit to long negotiations after four and one-half years of "hard routine." Horne realized that the postwar labor unrest was different from the past: Not only had union officials lost control over some of the rank and file, but a general expectation of job security and government intervention on the workers' side might well require a "general reform." Moreover, the government accepted the equity of workers' claims for decreased worktime. As Lloyd George admitted shortly after the Armistice: "It is not a question of whether the men can stand the strain of a longer day, but that the working class is entitled to the same sort of leisure as the middle class."[25]

Compared to the British, the French produced few strikes for hours reductions in the first quarter of 1919. This was more the result of much weaker unions and a more repressive war economy than less interest in free time. Still, by March 1919, French metal, dock, mine, and textile workers had demanded an eight-hour day. An alarmed Ministry of Interior reported CGT growth, especially in the white-collar sectors. Layoffs in war industries had stimulated eight-hour agitation. Moreover, "the fever of enjoyment and pleasure," often expressed in a "frenetic epidemic of dancing," could not be contained after over four years of sacrifice. A reduced workday surely had an enormous appeal in 1919. Indeed, police favored increased leisure as a means of "relaxing instincts too long suppressed."[26]

The CGT leadership eagerly exploited this situation. In early March, the CGT secretary, Léon Jouhaux, warned that "France is now on a volcano" and that he "declined all responsibility" if, by May Day, the parliament had not voted for an eight-hour bill.[27] Despite the CGT's threats of mass action, the reformist leadership was not sanguine that a political strike for the eight-hour day would succeed; they were, of course, afraid of unleashing the Bolshevik bogey on themselves. They supplemented the threat of insurgency with an Interfederal Cartel, inspired by the British unions. In March, the CGT formed this cartel from its strongest unions (transport, maritime, mines, metal, and construction) in order to coordinate bargaining for the eight-hour day and enforce a May 1 deadline. After ten days of negotiation, the Metalworkers won a national contract on April 17. In the face of strike threats for May Day and the growing movement for a forty-four-hour week, employers conceded a workday of eight hours (forty-eight per week). Similar negotiations in the rail and construction industries produced contracts by the first week of May. Most important, the threat of unleashing an insurgency loosely organized around the workers' Maypole was an effective weapon to mobilize the traditionally languid parliament to take action.[28]

Paralleling this Europeanwide pressure from below were efforts to make the eight-hour day an international law. Committed to this goal was a transnational network of reformers rather erroneously labeled "Wilsonians." Many in this group were linked to the International Association for Labor Legislation and the International Labor Office (ILO). Key British actors were George Barnes, a moderate former leader of the Amalgamated Society of Engineers and leader of the 1897 eight-hour strike, and H. B. Butler, a career functionary with wartime experience in the Ministry of Labour. Principle French leaders were Justin Godart, a radical deputy and chairman of the Chamber's Labor Commission, and Albert Thomas, a moderate socialist deputy, former administrator of war industries, and, after 1919, director of the ILO.[29]

This reformist network cooperated to incorporate this program in the peace treaty. George Barnes declared that the war had been a "great leveler." Advanced countries had now to establish an "international standard" for labor because "capital has no country." In order to "safeguard Dundee [we must] raise Calcutta." Justin Godart wrote in more idealistic terms: Because the world war "was a war of peoples, not of the mercenary," the treaty, "in place of the classic articles devoted to the prerogatives of dynasties or of the alliances of kings," must be "concerned with human interests." A treaty that included labor statutes not only would produce a more lasting peace but would guarantee an international labor standard and, with it, prevent economic competition from undermining these gains.[30]

The idea of an industrial peace treaty was not isolated to the liberal left establishment. On January 25, 1919, France's Clemenceau persuaded the Preliminary Peace Conference to create a Commission for International Labor Legislation partially to attract labor interest from Bolshevism and the revived socialist movement. With the American labor leader Samuel Gompers as its chairman, the commission was composed of major leaders from the reform network. It embraced Barnes's proposal for creating a permanent ILO to coordinate annual conferences that, in turn, would consider labor treaties or conventions. Agreeing that international action was needed in the face of "the nervousness of workers' opinion," the commission recommended on March 19 that an "Eight-Hour Convention" be drafted in Washington in October at the first International Labor Conference. These principles were enshrined in the Peace of 1919 (Part XIII): "Peace can be founded only on the base of social justice," which required the "application of the principle of the eight-hour day or 48-hour week." Despite this rather ambiguous commitment, in the spring of 1919 workers and even employers believed that the eight-hour day had international legal sanction.[31]

Both international insurgency and diplomacy were necessary backdrops to the spread of the eight-hour day. Eight-hour laws rapidly followed the decrees of revolutionary regimes in Central and Eastern Europe in Spain, Portugal, and Switzerland by June 1919, and in the Netherlands and Sweden by November. The connection between legislation and insurgency was no clearer than in France. Despite the snail's pace of prewar hours legislation, parliament took only eight days to pass an eight-hour law on April 23, 1919—in the shadow of threatened May Day demonstrations. The CGT leadership found temporary allies in the government, which was determined to contain labor militancy. Clemenceau, famous for breaking the 1906 eight-hour strikes, in January 1919 asked Louis Loucheur to convene an Interministerial Commission on International Labor Treaties consisting of notables from labor, management, and politics to help draft an hours law. After meeting merely five times between March 15 and April 7, the commission submitted a bill to the Chamber.[32]

While business representatives of the Loucheur Commission warned that with an eight-hour law, production would decrease, labor shortages emerge, and transportation and other costs would rise, the government pressed for legislation.[33] Defenders of the eight-hour bill (e.g., Godart and Thomas) were also key actors in the international reform movement and argued that an international eight-hour standard was inevitable and would prove to the soldiers that "something had changed." The law was a compromise, however, incorporating both the demands of the CGT (especially for no cut in pay as a direct result of hours reductions) and the pleading of management for exemptions, delays, and flexibility in the use of overtime.[34]

This trend was not limited to Europe. American textile workers and steelworkers struck for the eight-hour day in 1919, better-organized trades such as clothing and printing opted for the forty-four-hour week, and miners sought a six-hour day. This pattern closely followed the European strike wave. And twenty-eight American states passed hours legislation in 1919.[35]

Clearly, these concessions to labor were not freely granted by a modernizing group of corporate capitalists intent on coopting or domesticating labor into a "classless" consumer capitalism founded on increased leisure time. As David Roediger has shown, "Fordism" had few adherents. American steel, for example, successfully resisted government pressure to modify the two twelve-hour shifts during the war and defeated an eight-hour strike in the fall of 1919.[36] Instead, these eight-hour movements were the culmination of an international crisis in which shop-floor insurgency, coupled with the action of a network of reformers, led to general hours reductions throughout the Western world.

The United States and Britain were the only major industrial nations that failed to pass an eight-hour law. One might argue that the relative political impotence of American labor, the fragmentation of the American state, the power of a reactionary Supreme Court, and the relatively minor impact of the war on American society guaranteed the defeat of a federal law. This allowed the continuation of long days in the textile mills of southern states. In the British case, some have argued that "home rule for industry" or collective bargaining—after the TUC briefly flirted with legislative strategies in the 1890s—had won the adherence of major unions by 1918.[37]

Yet the exceptionalism of Anglo-American labor can be exaggerated. By 1920, the percentage of the workforce under the eight-hour regime in the United States (48 percent) was no smaller than in France, where procedural delays kept many, especially in retail, rural, or artisan trades, outside regulation until the late 1920s. In Britain, all heavy industry and 80 percent of the remaining industrial workers obtained the eight-hour day without a law. Moreover, neither the American nor British case lacked a political dimension. Semipublic corporatist bodies such as the American War Labor Board and the British Whitley Committee helped orchestrate short-hour collective bargaining. In France, the eight-hour law only sanctioned guidelines for hours standards that were set after the "advice" of labor and management. Often the state simply adopted the provisions of bargained labor contracts. The "voluntarism" of the Anglo-American world in comparison to the "statism" of the Continent was only relative. Despite significant national differences, the world war created the opening for an international labor offensive previously frustrated by the impotence of labor in the nation-states and by international economic competition.[38]

The significance of the international conjuncture of the postwar year is only confirmed by the regression of hours gains after 1919. The decline of the insurgency is evident in Europe by July 1919, and, with it, the number of new short-hour contracts rapidly dwindled in France and Britain. The American upsurge ebbed after the defeat of the steel strike in January 1920. As early as July 1919, French employers resisted contracts signed by their national employer associations (e.g., in metals), attacked the eight-hour day as a disaster to French economic recovery, and mobilized political support against it. Despite hopes of a general eight-hour law in Britain in the spring of 1919, that expectation disappeared by the end of the year, and British Conservatives led the opposition against an eight-hour law.[39]

When the insurgency that forced the eight-hour day on employers subsided, the internationalism that underpinned the shorter workday was itself weakened. In this context, the long-awaited Washington Conference of the ILO was convened in November 1919. The meeting was compromised from the start when the United States refused to participate officially. The British delegate, George Barnes, was shocked by the often hostile attitude of conservative senators, who viewed delegates as "Bolshevik agents." Jouhaux complained that "Americans only understand force and violence" in their rejection of the concept of international labor legislation.[40] Although the conference was officially an outgrowth of the Peace of Paris, the American rejection of the treaty guaranteed its ineffectiveness.

The result was a convention that was a study in moderation: A forty-eight hour week was to be applied only to transportation and industry (not commerce or agriculture), and it allowed wide latitude for exemptions, flexible workweeks, and overtime. Developing industrial countries, including India and Japan as well as several new Eastern European countries, were granted longer workweeks for a extended period. Although representatives of major nations (excluding the United States) signed the ILO's eight-hour convention in November 1919, Czechoslovakia was the only industrial country to ratify it.[41] Despite British leadership in the founding of the ILO and the writing of the Washington Hours Convention, Whitehall refused to endorse the agreement, citing technical problems. In reality, the British were unwilling to assume leadership in an experiment in labor diplomacy not joined by the United States. This gave permission to other major powers not to ratify, despite a decade of negotiation at the ILO. As the postwar insurgency waned with the division of the Left, so also did the influence of the international reformist elite (now institutionalized in the ILO). Neither the eight-hour day nor the international labor standard was free from powerful opponents, who attempted for another ten years to reverse the events of 1919.[42]

By the end of 1921, the expectation that the postwar recession would be followed by a boom encouraged competing national industries in Europe to press for an extended workday. For example, in 1922 Dutch workers lost the forty-five-hour week, which they had won in 1919 (raised to forty-eight hours by law); German employers eroded the eight-hour standard in steel and construction; and New England textile workers, facing the long hours of southern mills, found their workday under attack. The most dramatic, if temporary, attack on the eight-hour standard took place in Switzerland where the workweek was raised from forty-eight to fifty-three hours. This international assault by employers on worktime was symptomatic of the decline of working-class internationalism and a return to economic nationalism; employer groups did not argue in the rhetoric of classical liberalism against worktime regulation, but claimed that sacrifice (i.e., of time) was necessary for national economic survival and growth in the face of international competition. Each national business elite justified its efforts to erode the eight-hour standard with the claim that major competitors had already sabotaged it.

A conjuncture of factors, both national and international, institutional and "disruptive," created a unique reallocation of personal time in industrial Europe after World War I. The opportunity was very brief, lasting scarcely more than six months. It was followed by a closure when the extraordinary configuration of unstable alliances and constellation of national and international trends collapsed. Both economic and political circumstances facilitated this return to normalcy. The rapid disintegration of labor militancy in 1919 was in part the consequence of a weakening bargaining position when a postwar recession increased unemployment (especially in Britain).[43] Labor cohesion was quickly dashed over strategy and the schism resulting from communism.[44] Without the threat of labor militancy, neither reformist union officials nor middle-class political allies at home or around the ILO were capable of sustaining the momentum.

Despite the international reaction of employers and the impotence of labor, however, the eight-hour day generally held. A referendum reversed the Swiss fifty-three-hour-week law in February 1924, and attempts to modify the French eight-hour law failed by the end of 1922. When the American steel industry finally gave in to the three-shift, eight-hour day in 1923, the threat to this standard in the world steel industry subsided. Yet, everywhere, labor was on the defense throughout the 1920s over working hours. Not only did this issue play a central role in the disastrous British miners' strike in 1926, but during each economic upturn, employers agitated against the eight-hour ceiling.[45]

The eight-hour day not only was the key, and for many the only, tangilble social reform after World War I. Its proximate cause was an international political crisis facilitated by a fragile coalition of labor and reformers in the face of business opposition. Ultimately, it was the fruit of a generation of agitation for a new distribution of work and leisure.

## IV

With the normalization of the eight-hour day, leisure time became a central component in the ongoing social contest of the interwar period. Employers, governments, and mass-market industries sought to shape the utilization of leisure (e.g., as revealed in the attempts of the Fascists to organize recreational activities in the *dopolavoro*); trade unions and the Left in Europe also addressed the problem of workers' recreation and culture. In the tradition of prewar socialism, for example, the Austrian labor movement attempted to organize a complex of leisure and educational institutions specifically to advance workers' cultural, physical, and political needs. The question of the utilization of nonworktime also preoccupied the "neosocialism" of De Man and Albert Thomas, which played an important role in the 1920s in seeking more broadly based recreational facilities as alternatives to mass-market leisure. Moreover, in the decade following the eight-hour day, the demand for the annual paid vacation emerged. This goal was expressed not only in terms of democratizing the leisure enjoyed by the middle class and some white-collar employees but as a means of workers obtaining the extended time free from work that was necessary for the cultivation of family life and travel.[46]

The shrinkage of world markets in 1930–1931, however, brought a sudden resurrection of the short-hour movement in Europe and America. Many faced joblessness or, more often, part-time work (with corresponding reductions in pay). Others experienced overtime and more intense labor when employers sought to reduce unit costs and undercut competitors.[47] Employers blamed the slump on the world market (especially their inability to compete because of high labor costs), but organized labor attacked recent economic rationalization. A new consensus emerged on the Left that increased output per worker had not been balanced by either increased income or job security. The consequence was "underconsumption" and thus economic depression. The only solutions were salutary wage increases and job sharing by means of reduced hours.[48]

A British TUC report called for a forty-hour week with no reduction in pay as "one of the ways in which the workers may share in increased productivity." Even Harold Browden, an owner of the Raleigh Cycle Company, argued in October 1932 that employment was no longer a sufficient means of distributing purchasing power.[49] The only apparent solution to this dilemma was to find new mechanisms for allocating demand to balance supply. Trade unionists argued that the "problem of unemployment is in its essence a problem of undistributed leisure."[50]

In France, the CGT launched a forty-hour campaign in 1931. The new reduction of worktime was to solve the "disequilibrium of consumption and production" caused by "disorganized rationalization" and "overwork." "We must recognize that the industrial system creates two products: goods and leisure." There should be a balance between the two so that leisure did not become unemployment.[51] The communists agreed, going still further in resurrecting the Soviet example of the seven-hour day.[52]

Again, this was an international movement. The forty-hour week dominated the Stockholm meeting of the International Federation of Trade Unions in 1930. As Benjamin Hunnicutt details in this volume, sections of the American labor movement had advocated a forty-hour week in 1927, and at the depth of the depression, the AFL supported the introduction of the Black–Connery thirty-hour bill. While Europeans generally ignored the thirty-hour concept, they repeatedly referred to the American example in the hours provisions of the National Recovery Act of 1933.[53] And again a reformist network emerged to support the concept of job sharing: The International Association for Social Progress and the League of Nations Union favored the forty-hour week (with the maintenance of pay rates) as a means of expanding the home market.[54]

Nevertheless, the principle forum was the ILO. Its governing body, on the request of the Italian government, organized a Tripartite Preparatory Conference in January 1933, hoping to force the upcoming World Economic Conference to support an international reduction of worktime.[55] This plan was dashed by the implacable opposition of business representatives supported by Germany, Japan, and Britain. The proposal of the trade unions for forty hours without pay reductions failed when Italy and other governments refused to join. At the end of this meeting, the British employer representative, Forbes-Watson, took pleasure in reporting that short-hour advocates would have no influence on the World Economic Conference.[56]

Forbes-Watson was right. Instead of a general forty-hour convention, the ILO adopted a piecemeal program of special conventions for separate industries.[57] In any event, by 1937, the opportunity for international solutions to the depression had long passed. Instead, each nation adopted variations of a ''beggar thy neighbor'' approach to creating markets and jobs. Eventually, the fascist solution of war economy dominated.[58]

What had failed at the international level was not abandoned in the national arena. The British TUC continued to press for forty-hour standards through the normal channels of collective bargaining. The Iron and Steel Trades Conference proposed four six-hour shifts, and engineering unions pressed throughout 1934 and 1935 for an eight-hour/five-day week. Managers in some modern plants, where the Saturday half-holiday proved unprofitable, approved the latter plan. But the Engineering Employers' Federation held fast, as they had so often in the past, to the prevailing forty-seven hour standard.[59] Attempts by the Labour party to introduce a forty-hour week in municipal governments also met with little success.[60]

One of the great anomalies of British labor in the 1930s was its nearly complete inability to affect national economic policy. This was obvious in the failure of the unions to win a forty-hour week in any important sector. Britain had clearly lost its leadership in advancing the labor standard; the traditional tactic of collective bargaining was no longer effective.

On the Continent, hours reductions were more successful. In October 1934, Italy established a weak forty-hour statute (with corresponding reductions in pay); in June 1934, the Czechs adopted a forty to forty-two hour week with only a partial wage drop. By 1934, both wings of the French labor movement embraced the forty-hour week with no change in weekly wages. And in 1935, with the formation of the *Rassemblement Popular,* the forty-hour week became the cornerstone of an antideflationary economic program. Along with agricultural price supports and legal encouragement of collelctive bargaining, the forty-hour week was designed to increase purchasing power. Shortly after the election of the Popular Front government, a wave of strikes forced the enactment of a forty-hour law. Not only was this legislation modeled after the eight-hour law of 1919 but the origins of the two laws, during periods of social crises, were similar.[61]

The difference was that the 1936 law was passed in international isolation. Ironically, by 1938 the United States, which had abstained from the 1919 legislation, had adopted a forty-hour law. Yet the international coalescence of reform and insurgency, which had nourished the eight-hour movement of 1917–1920, was missing in the late 1930s. The surprising support of the Italian Fascists in 1932 for an international reduction of worktime proved to be short lived and was founded on wage-cutting principles opposed by the trade unions. In the spring of 1933, the destruction of the German labor movement, until then a strong supporter of international economic recovery through a worktime policy, severely weakened the prospects for the later success of the French Popular Front. Moreover, the political impotence of British labor sharply contrasted with the political climate of 1919. Finally, the failures of labor diplomacy at the ILO guaranteed an international context unfavorable to the reformist experiments of the Popular Front. As the French socialist governments would confirm in the 1980s, shop-floor or ballot-box victory in one country in the 1930s was insufficient to advance the labor standard in the face of the international market and hostile foreign policies.

As in 1919, the new French hours law was gradually implemented by decree. By the beginning of 1937, 3.5 million industrial workers enjoyed the forty-hour week, and by September 1938, it was, in theory, nearly universal except in agriculture and the professions.[62] Yet capital flight, declining productivity, and inflation helped produce trade imbalances in 1937 and 1938. While labor inspectors tolerated overtime, business opposition to "unilateral disarmament" of the French economy became unrelenting. Even the CGT leader René Belin had warned, in early 1937, that the forty-hour week would survive only if production rose. The collapse of the Popular Front by May 1937 was followed by a series of decrees in 1938 that suspended the law. Despite protest strikes in November 1938, the pressure to mobilize the economy in anticipation of the war undermined political support for the forty-hour week.[63]

Although the law was officially restored in February 1946, it again was suspended during the reconstruction. Indeed, it remained under a cloud for a generation. Economists and politicians have identified it with the failure of the Popular Front government to revive the French economy on the eve of war and prevent German conquest in 1940.[64] Yet it is surely simplistic to blame these calamities on the forty-hour week; it seems more reasonable to put the failure of the reform in context. In this century, any real improvement in a national labor standard has almost always occurred also on the international level. This was impossible in the 1930s.

The problem was also intellectual (as Benjamin Hunnicutt notes in an American context). Many Europeans associated the forty-hour week with economic Malthusianism. Of course, advocates claimed that the forty-hour week meant a demand-side economic recovery, an indirect means of deepening the home market. Supporters argued that productivity should and could increase with shorter hours. Still, the concept implied a sharing of work when not much was being produced—it seemed to deny economic growth. The very notion of distributing leisure as well as goods increased this suspicion. In a context of massive unemployment and diminished consumption, this seemed to suggest the opposite of obvious economic priorities.[65]

Moreover, there was a clear and (for some economists) superior alternative to the reduction of worktime: Government spending could stimulate demand. This had the advantage over job-sharing schemes of not imposing on capital the burden of redistributing demand. Neither option was acceptable to conservative British Treasury officials or business in Popular Front France. Nevertheless, the long-term solution would be predominately the Keynesian one. In the United States, the Roosevelt administration blocked the thirty-hour bill, opting instead for a number of fiscal measures. In France, the forty-hour week was quietly shelved in 1946 as incompatible with the "Battle of Production" and the Finance Ministry's plan for stimulating growth. In Britain, the immediate postwar demand for a forty-hour week was scrapped in 1946 for a more modest forty-four-hour week, and unions increasingly abandoned their traditional rejection of multiple shifts.

## V

This brief survey of the international movement for shorter hours between the origins of the Second International and the Popular Front suggests several conclusions. Leisure time remained a pent-up demand of workers in all industrializing nations. This objective was frustrated by economic competition and managerial resistance to the threat that reduced hours posed to its authority and capital accumulation. Time, not merely power and income, were at issue. And although freedom from work obviously had both economic consequences and affected authority relations between capital and labor, leisure was a distinct objective. Worktime diminutions across skill–trade lines became possible only in the context of a classwide international mobilization. In this process, reformists played an essential if often indirect and even unintentional role. These reforms cannot be dismissed as the manipulation of corporate liberals, and although the range of workers' objectives may be narrowed by the reforms, the laws themselves establish a platform of social right from which new struggles could be waged.[66]

Western European short-hour movements have been resurrected in the 1980s. In an era of increasing technological unemployment, reduced worktime becomes a means of sharing scarce employment; and in an age of feminist-inspired sex-role changes, shorter hours becomes a way of reducing the domestic burdens of two-income families. Yet, so far, efforts to lower the hours of worktime have largely been failures. Karl Hinrichs, Claus Offe, and others have suggested that the contemporary difficulties of winning reductions in worktime may be the result of the personalization of time-allocation needs; instead of working shorter days, most people prefer longer vacations and other extended blocks of time free from employment. As a result, there is little unity over a call for, say, a thirty-five-hour week.[67] If this is true, it reflects a trend that dates from the days of the Popular Front.

Yet the problem of shortening the workday may prove in the long run to have as much to do with the difficulty in forming an international movement for hours reductions as effective as that in 1919 (or even 1936) as it does with the cooptation of consumerism or the increasingly complex time-allocation problems of workers. The intensification of competition, especially between Third-World and Western labor, and the inability of workers (even when they have a foothold in the state) to break from the discipline of the international market continues to frustrate the shortening of worktime.

## NOTES

1. Although there is no comparative study of the eight-hour movement, some modern works deal with this topic in a major way at the national level. A very important American study is David Roediger and Philip Foner, *Our Own Time: American Labor and Working Hours* (Westport, Conn., 1988). Also important are David Montgomery, *Beyond Equality, Labor and the Radical Republicans, 1862–1873* (New York, 1967); and Benjamin Hunnicutt, *Work Without End: The Abandonment of Shorter Hours For the Right to Work* (Philadelphia, 1988). Some key studies of the European short-hour question are Maurice Dommanget, *Histoire du Premier mai* (Paris, 1953); Jean-luc Bodiguel, *La Réduction du temps de travail*

(Paris, 1969); M. A. Bienefeld, *Working Hours in British Industry: An Economic History* (London, 1972); Brian McCormick, "Hours of Work in British Industry," *Industrial and Labor Relations Review* 12 (1959): 423–433; August Geib, *Der Normalarbeitstag* (Leipzig, 1975); and Irmgard Steinisch, *Arbeitszeitverkuerzung und socialer Wandel. Der Kampf um die Achtstudenschicht in der deutschen und amerikanischen eisen- und stahlerzeugenden Industrie von der Jahrhundertwende zur weltwirtschaftskrise* (Berlin, 1985). Australian studies of the eight-hour day are particularly interesting because of Australia's success in winning the shorter workday in some industries in the 1850s. See, for example, John Niland, "The Birth of the Movement for an Eight-hour Day in New South Wales," *Australian Journal of Politics and History* 14, no. 1 (1968): 75–87; and H. Hughes, "The Eight Hour Day and the Development of the Labour Movement in Victoria in the Eighteen Fifties," *Historical Studies of Australia and New Zealand* 9 (May 1961): 396–412.

2. Note James Cronin and Carmen Sirianni, ed. *Work, Community, and Power, The Experience of Labor in Europe and America, 1900–1925* (Philadelphia, 1983).

3. For Britain, see Richard Price, *Masters, Unions, and Men* (New York, 1980); and James Hinton, *The First Shop Stewards Movement* (London, 1973). See also Charles Tilly and Edward Shorter, *Strikes in France* (New York, 1974), especially pp. 66–68, 190; and Eric Hobsbawn, *Laboring Men* (New York, 1964), pp. 371–386.

4. Michael Anderson, *Family Structure in Nineteenth Century Lancashire* (London, 1971); Tamara Hareven, *Industrial Time and Family Time* (Cambridge, Mass., 1982); and Joan Scott and Louis Tilly, *Women, Work, and Family* (New York, 1978), deal with the interaction of work and family. Recent studies concerned with working-class leisure are Roy Rosenzweig, *Eight Hours for What We Will, Workers and Leisure in an Industrial City* (New York, 1983); and Standish Meacham, *A Life Apart* (Cambridge Mass., 1977).

5. Bienefeld, *Working Hours in British Industry*, pp. 122–126; George D. H. Cole, *A Short History of the British Working Class Movement* (London, 1948), p. 249; Hugh Clegg, *A History of British Unions Since 1889* (London, 1964), pp. 53–54; John Burnett, *The History of the Nine Hours Movement at Newcastle and Gateshead* (London, 1872); Ministère du Commerce, France, *Enquête sur les modifications à apporter aux lois du 9 octobre 1848 et du 19 mai 1874 sur le travail dans l'industrie* (Paris, 1885), p. 129; Michelle Perrot. *Les ouvriers en grève* (Paris, 1974). 1:260–267.

6. Dommanget, Chap. 3; Bodiguel, *La Réduction du temps,* pp. 3–69; M. Lecoq, *La Journée de huit heures* (Paris, 1907): and E. A. P. Duffy, "The New Unionism in Britain, 1889–1890, a Reappraisal," *Economic History Review* 14 (1961): 309–325.

7. Monica Hodgson, "The Working Day and the Working Week in Victorian Britain, 1840–1900," Master's thesis University of London, 1974, pp. 69–84; (TUC) Trades Union Congress *Report of the Proceedings* (1887), p. 42. Numerous sources deal with union politics behind the eight-hour movement. Note, especially, Duffy, "New Unionism"; and E. A. P. Duffy, "The Eight Hour Day Movement in Britain, 1836–1893," *Manchester School of Economics and Social Studies* 36 (1968): 203–

222, 345–363; and Eric Hobsbawm, *The Turning Point of Labour, 1880–1900* (London, 1977). See also the sources listed in note 9.

8. Great Britain, *Royal Commissions on Labour:* 1892, vol. 1, pt. C, pp. 338–339; 1894, vol. 3, pt. B, pp. 200, 221, 472–473.

9. A few useful sources are Dommanget, *Histoire de Premier mai*; Duffy, "Eight Hour Day"; and Gosten Langenfelt, "The Eight Hours' Day: A History and a Legend," *Zeitschrift fuer Anglisik und Amerikanistik* 13 (1965): 167–173. See also the journal *The Eight Hours Working Day,* published in Berne, 1889–1890.

10. Beyond this well-known struggle between advocates of direct action and legal reform, the anarchist journal *La Révolt,* February 1, 1886, argued that an eight-hour day would only lead to further mechanization and an "aggravation of misery in real society."

11. TUC, *Report of Proceedings* (1887), p. 36.

12. Tom Mann, *What a Compulsory Eight Hours Working Day Means to Workers* (London, 1886); Tom Mann, *Memoirs* (London, 1923), pp. 58–60; TUC, *Report of the Proceedings* (1889), pp. 47–57; and TUC, *Report of the Proceedings* (1890), p. 53. See also Duffy, "Eight Hour Day"; and Brian McCormick, "The Miners and the Eight Hours Day, 1863–1910," *Economic History Review* 35 (1959): 238–250.

13. Sidney Webb and Harold Cox, *The Eight Hours Day* (London, 1891), pp. 118–120; and Mann, *Compulsory Eight Hours Day.* See also Dommanget, *Historic du Premier mai,* pp. 52–180; H. H. Champion, "An Eight-Hours Law," *Nineteenth Century* 26 (1889): 509–522; Henry M. Hyndman, "Eight Hours, the Maximum Working Day," *New Review* 1 (1889): 266–287; and Jules Guesde, "La Journée de huit heures," *L'Ere nouvelle* 3 (1894): 231–234.

14. H. A. Phelps-Brown, *The Growth of Industrial Relations* (London, 1955), pp. 181–190; Duffy, "Eight Hour Day," pp. 346–352; Dommanget, *Histoire du Premier mai,* pp. 180–200; and Foner and Roediger, *Our Own Time,* Chap. 8.

15. See Chap. 4 in my forthcoming book, *The Quest for Time: Reduction of Work in Britain and France, 1840–1940;* and Kathyrn Sklar's chapter in this volume.

16. I develop this theme in my "The Quest for Leisure: Reassessing the Eight-Hour Day in France," *Journal of Social History* 18 (Winter 1984): 195–216.

17. For example, see Robert Gibbons, *A Shorter Working Day* (London, 1892); and Office du Travail, France, *Notes sur la journée de huit heures dans les établissements industriels de l'état* (Paris, 1906).

18. Todd Nigel, "Trade Unions and the Engineering Industry Dispute at Barrow-in-Furness, 1897–98," *International Review of Social History* 20 (1975): 33–47; Jonathan Zeitlin, "The Labour Strategies of British Engineering Employers, 1890–1922," in *Managerial Strategies and Industrial Relations,* Howard Gospel and Craig Litter editors (London, 1983); Steven Tolliday and Jonathan Zeitlin, *Shopfloor Bargaining and the State, Historical and Comparative Perspectives* (New York, 1985); and Judith Stone, *The Search for Social Peace: Reform Legislation in France, 1890–1914* (Albany, 1985), Chap. 1.

19. A summary is provided in British Parliamentary Papers, Health of Munitions

Workers' Committee, *Final Report*, 1918, vol. 12, pp. 40–42. Lengthy documentation is offered in Cross, *Quest for Time*, Chap. 5.

20. Some basic studies include Bernard Mottez, *Systèmes de salaire et politiques patronales* (Paris, 1965); Aimée Moutet, "Les origines du système de Taylor en France. Le point de vue patronal (1907–1914)," *Le Mouvement social* 93 (October–December 1975): 15–49; George Humphreys, *Taylorism in France, 1904–1920* (New York, 1986); Michelle Perrot, "Le Regard de l'autre: Les patrons français vue par les ouvriers (1880–1914)," in *Le Patronat de la seconde industrialisation*, ed. Maurice Levy-Leboyer (Paris, 1979), pp. 293–306; Anson Rabinbach, "The European Science of Work: The Economy of the Body at the End of the Nineteenth Century," in *Work in France*, ed. Steven Kaplan and Cynthia Koepp (Ithaca, N.Y., 1986), pp. 475–513; E. Wigham, *The Power to Manage: A History of the Engineering Employers' Federation* (London, 1973), pp. 38–43; and Howard Gospel, "The Development of Management Organisation in Industrial Relations," in *Management Strategy and Industrial Relations*, ed. Keith Thurley and Steven Wood (Cambridge, 1982). See also D. Roediger's Chapter in this volume.

21. In addition to Roediger and Foner's thorough treatment (see note 1), see David Montgomery, *Workers' Control in America, Studies in the History of Work, Technology, and Labor Struggles* (New York, 1979). See also my "Redefining Workers' Control: Rationalization, Labor Time, and Union Politics in France, 1900–1928," in Cronen and Sirianni, eds., *Work, Community, and Power*, pp. 142–168.

22. See Stephen Bauer, *Der Weg zum achtstundentag* (Zurich, 1919). For an interesting description of hours militancy on the part of French women during the war, see James McMillan, *Housewife or Harlot: The Place of Women in French Society, 1870–1940* (London, 1981), pp. 133–161.

23. Summaries are in A.A. Evans, "Work and Leisure, 1919–1969," *International Labor Review* 91, no. 1 (January 1969): 45–69; and Stephen Bauer, "The Road to the Eight Hour Day," *Monthly Labor Review* 2 (August 1919): 4–65. Greater details are in *Archives nationales de la France* (AN): $F^{22}$ 318, "Recueil des Actes de la Conférénce de la Paix: Commission de legislation international du travail" (1922); $F^{22}$ 401, "Report of Commission de legislation international du travail" (n.d.), $F^{22}$ 402, Ministry of Labor report (November 19, 1921); and 41 AS 12, Circulars of the Union des industries métallurgiques et minières, Nos. 1112–3 and 1136.

24. Public Records Office (PRO), CAB 24/71, "Labour Situation," November 27 and December 2, 1918; PRO, CAB 24/72. "Labour Situation," December 18, 1918; and *Daily Herald*, December 11, 1918.

25. PRO, CAB 24/71, Memo from Food Controller, December 6, 1918, and from Home Office, December 2, 1918, regarding the need for more and stronger beer was supported in the War Cabinet on January 24, 1919. See PRO, CAB 24/76, March 1, 1919, Memo; PRO, CAB 24/73, "Labour Situation," January 1 and February 19, 1919, for Horne's views. PRO, CAB 23/8, December 6, 1919, meeting cited in Keith Middlemas, *Politics in Industrial Society* (London, 1979), pp. 142–143.

26. AN, F⁷ 13576, Ministry of Interior report, April 10, 1919; and Archives de la Prefecture du Police, Ba 1614, Commissaire divisionnaire reports, March 1919.

27. AN, F⁷ 13576, "CGT note," March 19, 1919.

28. AN, F⁷ 13576, CGT Commission Administratif, March 18, April 4, and April 16, 1919; AN, F⁷ 13273, Comité confédéral, March 23 and April 7, 1919; *France libre*, February 7, 1919; AN, F⁷ 13293, Interior Ministry report, April 18,1919; AN, F²² 420, Ministry of Labor report, April 29, 1919. See also Fédération des ouvriers des métaux et similaires de France, *Pour la défense de la journée de huit heures* (Paris, 1922).

29. George Barnes, *History of the International Labour Office* (London, 1926), pp. xi–xii, 39, 59; PRO, CAB 24/78, "Labour Situation," April 23 and May 7, 1919; PRO, LAB, 2 771/12. See also Justin Godart, *Les Clauses du travail dans la traité de Versailles* (Paris, 1920) pp. 5–6, 10–13.

30. Barnes, *History of ILO*, pp. 36–37; Godart, *Clauses*, pp. 32, 65. See also Louis Pasquet, *La Loi sur la journée de huit heures* (Lyons, 1921), pp. 20–21.

31. AN, F²² 319, "Note sur les conditions internationales de travail," January 24, 1919; AN, F²² 318, "Commission de législation internationale du travail," February 2, 1919–March 14, 1919; and International Labour Office (ILO), "Report Presented to the Peace Conference by the Commission on International Labour Legislation," Geneva, 1920; Bureau International du Travail, *Clauses de Traités de Paix relatives au travail* (Geneva, 1920), pp. 1–2; *Voix du peuple*, April 1919, p. 233.

32. *Bulletin du Ministère du Travail*, June–August 1919, pp. 288–289; and *Information ouvrière et sociale*, January 26, 1919. See also Jacques Julliard, *Clemenceau, briseur de greves* (Paris, 1965); *Le Peuple*, January 13, 1919; and *Le Journal*, January 17, 1919. Minutes of the"Loucheur Commission" are in AN F²² 401.

33. *Information ouvrière et sociale*, March 6 and April 14, 1919; AN, F²² 401, "Loucheur Commission," March 15, 21, and 27, 1919. For the "Minority Report," see Chambre des députes, *Annales, Documents parlementaires*, No. 5980, April 19, 1919, p. 1185.

34. In fact, it was merely an enabling act; hours reductions became legal only after decrees were promulgated for each industry in a complex and slow process. The law's authors hoped that this legislation would induce the French to adopt English-style collective bargaining. Until early June, all went well as national eight-four contracts were signed in the metal, railroad, textile, printing, leather, shoe, and construction industries. Collective bargaining éven yielded reduced hours for some retail clerks. Largely because of the eight-hour law, 1919 was an unprecedented year for collective bargaining. Some 557 contracts were signed (compared to the prewar high of 252 in 1910), 331 of which included hours reductions. See Chambre des députes, *Annales, Documents parlementaires*, No. 5980, April 10, 1919, pp. 1183–1189; *Débats parlementaires*, April 16–17, 1919, pp. 1801–1842; AN, F²² 420, "Avant-projet relatif à la journée de huit heures," April 1919, and *Information ouvrière et sociale*, April 12 and 23, 1919. For the law, see *Journal officiel* (France), April 25, 1919, p. 4266. For collective bargaining in the interwar period, see Pierre Laroque, *Le conventions collectives de travail* (Paris, 1934).

35. Arno Mayer discusses this insurgence in his classic *Politics and Diplomacy*

*of Peacemaking: 1918–1919* (New York, 1967). For a specific case, see Harry McShane, *Glasgow 1919: The Story of the 40 Hours Strike* (London, n.d.).

36. See Gerald Eggert's treatment of the eight-hour struggle in American steel, *Steel Masters and Labor Reform, 1886–1923* (Pittsburgh, 1981). Note also Steinisch, *Arbeitszeitverkuerzung*, who compares the introduction of the eight-hour day in German and American steel.

37. Note, for example, Rodney Lowe, "The National Industrial Conference, 1919–1921," *Historical Journal* 2 (1978): 649–675; and Duncan Gallie, *Social Inequality and Class Radicalism in France and Britain* (Cambridge, 1983), pp. 224–251.

38. In addition to Roediger and Foner (see note 1), see Rodney Lowe, "Hours of Labour: Negotiating Industrial Legislation in Britain, 1919–1939," *Economic History Review* 35 (1982): 254–271; E. H. Phelps Brown, *The Growth of British Industrial Relations* (London, 1955); Frank Wilkinson, "The Development of Collective Bargaining in Britain to the Early 1920s," paper for the Shop Floor Bargaining Seminar, King's College, Cambridge University, March 1981.

39. Lowe, "Hours of Labour"; and Bernard Abherve, "Les origines de la grève des Métallurgistes parisiens," *Le Mouvement social* 93 (October–December 1973): 75–81.

40. AN, F$^{22}$ 404, Bureau international du travail, "Rapport sur les huit heures," June 1923; AN, F$^7$ 13577, report on CGT, January 7, 1920; PRO, CAB 24/95, report on the Washington Conference by G. Barnes, December 30, 1919; PRO, LAB, 2 698/1, undated (1921?) report on the Washington Conference.

41. Comité d'organisation de la Conférénce internationale de travail, *Rapport sur la journée de huit heures* (Geneva 1919), pp. 117ff.; and International Labor Conference; *First Annual Meeting* (Washington, D.C., 1920), pp. 222–227. See also James Shotwell, *The Origins of the International Labor Organization*, 2 vols. (New York, 1934); and H. Solano, ed., *Labour as an International Problem* (London, 1920).

42. Roger Picard, "La Journée de huit heures à l'étranger, *Les Documents du travail*, March 1922, pp. 1–14.

43. PRO, CAB 24/97 "Labour Situation," January 28, 1920; PRO, CAB 24/125, Ministry of Labour memo, May 14, 1921; PRO, CAB 24/128, "Labour Situation," October 1, 1921; *British Trade Union Review*, November 1919, p. 3, January 1922, pp. 9–11 and February 1922, pp. 3–5; TUC, "Wages and Hours of Labour," December 12, 1921; and *FBI Bulletin*, March 31, 1919, p. 14.

44. See evidence of the growing split in CGT, *Congrès corporatif* (Paris, September 1919), pp. 208–210, over hours strategy; and *Journal du peuple*, October 16, 1919.

45. Rodney Lowe, "The Erosion of State Intervention in Britain, 1917–1924," *Economic History Review* 31 (1978). On the 1926 strike, see, for example, G. E. Noel, *The Great Lockout of 1926* (London, 1976); and G. Skelley, ed., *The General Strike* (London, 1976).

46. Victoria De Grazia, *The Culture of Consent: Mass Organization of Leisure in Fascist Italy* (New York, 1981); and "La politique sociale du loisir: 1900–1940,"

*Les Cahiers de la recherche architecturale,* no. 15–17 (1985): 24–35; Anson Rabin-bach, *The Crisis of Austrian Socialism* (Chicago, 1982); Robert Goldman and John Wilson, "The Rationalization of Leisure," *Politics and Society* 7 (1977): 157–187; and Patrice Boussel, *Histoire des vacances* (Paris, 1961).

47. Allen Hutt, *The Condition of the Working Class in Britain* (London, 1933), pp. 22–23, 30, 61–65, 169–170; Walter Southgate, *That Was the Way It Was, 1890–1950* (London, 1972), Chap. 25; Odette Hardy-Hémery, "Rationalisation technique et rationalisation du travail à la compagnie des Mines D'Anzin (1927–1938)," *Mouvement social* 72 (July–September 1970): 3–48; Marie-Antoinette Bou-det, *Le Semaine de 40 heures* (Paris, 1935), pp. 85–88, 101–108; and Adolphe Hodée, *Les travailleurs devant la rationalisation* (Paris, 1934).

48. Michelle Collinet, *La Condition ouvrière* (Paris, 1951), Chaps. 1, 2. Ex-amples of the reformist French disillusionment with rationalization include *Informa-tion sociale,* April 30, 1930; CGT, *Congrès national corporatif* (Paris, 1931), pp. 43–51; and *Le Peuple,* September 12 and 15, 1931. Communist views are summa-rized in CGTU, *Congrès national ordinaire* (Paris, 1931), pp. 39–40, 128–129; 153–158, 450, 458. British sentiments are expressed in the *Proceedings at a Meeting between Engineering and Allied Employers' National Federations and Various Trade Unions, 40 Hours Week* (London, February 1934), pp. 1–5, 8–9, 11–12; and Inter-national Association for Social Progress, *Inquiry into the Hours Problem* (London, 1933), pp. 48–51.

49. *Times,* (London) October 27, 1932; and Josiah Stamp, *The Present Position of Rationalisation* (London, 1932).

50. *Proceedings between Engineering and Various Trade Unions,* p. 15; TUC, *Annual Proceedings* (1933), p. 71.

51. Jouhaux's speech at Lille, February 26, 1933, cited in Boudet, *La Semaine de 40 heures* p. 162; CGT, *La Semaine de quarante* (Paris, 1932), p. 4.

52. CGT, *Pourquoi la semaine de 40 heures* (Paris, 1933), pp. 7–15; *Congrès Confédéral* (Paris, 1933), pp. 43–44; *Le Peuple,* June 10, 1933; *Voix du peuple:* January 1934, p. 36, September 1934, pp. 549–550, December 1934, p. 778; M. Lescure, *Les Crises générales et periodiques de surproductions* (Paris, 1934). For the communist view, see Jacques Doriot, *Journée de sept heures avec salaire de huit heures* (Paris, 1932).

53. See Benjamin Hunnicutt's chapter in this volume. See also Harold Moulton, *The 30-Hour Week* (Washington, D.C., 1935); and R. C. Wallhead, *A Six Hour Working Day* (London, 1933).

54. International Association for Social Progress, *Inquiry,* 1933, pp. 3, 5–6, 14–17, 21–24; C. A. Macartney (League of Nations Union Conference), *Hours of Work and Employment* (London, 1934), pp. 10–16, 26–27, 31–33, 38, 40–45, 51; M. Steward (New Fabian Research Board), *The 40 Hours Week* (London, 1937), especially pp. 25–31; *Industrial Welfare,* October 1934, pp. 42–43; Ernest Bevin, *My Plan for 2,000,000 Workless* (London, 1936); and H. M. Vernon, *The Shorter Working Week with Special Reference to the Two-Shift System* (London, 1934).

55. ILO, *Hours of Work and Unemployment. Report to the Preparatory Confer-ence* (Geneva, 1933), pp. 1–2, 8–9, 17–19, 28–29, 48–65; and Lello Gangemi, *Il*

*Problema della durata del Lavoro* (Florence, 1929). For additional background, see Boudet, *Le Semaina de 40 heures,* Chap. 1.

56. ILO, *Hours of Work and Unemployment. Report of the Preparatory Conference, January 20 to 25, 1933* (Geneva, 1933), pp. 8–10, 12–13, 22–23; PRO, LAB 2 1008 IL 13/1933, reports on the ILO conference in January 1933, especially the report by Forbes-Watson, February 7, 1933.

57. While Italy continued to support an international hours standard, when the ILO staff introduced the idea of wage stabilization into an inquiry in 1934, Mussolini's delegates withdrew their support. The Fascist objective was to "share the misery," not to impose a burden on profit by raising the wage bill. In the following year, Mussolini, like Hitler before him, abandoned the ILO and international solutions to the employment problem. While the ILO plodded on, passing special forty-hour conventions for mining, textiles, and other industries in 1937 and 1938, these measures were delayed, and few nations ratified them. In addition to the publication of the International Labour Conferences of 1933–1938, which are replete with hours matters, note, among the numerous documents dealing with the ILO 40-hour issue, PRO, CAB 24/235, Labour memo, December 19, 1932; PRO, CAB 24/247, Labour memos, February 6 and 7, 1934; PRO, CAB 24/255, Labour memo, May 18, 1935; PRO, CAB 24/256, Labour memo, December 13, 1935; PRO, LAB 2 IR 409/1933, report on meeting of Treasury concerning the 40-hour week, April 29, 1933; PRO, LAB 2 10008 IL 173/2, Labour memo, February 13, 1934. See also the thorough study of Boudet, *Le Semaine de 40 heures,* especially pp. 275–276, 341.

58. The classic discussion of international economic policy during the depression is Charles Kindleberger, *World in Depression* (Berkeley, 1978).

59. TUC, *Proceedings:* (1933), p. 243–249; (1935), pp. 70–71, 138–142, 161–163, 171–174, 314–316; (1936), pp. 71, 171–173, 341–344; PRO, LAB 2 2047 IL 1935, Minister of Labour memo, July 27, 1933; and *Labour Magazine,* March 1935, p. 159, and August 1937, p. 294.

60. *Labour Magazine,* November 1933, p. 70; Manchester City Council, "Reports of the Establishment Committee and the Finance Committee on the Financial Effect of the Establishment of a 40 Hour Week for All Manual Workers in the Employment of the Corporation" (Manchester, 1936), in the TUC Archives, HD 5165. See also Stephen Jones, The Trade Union Movement and Work-Sharing Policies in Interwar Britain," *Industrial Relations Journal* 16 (1985): 57–69.

61. A summary is in CGT, *Congrès Confédéral:* 1935, p. 74–84; 1938, pp. 65–66. See also *Voix du peuple,* June 1936, pp. 365, 388. A fine recent analysis of the period is Julian Jackson, *The Politics of Depression in France* (New York, 1985).

62. René Belin, *La Semaine de quarante heures et la réduction du temps de travail* (Paris, 1937), pp. 1–14; Jean-Charles Asselain, "Une Erreur de politique économie, La Loi de quarante heures de 1936," *Revue économique* 25 (1974): 690–691.

63. Belin, *La Semaine de quarente heures,* pp. 25–26.

64. Asselain, "Une Erreur de politique économie," pp. 672–705; and Michael

Seidman, "The Birth of Weekend and the Revolts against Work during the Popular Front, 1936–1938," *French Historical Studies* 12 (Fall 1982): 249–276.

65. Note John Hobson's rejection of shorter hours for increased purchasing power through taxation and fiscal policy in *Rationalisation and Unemployment, an Economic Dilemma* (London, 1930), p. 123.

66. For a different view, see Seidman "Birth of the Weekend." Note also Ronnie Steinberg, *Wages and Hours, Labor and Reform in Twentieth Century America* (New Brunswick, 1982).

67. Karl Hinrichs and Helmut Wiesenthal, "Arbeitswerte and Arbeitszeit: Zur Pluralisierung von Wertmustern und Zeitverwendungswünchen in der modernen Industriegesellschaft," in *Artbeitszeitpolitik. Formen und Folgen einer Neuverteilung der Arbeitszeit,* ed. Claus Offe, Karl Hinrichs, and Helmut Wiesenthal (Frankfurt, 1982) pp. 116–136; and Karl Hinrichs, William K. Roche, and Helmut Wiesenthal, "Working Time Policy as Class-Oriented Strategy: Unions and Shorter Working Hours in Great Britain and West Germany," *European Sociological Review* 2 (1986).

# 9

# Worktime and Industrialization in the U.S.S.R., 1917–1941

## William Chase and Lewis Siegelbaum

### I

DURING THE first four decades of the twentieth century, Russian workers experienced a host of profound transformations in their working, familial, and private lives. Among the most important but least investigated changes were in the workday's duration and structure. These changes were especially significant after the 1917 revolution. Not only did the Soviet government introduce the eight-hour (and in 1927, the seven-hour) workday, but it also strove to inculcate new attitudes toward the use of time. In factories, the government struggled to intensify the shortened workday in order to boost industrial production. Outside the factories, it sought to extend education, to make various forms of culture available to all, and to socialize certain domestic tasks. The latter effort aimed at restructuring the use of leisure time so as to liberate the individual and create the new Soviet man.

The government's success in redefining and restructuring time was mixed. Although the duration of worktime changed dramatically between the world wars, the "proper" use of that time remained an illusive goal. The same was true for leisure time, which increased substantially for males, but remained a dream for the vast majority of females. In its struggle to redefine time, as in many other areas, the Soviet government found it easier to decree change than to alter traditional values and behaviors.

### II

To appreciate the changes wrought by the revolution, let us briefly examine the workday's duration in the late imperial period. Before 1897, many

183

workers, both industrial and artisanal, worked 14, 15, even 16 hours a day. Because no effective labor legislation existed, factory owners were free to determine the workday's length. The upsurge of labor unrest in 1896–1897 forced the government to enact a decree limiting the workday to 11.5 hours. The workweek was 6 days long; the average workyear was 264 days. As the latter figure implies, what mitigated the workday's exhausting length was the existence of many holidays: There were 91 official holidays, excluding those of local significance that many workers observed. Taking into account holidays and absence, the average worker in 1900 worked 251 days and 2810 hours per year.[1]

Between 1897 and 1905, the average workday contracted slightly to an estimated 10.5 hours (excluding overtime), but this change occurred on a piecemeal basis. During the 1905 revolution, labor unrest forced the shortening of the legal workday to 10 hours. Nonetheless, workers continued to demand a shorter workday; one-quarter of all strike demands in 1905 called for an 8-hour day. During the mounting labor unrest on the eve of World War I, the issue was no less evident; almost half of all strike demands in 1914 called for the 8-hour workday.[2] Although the average workday in 1913 is estimated to have been 9.7 hours, the 10-hour day, 6-day week, and 264-day year remained the legal norm until the revolution. Despite the increased industrial demand created by the war, the length of the average workday and workyear hardly changed between 1914 and 1917 (see Table 9–1).[3]

With the overthrow of the tsar in February 1917, worker demands for the 8-hour day erupted nationwide. During the revolution's first halycon weeks, many workers simply forced the 8-hour day on management. The effect was immediate and dramatic in places such as Petrograd *guberniia* where, in January 1917, the average workday (without overtime) was 10.1 hours; by March, it had dropped to 8.4 hours. Faced with widespread unilateral enactment of the 8-hour day, the Petrograd Society of Factory and Works Owners had little choice but to agree to the reduction. The Provisional Government, however, after stating its intention in March to legislate the shorter workday, bowed, to pressure from disgruntled owners and chose instead to establish a commission to study the proposal. Workers also demanded a reduction (and in some cases, the abolition) of overtime work. Settlements regarding overtime were decided on a case-by-case basis in the factories through the newly established conciliation boards. Although neither the 8-hour day nor the elimination of overtime became universal in 1917, that year witnessed a reduction in the length of the average workday from 9.7 hours in 1916 to 8.8 hours.[4] The workyear in 1917 shrank to between 238 and 249 days,[5] a reduction caused primarily by political activism. Cities and factories buzzed with political activities in 1917; meetings of trade unions, factory committees, and local soviets, as well as strikes and demonstrations, drew workers away from the bench. Workers' growing sense of class power and their concomitant diminishing fear of bosses' powers, as well as shortages of raw materials and fuel, also contributed to this shortening of the workyear.

Four days after the October Revolution, the new Soviet government decree the establishment of the eight-hour day. That first labor decree, which remained the cornerstone of all subsequent Soviet labor legislation, set firm guidelines on the duration of work. The decree stipulated a maximum of eight working hours a day and forty-eight hours a week, banned night work for women and juveniles under the age of eighteen, limited the workday of juveniles to six hours, restricted overtime to four hours in two days and fifty days a year for each worker, mandated the shortening of the workday (to six or seven hours) in occupations designated as unhealthy and dangerous, and recognized Sundays and official holidays (including holy days) as days off from work.[6] The December 1918 Labor Code made only minor changes in this decree and these were to the benefit of the workers; it reduced worktime on Saturdays to six hours and the workweek to forty-six hours, mandated a weekly rest period of at least forty-two consecutive hours, and guaranteed a two-week vacation after six months of continuous work and a one-month vacation after a year's work.[7] With the 1918 Labor Code, the Bolshevik party hoped to realize "the introduction of a normal working day and of a normal intensity of labor."[8]

This labor legislation was the most progressive in the world at the time and radically redefined the duration of worktime and hence the amount of leisure time. As important as it was, the realities of the economic collapse that engulfed Russia from 1917 until the early 1920s proved far more crucial in defining how workers spent their time than did any legislation. The economic strains of three years of war, the shortening of the workday, high rates of worker absenteeism, and the closing of factories in late 1917 all contributed to the sharp decline in industrial production and productivity in that year. By one estimate, the value of the average worker's output in 1917 declined by almost 40 percent compared to 1916. Between 1918 and 1921, dire shortages of food, fuel, raw materials, replacement parts, tools, machinery, and skilled workers hastened the collapse. By 1921, the average worker's productivity stood at 29 percent of the 1913 level, thousands of factories and mines had closed, and more than half of the rail system was inoperative. The economy had ground to a virtual halt.[9]

The Bolsheviks and their supporters clearly understood the consequences and implications of economic collapse for their government and took measures to stem it. With regard to time, the young state pursued a two-pronged strategy: It issued decrees and laws to create a "normal working day" and simultaneously urged workers to make more efficient use of the shorter day.

In this way, it hoped that higher hourly productivity would offset the reduction in working time. The Soviet struggle for a more intensive use of the workday dates from early 1918 and continues today.

For our purposes, two complementary sets of labor policies are especially important: the drive to improve labor discipline, and the effort to increase productivity by intensifying labor. In Soviet parlance, labor discipline includes a wide variety of traits: arriving at work on time, working a full day, taking only authorized breaks, sobriety, and minimizing absence from work. Unfortunately, few Russian workers in 1918–1921 possessed these traits. Sometimes this was because, as Lenin stated, "The Russian worker is a bad worker compared with people in advanced countries." [10] Given the mass exodus of experience and skilled workers into the Red Army and new state, party, and union bureaucracies, and the influx (on a much smaller scale) into the working class of inexperienced and unskilled youth, women, and *déclassé* elements, the relative proportion of such workers by 1921 was probably considerable. [11] Even if all workers had possessed the prescribed desirable traits, maintaining labor discipline in the midst of mounting economic collapse, shortages of food and home fuel, and epidemics would have been difficult.

The fledgling Soviet government was not alone in attempting to improve the quality of work. In early 1918, many factory committees and unions passed resolutions calling for better labor discipline and higher worker productivity. To achieve the former, these bodies urged their constituents to adopt a host of desirable traits. The following rules, adopted by the All-Russian Central Council of Trade Unions (VTsSPS) in July 1918, represented those passed by lower-level bodies during the previous nine months. The rules urged workers to arrive at work on time and not leave work early; not to be absent from work or leave without permission; to cease revelry, card playing, and other games on the job; to arrive at work sober and not drink on the job; to follow instructions; to halt the theft of materials; to halt damaging and careless treatment of machines and instruments of production; and to cease beating up managerial and technical personnel. [12]

Although instances of assault and battery against their bosses declined over time, too few workers adopted the other rules recommended by VTsSPS. This was especially true of absenteeism. Systematic data on absenteeism and its causes do not exist for 1917–1919. But according to one source, the average worker worked 238 days in 1917, 219 days in 1918, 183 days in 1919, and 228 days in 1920. Put another way, the average number of hours worked in 1919 was 41 percent fewer than in 1918. Data from 1920 indicate the reasons for the shorter workyear. That year, there were 295 prescribed workdays, but the average worker actually worked only 228 days. Eight days were lost as a result of factory idleness for want of fuel, raw materials,

**TABLE 9–1.**
**Utilization of Worktime in Large-Scale Industries in the U.S.S.R.**
**(in days per year)**

| Year | Days Worked | Rest Days | *Reasons for Days Not Worked* | | | | | Total Not Worked |
|---|---|---|---|---|---|---|---|---|
| | | | Idleness | Vacation | Illness and Family | Valid Reasons | Absence | |
| 1913 | 257.4 | 88.6 | 6.4 | — | 5.7 | 2.8 | 4.6 | 12.6 |
| 1920 | 228.3 | 59.3 | 7.7 | 5.8 | 22.7 | 18.9 | 23.6 | 71.0 |
| 1921 | 221.5 | 61.4 | 8.4 | 12.5 | 18.3 | 22.3 | 20.6 | 73.7 |
| 1922 | 257.9 | 59.7 | 3.7 | 10.3 | 14.7 | 8.4 | 10.3 | 43.7 |
| 1923 | 260.9 | 60.8 | 1.9 | 12.7 | 13.8 | 5.1 | 9.8 | 41.4 |
| 1924 | 262.8 | 61.2 | 1.2 | 12.9 | 14.7 | 4.4 | 8.8 | 40.8 |
| 1925 | 261.9 | 61.6 | 0.8 | 13.9 | 15.6 | 3.8 | 7.4 | 40.7 |
| 1926 | 261.4 | 60.1 | 1.9 | 14.0 | 15.9 | 3.9 | 7.8 | 41.6 |
| 1927 | 260.9 | 63.3 | 1.7 | 14.0 | 14.8 | 3.5 | 6.9 | 39.2 |
| 1928 | 263.0 | 62.3 | 1.9 | 14.2 | 15.3 | 3.6 | 5.7 | 38.8 |
| 1929 | 264.2 | 62.4 | 1.9 | 14.0 | 15.4 | 3.6 | 4.1 | 37.1 |
| 1930 | 252.7 | 68.6 | 4.9 | 14.0 | 15.2 | 5.1 | 4.5 | 38.8 |
| 1931 | 253.2 | 69.6 | 1.2 | 14.2 | 15.6 | 5.2 | 6.0 | 41.0 |
| 1932 | 257.2 | 67.1 | 1.2 | 15.1 | 14.2 | 5.2 | 6.0 | 40.5 |
| 1933 | 265.9 | 64.9 | 1.8 | 13.7 | 13.0 | 4.8 | 0.9 | 32.4 |
| 1934 | 265.4 | 65.8 | 1.8 | 14.3 | 13.5 | 3.5 | 0.7 | 32.0 |
| 1935 | 266.2 | (65.8) | 1.6 | — | — | — | — | 30.4 |

**Source:** S. G. Strumilin, "Rabochee vremia promyshlennosti SSSR (1897–1935 gg.),"
p. 367.

parts, repairs, or food. Another 65 days were lost because of absenteeism: Illness and familial responsibilities accounted for 23 lost days; but for 24 missed days, workers offered no excuse[13] (see Table 9–1). That the average worker in 1920 missed upward of 23 days due to illness underscores the importance of disease, especially epidemic diseases, in frustrating official efforts to reduce absenteeism.

But a more important factor for high absentee rates was the food shortage. From 1917 to 1921, the quantity and quality of food deteriorated sharply and steadily. Food shortages were greatest in the northern industrial cities. In Moscow in 1919, the official daily bread ration was a mere 80 grams; in early 1921, the average worker consumed less than 1800 calories a day.[14] In search of food, workers skipped work or arrived late so as to stand in line for rations or ferret out food in the city's black markets. The timing of absences further underscores the importance of food as a factor. In 1920, the highest absentee rates occurred in July and August, when workers extended their weekend visits or vacations to remain in the villages, where food was relatively abundant.[15] While shortages of fuel and raw materials and mechanical disrepair undoubtedly contributed to the problems of high worker absenteeism and low productivity, hunger may have been the most important reason. As the economist S. G. Strumilin observed in early 1921, "The human organism, like a machine, can not create energy from nothing."[16]

To counter rising absentee rates, in April 1920 the Council of People's Commissars (Sovnarkom) issued a decree that fixed specific penalties for unwarranted absence. The decree stated that for one day of unauthorized absence a month, workers would forfeit 15 percent of their monthly bonus in money or kind; for two days, 25 percent of that bonus; and for three days, 69 percent. Absenteeism in excess of three days was considered sabotage and was to be dealt with by disciplinary courts. The worktime lost had to be made up after work or on free days.[17] Factory committees and workers' comradely courts within factories were empowered to mete out the prescribed punishments, but one wonders how assiduously they did so. Given that all workers suffered severely from the economic collapse and food shortages (bonuses were often paid in food) and that experienced laborers were scarce, worker solidarity and management's desire to retain workers may have mitigated the decree's harshest penalties. There is some circumstantial evidence to support this hypothesis. Data from the Moscow comradely courts in May and June 1920 indicate that only 1800 workers (out of about 100,000 in the city) appeared before the courts on charges of unauthorized absence or tardiness.[18] National data on absenteeism reveal that unauthorized absences dropped only slightly after the decree (see Table 9–1).

Although the 1918 Labor Code set clear limits on overtime, the demand for goods to sustain the Red Army led officials to permit overtime in excess of the recommended norms. Precise serial data on overtime work during the civil war years are lacking. But in April 1920, more than 107,000 workers reportedly worked ten-hour days on a regular basis, and another 45,000 workers routinely worked twelve-hour days. Some factories reported even longer workdays. At the Goznak factory in Moscow, more than 3000 workers labored an average of sixteen and a half hours a day. Although overtime work did occur during these years, one must be cautious in accepting such data because, in many instances, the reported overtime work was fictitious, a device used by management and workers to increase rations. Some of this overtime may also reflect workers making up lost time, as recommended by the April 1920 Sovnarkom decree.[19]

The above data suggest that the new government sought to counter the sharp decline in production and productivity by extending the workday. But the government and other organizations also sought to intensify the workday. Although these efforts generally came to naught, they had considerable significance as portents of subsequent initiatives that were to prove more successful. Not long after the October 1917 revolution, numerous factory committee and trade union organizations passed resolutions urging their constituents to increase productivity now that the workday was shorter. The various resolutions made it clear that if workers' economic demands were to be realized and the spiraling economic collapse that threatened the revolutionary government was to be reversed, workers had to adopt greater labor discipline and to be more productive. Toward the latter goal, many factory and union organizations urged the reintroduction of piece-rate wages and the creation of special commissions to establish production norms for each shop and category of worker.[20] Given that in 1917 many workers had demanded payment of time-based wages in order to minimize the exploitation that accompanied piece rates, the extension of the latter form of payment, like the improvement of labor discipline, often remained a dead letter, and for good reason. The rapid deterioration of productive forces from 1918 to 1921 spelled an increase in the level of exertion without a concomitant increase in remuneration. According to the August 1918 industrial census, only 31 percent of the nation's workers received piece-rate wages; by January 1920, the figure for Moscow workers was a mere 7 percent.[21]

A temporary solution to the problem of productivity was found in March 1920 when the government urged the wider introduction of the bonus system. Workers who exceeded the established output norms received bonuses, usually consisting of food, clothing, or fuel. Given the scarcity of these commodities, the policy's impact was swift and dramatic. For example, whereas in January 1920 about 48 percent of Moscow's workers received either piece-rate (7 percent) or bonus (41 percent) wages, by December the proportion had risen to 85 percent. For the first time in four years, worker productivity rose.[22]

By the end of the civil war, the Soviet government's hopes of introducing a "normal working day" during which workers exerted a "normal intensity of labor" had failed to materialize. The eight-hour workday was the law, but high rates of absenteeism and forced idleness, as well as overtime work, meant that the law was honored more in the breach than in the observance. Amid unabated economic collapse, the workyear also contracted well below that prescribed. Nor had the government's hopes that the shorter workday be counterbalanced by more intensive labor come to fruition. Lenin had warned his comrades that "the working out of new principles of labor discipline by the people is a very protracted process,"[23] but the deterioration of labor discipline (and productivity) made a mockery of that warning.

Precisely how workers used the increased free time that the law permitted, and their actions created, is not clear. Considering the dire shortages of food, fuel, and other necessities, much of this "free time" was probably spent searching for these goods. Some people worked two jobs so as to increase their rations. In addition, many workers availed themselves of the new educational and cultural activities offered by various organizations such as Proletkul't, the Commissariat of Enlightenment, and others. Clearly, during these trying years, workers' time had become both more and less dictated by life's realities. Like the government, workers hoped for a normal division and use of time; beginning in 1921, both quests commenced anew.

## III

At the Tenth Congress of the Russian Communist party in 1921, the transition from War Communism (as the policies of 1918–1921 were called after the fact) to the New Economic Policy (NEP) began. During the NEP, that is, from 1921 to 1929, government, party, union, and managerial officials continued to pursue the two-pronged policy begun during the civil war. For analytic purposes, however, it is best to examine this policy in two periods: from 1921 to mid-1924, during which time economic hardship and rampant inflation frustrated official efforts; and from mid-1924 to 1928, NEP's "good years," when the official two-pronged policy was vigorously pursued and began to yield results.

From 1921 to mid-1924, efforts to increase the number of days worked and reduce absenteeism, tardiness, and overtime, that is, to institute a "normal workday," proved reasonably successful. As Table 9-1 indicates, during 1921 the number of days worked reached a historic low (211.5 days) for the Soviet period. Absences caused by idleness and unexcused absences remained very high, but one omen of better days appeared: The number of vacation days increased to 12.5. Considering the dire conditions in industry, continued food shortages caused by the famine of 1921–1922, and the continuation of epidemic diseases, the low amount of time spent at work in 1921 is hardly surprising. Between 1922 and 1924, all indices of worktime improved. The average number of days worked rose to almost 90 percent of the actual number of workdays, absenteeism (especially unexcused absence) and idle time dropped sharply, and the number of vacation days approached the prescribed norm.[24] During these years, the length of the average workday also dropped—from 7.8 hours to 7.6 hours for 1922–1924. While these data suggest that the struggle to realize a "normal workday" made significant strides, substantial problems remained: The average worker in 1924 was absent 27 days a year (9 without an excuse), and tardiness remained common.

There were several reasons for the improved statistics. Chief among them was that the state took drastic measures to reduce absenteeism. A November 1921 decree mandated the loss of a day's wages for every day of unauthorized absence, as well as the payment of fines; four straight days of unexcused absence or four such days a month could lead to dismissal.[25] Given that unemployment (as a result of official policies and excessive rural–urban migration) was a significant problem, the threat of dismissal was a menacing one for many workers.[26]

Improvements in the well-being and composition of the workforce were also significant factors in reducing absenteeism. Increased food supplies from 1922 provided workers with a more adequate diet. The elimination of epidemic diseases by 1924 and increased accessibility to health care also benefited workers, although it must be noted that Russian workers' physical well-being remained precarious throughout the 1920s. The replacement of the less experienced and less disciplined workers, who staffed the factories from 1918 to 1921, with more experienced and disciplined former workers returning from the Red Army and villages further contributed to the improved statistics.

The systematic enactment of economic and labor policies also played an important role in the quest for a "normal workday." With regard to industry, the state enacted a series of stringent fiscal policies aimed at lowering production costs. The state reduced, and in some instances eliminated, subsidies to industry, ordered enterprises to introduce cost-accounting procedures and balance their budgets, and closed inefficient enterprises. Factory managers responded in turn by firing workers, altering their hiring practices so as to maximize productivity and reduce the labor bill, fining (or firing) workers for unauthorized absences and tardiness, and mechanizing and rationalizing production wherever possible. In general, these managerial efforts received the support of union and party officials in the factories. The Komsomol, the party's youth organization, was especially active in the struggle to reduce absenteeism and idleness and to intensify labor. In some factories, the Komsomol organized processions to mock slackers, idlers, and loafers.[27]

Parallel with these measures to improve work discipline and intensify labor, the government sought to enact the scientific organization of labor (*nauchnaia organizatsiia truda,* NOT) so as to train generations of workers to make better, more productive use of worktime. The adoption of certain aspects of Taylorism presented less of a political dilemma for communists than one might initially suspect. For NOT advocates such as Lenin and Aleksei Gastev, what distinguished Taylorism from NOT was the context in and purpose for which the practices were enacted. In capitalist countries, they argued, the purpose of Taylorism was to put scientific analysis of the work process in the service of greater worker exploitation so as to increase profits. For the Soviets, the scientific organization of labor promised, not to exhaust workers, but to reduce fatigue by teaching workers how to synchronize their movements to those of the machine. By so doing, they argued, workers would be less tired and more productive, and the profits thereby generated would enrich the society as a whole. To enable researchers to determine optimal work methods, the government created the Central Institute of Labor (TsIT), headed by Gastev, which both conducted time–motion studies and trained workers to work more efficiently.

The TsIT was not without its critics. But what the critics disliked about the institute was the narrowness of its prescribed tasks. This was the main complaint of the *Liga vremia* (Time League), the most organized and prominent of Gastev's critics. The *Liga* sought to inculcate in all Soviet citizens a new sense of time—how to organize it and use it most effectively and efficiently. For these communists, the scientific organization and use of time was a means of achieving greater personal advancement and freedom. Although the group lost its political struggle to control the NOT movement, many prominent Soviet officials adopted its views.[28] One such person was Strumilin, whose time–budget studies (discussed below) were infused by a deep commitment to rationalize the use of time so as to permit people greater opportunities to pursue personal interests and improve themselves.

Parallel with the TsIT's efforts to determine the optimal, scientific methods of labor was a campaign to involve managerial and technical personnel and workers in organized discussions of how to make the best use of the workday and how to increase efficiency and productivity in the factories. Begun in late 1920, the production propaganda circles, which later became known as NOT circles, were a failure. Instead of becoming forums at which workers and bosses exchanged ideas on these issues, they proved to be poorly organized, boring meetings at which managerial and technical personnel spoke to each other; few workers attended or even knew of their existence.[29] Despite their lack of success, these early efforts to devise a scientific organization of labor and the workday provided the organizational bases for later, more successful efforts.

In mid-1924, the tenor of economic life began to change. The introduction of a gold-backed currency dramatically reduced inflation, factory production increased, and the flow of raw materials and products became more regular. Yet problems endured: Labor costs were high; labor productivity was low; absenteeism and idle time, although they were declining, remained unsatisfactorily high. Buoyed by the successes and determined to reduce these problems, the government from mid-1924 embarked on a renewed campaign to reduce costs and raise productivity. Chief among the campaign goals was the intensification of the workday and the reduction of absenteeism. The campaign's first phase, from mid-1924 to mid-1926, was labeled the *rationalization campaign;* the second phase, from mid-1926 to 1929, was dubbed the *regime of economy,* although the former appellation continued to be used.

Urged on by a barrage of party and government resolutions during late

1924, factory managers devised ways to raise labor productivity. Managers introduced time–motion studies, empowered norm-setting bureaus to raise output norms, and increased the number of machines that workers operated. These activities were especially pronounced in the textile industry, the goods of which were in high demand. During the first half of 1925, output norms there were raised by 10 to 20 percent, the number of weavers working three or four looms jumped from 99 to 33,628, and the number of spinners working three or four spindles increased from 202,552 to 3,313,417. Although less dramatic, other industries' workers also experienced an intensification of the workday.[30] Workers' reactions to the shift differed. Some, especially older workers and some skilled workers, went on strike and denounced the party for renouncing the ideas of Marx. But others, particularly younger workers and party and Komsomol members, often welcomed the change. Given their age and lack of skills, young workers were most apt to benefit from intensification in terms of an increase in their wages and job opportunities.

In 1927–1928, officials renewed the drive to intensify labor by utilizing the same tactics. Again, output norms rose, as did the number of machines workers operated. And again, while older and some skilled workers vowed to fight the shift, young and politically active workers were in the forefront of the transition.[31] The government and management prevailed. By the end of the NEP, workers in all industries labored more intensively than they had in 1922 or 1923.

From 1924 onward, officials also struggled to reduce absenteeism and tardiness and to instill new attitudes toward punctuality and labor discipline. In this battle, official efforts proved to be less successful. The levying of fines for absenteeism remained in effect, and the government passed decrees to ensure that the workday was devoted to work—meetings were to be conducted after work, as were medical examinations and treatments.[32] While decrees could mandate how the workday was to be used, they could not easily instill time discipline and sobriety in the masses of rural migrants who entered the factories in increasing numbers after 1925.[33] Although nationally the average number of days absent per worker declined slightly from 1924 to 1929, (see Table 9-1), in factories that hired large numbers of peasants, the reverse occurred.

Rising absentee and tardiness rates in those factories resulted from two factors. First, peasants who entered the industrial workforce brought with them different conceptions of time and labor discipline than those expected in industry. Accustomed to organizing their rural work around the sun and seasons, they found the discipline imposed by the clock difficult to adopt. Such workers were also most likely to miss Mondays and the day after holidays because they extended their trips to their villages. On the job, new workers displayed the absence of discipline in other ways, such as smoking and talking on the job, walking around during work, and reading newspapers. But peasant workers were not the only ones who punctuated their workday with such unauthorized breaks. Older workers and some skilled workers, accustomed to behavior designed to mitigate the length of the pre-revolutionary workday, also did so. While this may have been conscious behavior to frustrate the speed-up and intensification of labor, contemporaries viewed it as simply poor work habits and discipline.

The second factor that accounted for rising absentee and tardiness rates in many factories was drunkenness. To contemporaries, drunkenness was becoming an increasingly alarming problem that was at the root of a host of menacing industrial problems: increasing absenteeism, tardiness, accidents, waste, and breakage. Evidence of the impact of drunkenness abounds. On "blue Mondays" and the days after paydays or holidays, unauthorized absences were between 33 percent and 70 percent higher than on other days.[34] From 1926, the party and trade unions launched a concerted campaign to reduce tardiness and absenteeism; the struggle against drunkenness was central to the campaign.[35] Nonetheless, problems continued. In November 1928, the Central Committee listed among the reasons for the recent drop in productivity the following problems: drunkenness, unauthorized absence and tardiness, sleeping on the job, and not coming to work on religious holidays.[36]

Another method employed in the campaign was the convoking of production meetings. Decreed into existence in late 1923, these heirs to production propaganda and NOT meetings were supposed to tackle a wide range of problems facing factories. But not until 1926 did production meetings begin to develop their own identity and behavior, and to attract significant numbers of workers. Discussions of and resolutions on how to reduce absenteeism and tardiness were common. Reports on such meetings clearly suggest that, from 1926 to 1929, they became forums in which intrafactory tensions and divisions were aired and sharpened.[37] Among them was the tension between urbanized workers, who possessed greater time and labor discipline, and new workers, especially recent rural migrants, who lacked these traits.[38]

Although officials waged a concerted campaign to intensify the workday, the exploitation of the workforce by means of excessive overtime was anathema to policymakers. As data in Table 9-2 indicate, overtime work peaked in 1920 and then declined steadily and sharply throughout the decade. Nevertheless, while other contemporary reports confirm that there was a systematic lowering of overtime work and the percentage of workers working overtime,[39] the data mask certain problems. Throughout the decade, the press reported continual violations of laws regarding worktime and overtime

**TABLE 9–2.**
**Average Workday and Workyear in Soviet Industry**

| Year | Workday in Hours | | | Percentage of 1913 Workday | Workyear in Hours | | Percentage of 1913 Workyear |
|------|--------|----------|----------------|--------|---------------|---------------|--------|
|      | Normal | Overtime | Total Hours |  | Total Days | Total Hours |  |
| 1913 | 9.7 | 0.3 | 10.0 | 100 | 257.4 | 2574 | 100 |
| 1914 | 9.5 | 0.2 | 9.7 | 97 | 244.8 | 2375 | 92 |
| 1915 | 9.5 | 0.2 | 9.7 | 97 | 240.7 | 2335 | 91 |
| 1916 | 9.7 | 0.2 | 9.9 | 99 | 257.8 | 2552 | 99 |
| 1917 | 8.8 | 0.1 | 8.9 | 89 | 237.8 | 2116 | 82 |
| 1918 | 8.1 | 0.4 | 8.5 | 85 | 219.0 | 1861 | 72 |
| 1919 | 7.9 | 0.4 | 8.3 | 83 | 183.0 | 1519 | 59 |
| 1920 | 7.8 | 0.8 | 8.6 | 86 | 228.3 | 1963 | 76 |
| 1921 | 7.8 | 0.7 | 8.5 | 85 | 221.5 | 1883 | 73 |
| 1922 | 7.6 | 0.3 | 7.9 | 79 | 257.9 | 2037 | 79 |
| 1923 | 7.6 | 0.2 | 7.8 | 78 | 260.9 | 2035 | 79 |
| 1924 | 7.6 | 0.2 | 7.8 | 78 | 262.8 | 2050 | 80 |
| 1925 | 7.4 | 0.2 | 7.6 | 76 | 261.7 | 1989 | 77 |
| 1926 | 7.3 | 0.1 | 7.5 | 75 | 261.4 | 1961 | 76 |
| 1927 | 7.4 | 0.1 | 7.5 | 75 | 260.9 | 1957 | 76 |
| 1928 | 7.3 | 0.1 | 7.4 | 74 | 263.0 | 1947 | 76 |

**Source:** S. G. Strumilin, "Rabochee vremia promyshlennosti SSSR (1897–1935gg.)," p. 365.

in privately owned factories.[40] Also, during the late 1920s, reports critical of labor inspectors' failure to punish violators of the overtime law and even to report overtime work suggest that managerial efforts to increase productivity and reduce the labor bill resulted in many violations of the overtime restrictions. One report, which sharply criticized the "insufficiently energetic" struggle against overtime by labor inspectors, stated that at Moscow's Frunze Factory the number of overtime hours worked exceeded that allowed by 100 percent.[41] Still, both legal and illegal overtime became less and less common during the 1920s.

# IV

To this point the discussion has centered on worktime, yet workers spent only about one-third of their day commuting to or at work. Fortunately, how workers spent their time greatly interested S. G. Strumilin, who conducted time–budget studies of workers' families in 1922 and 1923–1924.[42] Before discussing his findings, it is worth noting that Strumilin used these studies as a vehicle to express his belief that the poorly developed social-service sector meant that all Soviet citizens, especially women, devoted unnecessary and inordinately long hours performing tasks that could be accomplished more efficiently by communal services, such as public dining halls, laundries, day-care centers, and the like. To communalize such daily tasks, he argued, would free citizens (again, especially women) to engage in cultural, educational, and political activities that would enhance self-improvement and give them more time for recreation. Strumilin was but one of many Soviet citizens who viewed the communalization of daily life *(byt)* not in utopian terms but as a means of freeing individuals to reach their full potential.

His arguments and those of the *Liga Vremia* together represent the widely held belief among many Soviet citizens that the key to creating the new Soviet man rested with the rational and scientific organization of time. In the late 1920s, certain groups and individuals pushed this belief even further when they built into their visionary plans on the restructuring of cities and housing recommended time schedules in which every normal daily activity was fit into prescribed time slots.[43] Yet, despite the new conceptions of time current among certain groups of intellectuals and officials, the realities of daily life defined the average worker's day in terms that were considerably less than optimal or utopian.

Because Strumilin's 1923–1924 study is based on a larger and more geographically and occupationally diverse set of data than the 1922 study, and because the results of the two do not differ significantly, this discussion focused on the later study. In 1923–1924, the average worker daily devoted about nine hours to work, including the regular job, overtime, commuting, and a part-time second job. The difference between the sexes when both spouses worked was minimal. Such equality was not the case at home where females daily devoted more than four hours to preparing meals and taking care of clothes, children, and housework; males devoted about one hour. The most time-consuming tasks for females were preparing meals (two and a half hours as opposed to a half hour for males). When males performed domestic work, it was usually confined to tasks such as chopping and carrying wood and doing jobs around the apartment. Taken together, among working couples, the workday (wage and domestic labor combined) for women was more than fourteen hours long; for men, eleven hours. (For housewives, it was thirteen hours long.) Consequently, women slept an hour less than men and devoted considerably less time to eating, personal care, political and social activities, and self-education (i.e., reading books and newspapers, attending lectures, visiting museums, etc.).

These budget studies reveal several striking aspects of workers' use of time. The most obvious is that females devoted far more time to domestic work and far less time to personal edification than did males. That is hardly surprising. The Soviet government could legally decree the equality of the sexes, but the deep-seated patriarchal attitudes of Russian society could not be decreed away. In fact, budget studies conducted during the 1930s revealed that the division of domestic labor between the sexes became even starker as females devoted more and males few hours to preparing food, shopping, looking after children, cleaning clothes, and repairing their dwellings.[44] Precisely why this pattern intensified deserves further investigation. Two reasons suggest themselves. From the first Five-Year Plan, rural-born migrants, who possessed long-held patriarchal attitudes, inundated the workforce. Second—and here cause and effect are less clear—the government adopted and espoused traditional, patriarchal attitudes.

The second point to emerge from the time–budget studies is that for want of electricity, running water, and communal services, Soviet citizens devoted long hours to chopping and carrying fuel, carrying water from outside pumps or rivers, doing laundry by hand, and preparing meals on primus stoves. Clearly, the lack of extensive municipal infrastructures, social services, and domestic appliances doomed efforts by groups such as *Liga vremia* to inculcate in workers a mastery and efficient use of time.

## V

On the eve of the October Revolution's tenth anniversary, the party's and government's struggle to introduce a "normal working day" during which workers expended a "normal intensity of labor" had yielded considerable gains but continued to confront formidable obstacles. The introduction of the eight-hour workday and forty-two-hour workweek meant that the average worker worked 25 percent fewer hours in 1927 than in 1913. Although the elimination of many religious and tsarist holidays meant that workers worked six more days per year than in 1913, the number of hours worked per annum declined by a quarter. Laws limiting overtime work and mandating forty-two-hours of continuous rest per week existed and were generally observed. In short, the revolutionary government's laws and decrees had radically altered the duration of worktime and thereby gave workers, especially males, the opportunity to structure their leisure time in new ways. Nonetheless, one need only read the labor press during the period to realize that the official definition of a "normal working day" and "normal intensity of labor" was not universally shared. Many older workers and some skilled workers continued time-honored behaviors, such as taking unauthorized breaks, and recent migrants from the villages possessed few of the officially mandated traits of time and labor discipline. It proved much easier to pass laws than to inculcate new attitudes and values. Such was equally true at home.

These, then, were the circumstances in which the government took a bold step with regard to worktime. On October 15, 1927, the Central Executive Committee (TsIK) issued a manifesto that announced its intention gradually to introduce a seven-hour workday for all industrial workers, without any reduction in their wages. Coming on the eve of the revolution's tenth anniversary, great fanfare accompanied the manifesto. In Leningrad, where TsIK held it jubilee session, demonstrations of support and a parade reviewed by party leaders took place, and factory meetings throughout the country passed resolutions approving the measure.[45]

Strange as it may seem, this momentous decision, which was to provide Soviet workers with the shortest workday in the world, was made with virtually no prior discussion either in the press or in the plenary sessions of party, governmental, or trade union organs.[46] No mention of it appeared in any of the drafts of the Five-Year Plan then being considered. An article on the reduction of worktime by a member of the State Planning Commission (Gosplan) had appeared earlier in 1927. Its consideration of a six-hour workday was purely hypothetical, however, and was predicated on implementation no earlier than 1940.[47]

The unexpectedness and the timing of TsIK's announcement have been interpreted by several historians as an indication of its essentially demagogic character. Trotsky, Zinoviev, and other Oppositionists, who were then locked in desperate combat with Stalin and his supporters, regarded the measure as such, and voted against it a few days later in the party's Central Committee.[48] But whatever the party leadership's political calculations, and however much it exploited the announcement to the discomfit of the Opposition, the inner party struggles were hardly the sole factor involved.

The reduction of the workday to seven hours was not a gift to industrial workers, or at least not a free gift. As the manifesto stated, its introduction was predicated on "the renewal of equipment, rationalization of enterprises, and increased productivity of labor."[49] Simply to make up for the loss of one hour of production time per worker, labor productivity would have to rise by 12.5 percent. Such an increase would only bring industry back to the status quo ante and was therefore inadequate.

The real context for the reform was the impatience of both party leaders and industrial officials with existing measures to increase industrial output and lower production costs. Despite vigorous efforts to improve labor discipline and promote rationalization, the increase in labor productivity in the economic year 1926–1927 was smaller than the previous year, while wages had risen faster than previously.[50] Exacerbating official concern was the difficulty then being experienced with grain collections. Short of squeezing the peasantry—the Left's solution and one that Stalin soon would apply with a vengeance via the "Urals–Siberian method"—the only feasible way of extracting more grain was to put more manufactured goods, particularly textiles, on the market.

What the seven-hour day did was to permit the addition of an extra shift. Three shifts were already common in the extractive industries and some producer goods industries (e.g., oil, coal and ore extraction, chemical, and metallurgy). In textile manufacturing and other industries heavily dependent on female labor, however, they were rare, owing to legal restrictions against night work for women.[51] To waive these restrictions on a massive scale and without compensation would have violated the Labor Code and played into the Opposition's hands. Yet it was precisely the presence of cotton goods on the market that could forestall a peasant grain strike.

Thus, at least in part, the introduction of the seven-hour day was a means of facilitating the implementation of the three-shift system and thereby increasing productivity. Carr and Davies indicate that this "had been from the first in the minds of those who propounded the scheme," and cite as evidence statements made in September and early October by several prominent economists in which a reduced workday and three-shift production were linked.[52] Three days after the manifesto was issued, an editorial in *Pravda* also made the connection. The seven-hour day, it noted, would be "linked in a number of branches of industry with an increase in the number of working shifts, and with a diminution of unemployment."[53]

*Pravda*'s claim that the three-shift system would reduce umemployment was not gratuitous and may well provide another motive for the introduction of the seven-hour day. Throughout the 1920s, unemployment rose steadily as a result of government economic policies and high rates of rural–urban migration. In 1927, 17.3 percent of trade union members were reported as unemployed, and the number of union and nonunion members registered as unemployed stood at 1.29 million.[54]

The seven-hour day and three-shift system was first introduced in the textile industry. Conversions began in January 1928 on the basis of a schedule devised by a special governmental commission that included members of VTsSPS. By October 1, twenty cotton mills with 113,712 workers and four woolen factories with 4910 workers (22.4 percent of all cotton workers and 7.7 percent of woolen workers) had gone over to three shifts of seven hours each.[55]

As a rule, workers were on the job for seven hours. The first shift began at 4:00 A.M. and ended at 11:00 A.M., the second shift worked from 11:00 A.M. until 6:00 P.M., and the third from 6:00 P.M to 1:00 A.M., leaving the remaining three hours for maintenance, cleaning, and repairs. Alternatively, a split-shift system was applied whereby the workday was divided into two three-and-a-half-hour stints with a break of several hours in between.[56]

Simultaneously, as noted earlier, the authorities made a serious effort to intensify production by increasing the number of machines tended by each worker. Whereas before conversion to the seven-hour day, 67.5 percent of cotton weavers had worked two looms at a time, by September 1928, only 36.6 percent did so. The proportion tending three looms increased from 29.3 percent to 35.5 percent, while those operating four looms accounted for 24.6 percent, as compared to only 1.4 percent in December 1927. These figures somewhat mask the full magnitude of the change, since approximately two-thirds of the new workers hired in the interim were assigned to two machines.[57]

The twenty cotton enterprises in which the seven-hour day was introduced showed some positive results in the new system's first year. Thanks to the additional shift, the number of hours that the spinning and weaving machines were in use increased by 30.1 and 32.8 percent respectively; the volume of output rose as well, by 30.3 percent in the spinning mills and 23.9 percent in the weaving mills. Some, but only a small proportion, of the increase may be attributed to new machinery installed in the course of the year. In any event, the results were far more impressive than among enterprises retaining eight-hour shifts.[58]

Other indices were not so encouraging. Hourly output of machinery dropped; in mid-1929, that is, a year an a half after the change, it was still below what it had been at the outset.[59] The daily output per worker rose by 10 to 15 percent in eight of the enterprise, but fell by an average of 9 to 10 percent in the remaining sixteen. The addition of approximately 20,000 inexperienced and unskilled new workers and the unfamiliarity of night work account for some of the decline. But, as was admitted at the time, "in quite a few cases, the hourly productivity of labor, against all expectations, fell for older workers."[60]

Workers' reactions are not easy to ascertain, but many were clearly dissatisfied with some aspects of the new system. Split shifts were very unpopular. The textile workers' union lodged a formal complaint against the enterprises where it was practiced. The Commissariat of Labor upheld the complaint, but nonetheless split shifts persisted throughout 1928.[61] The prohibition against night work for women was revised in January 1928 to apply only to women who were more than five months pregnant and to nursing mothers for seven months after the birth of a child.[62] Accommodating these workers in day shifts proved difficult, however, and according to at least one reliable source, "the women in question often opposed such an arrangement very forcibly . . . either because they feared their earnings might drop . . . or because they wished to work on the same shift as their husbands, or sometimes because of a false sense of solidarity."[63]

The deleterious effects of the new system on the health and safety of workers were widely reported at the time. As several labor hygienists concluded, the problem was not so much the intensified pace of work as the deterioration of working conditions that resulted from it. The irregularity of supplies of raw cotton, the poor quality of thread, and the running down of machines were cited as major irritants to workers whose wages were based on piece rates. Operating around the clock, the mills heated up, particularly in the third shift when the temperature could be as high as 40 degrees Celsius. Lighting was often inadequate. In addition, some workers' living conditions were disrupted. According to one account, factory barracks were filled with noise day and night as occupants left for and returned from work. In the words of another, "The presence in the same room of those working on different shifts . . . deprives workers of the possibility of having normal rest."[64]

Not surprisingly, absenteeism, illness, and accident rates rose. Among the fourteen cotton factories converted in January 1928, absences increased 6.5 percent by April and 7.3 percent by July compared to the last quarter of 1927.[65] The accident rate in the same factories was reported to be 35.7 percent higher in the second quarter of 1928 than during the same base period.[66] Among the eight-hour factories in Moscow *guberniia*, absences due to illness generally declined in 1928, but the reverse was true in the majority of those that had converted to the seven-hour day.[67]

Having hastily launched the seven-hour day, the central authorities seemed incapable of solving the problems generated by it. The Commissariat of Labor admitted that the absence of breaks for meals was a contributing factor to fatigue, accidents, and a decline in hourly productivity. Yet it restricted itself to sending a circular to seven-hour plants proposing that meal breaks be introduced.[68] It also allocated additional funds to the appropriate trust to improve safety, but had little success checking on how such funds were actually spent.[69]

Still, by the end of 1928, there were definite signs of improvement. Accident rates declined and productivity per work-hour rose substantially in the last quarter of the year. Whether it was such developments that account for the expansion of the seven-hour day to other industries, or simply the determination to push forward with the reform come what may, on January 2, 1929, the TsIT and the party's Central Committee decreed that all production enterprises convert to the seven-hour day by the end of the first Five-Year Plan. The initial timetable for conversion and upwardly revised version that was incorporated into the plan are presented in Table 9-3.

By the end of the 1928–1929 economic year, 257,000 workers were on a seven-hour workday schedule. Of these, 145,000 were employed in heavy industry and 112,000 in light industry, representing respectively 15.5 percent and 23 percent of the total number of workers in those sectors.[70] The

**TABLE 9–3.**
**Projected Percentages of Industrial Workers on Seven-Hour Day**

| | Heavy Industry | | Light Industry | | All Industry | |
|---|---|---|---|---|---|---|
| Year | Projected | Revised | Projected | Revised | Projected | Revised |
| 1928–1929 | 13.4 | — | 23.8 | — | 18.3 | — |
| 1929–1930 | 40.0 | 48.5 | 40.0 | 51.9 | 40.0 | 50.0 |
| 1930–1931 | 58.8 | 83.9 | 53.7 | 75.0 | 56.3 | 80.0 |
| 1931–1932 | 81.6 | 100.0 | 80.1 | 100.0 | 80.9 | 100.0 |
| 1932–1933 | 100.0 | — | 100.0 | — | 100.0 | — |

**Sources:** Solomon M. Schwarz, *Labor in the Soviet Union* (New York, 1952), p. 226; Lev. Edvard, *Semichasovoi rabochii den'* (Moscow, 1930), p. 25.

pace of conversion thereafter appears to have fallen somewhere between the original and revised schedules. By January 1931, 1.58 million, or 58.7 percent, of all industrial workers were employed on seven-hour schedules—one million (57.4 percent) in heavy industry and 677,000 (59.7 percent) in light industry. A year later, the proportions were 83.1 percent for heavy industry and 83.7 percent in light industry; by July 1932, the last date for which such information is available, they were 86.4 percent and 92.3 percent respectively.[71]

The experiences of enterprises converting to the seven-hour day in these years were as varied as those that had made the transition earlier. Generally, when advance notice was short, preparations minimal, and the number of new workers large, the difficulties were greatest and of longest duration. Nonetheless, the results of the reform were unmistakably clear: An increasing number of workers worked a seven-hour day, the world's shortest prescribed workday, and during those hours, workers labored more intensively than they had in 1927. In this respect, the seven-hour day, three-shift system represented a continuation of the two recurrent themes in Soviet labor policy.

# VI

After the middle of 1929, however, it is impossible to assess precisely the seven-hour day's impact because it was overshadowed by a far more ambitious scheme: the continuous workweek (*nepreryvnaia nedelia,* often abbreviated to *nepreryvka*). If the seven-hour day and three-shift system reflected official impatience with the modest pace of industrialization under NEP, the continuous workweek was typical of the utopian optimism that was rampant during the early stages of the first five-year plan. Its basic premise was that while workers required days off, machines did not. As V. V. Kuibyshev, chairman of the Supreme Council of the National Economy (Vesenkha), put it to a meeting of electrical power workers: "One fifth of the time in the course of a year, machines—that is, our mechanical slaves— stand [idle] and do not work. It is completely natural that man must rest, buy why must these mechanical slaves rest?"[72]

The solution was to arrange work schedules so that on any one day, only a fraction of an enterprise's workforce would not be on the job. Continuous production for all 365 days of the year, minus five days for general observance of revolutionary holidays, could thus be assured. A variety of work schedules was possible, and indeed by December 1929 some fifty schedules were counted, but the most common arrangement was the so-called five-day week, that is, four days on followed by one day off.[73]

The idea for the *nepreryvka* first surfaced at the fifth All-Union Congress of Soviets in May 1929 when Iu. M. Larin, characterized by Carr and Davies as "a notorious eccentric," proposed it. None of the other speeches at or resolutions of the congress mentioned continuous production. Yet by mid-June, the press was hailing it as a "great socialist idea," and Vesenkha was deliberating about how to expedite its introduction. Based on Vesenkha's reports, Sovnarkom proposed on August 26 that systematic preparations for the transition to continuous production be undertaken during the economic year 1929–1930.[74]

As it turned out, this was a modest proposal. By April 1930, it was reported that 63 percent of all industrial workers had gone over to the continuous workweek (71.6 percent of workers in heavy industry and 46.5 percent in light industry). Since additional quantities of fuel and electrical power were required, these were the first industries in which the entire workforce was thus converted.[75] What might have been considered eccentric in other circumstances came to be regarded as minimally acceptable in the context of the first Five-Year Plan's "passion for construction."

As Table 9-1 indicates, the *nepreryvka* made little difference in terms of the actual number of days worked. Previously, the norm was 79 days off per year, consisting of 52 Sundays, 13 holidays, and 14 days composed of the two hours off workers received on Saturdays and before holidays. With the introduction of the 5-day workweek (4 days on and one day off), workers had 73 days off plus 5 revolutionary holidays, or a total of 78 days. In cases where workers had one common day off per month to allow for repairs and cleaning (*remontnyi* or *sanitarnyi den*), a 6-day system applied. This gave them 61 days off, plus 5 holidays, plus 11 or 12 days when the factory ceased production operations.[76]

The problem, as far as many workers were concerned, was not fewer days off but the absence of common days off, particularly Sundays and religious holidays. Schwarz claims that official propaganda exaggerated the antireligious significance of the continuous workweek so as to intimidate its opponents and that workers' dissatisfaction was "due chiefly to social reasons."[77] But it is not as easy to separate religious from social reasons as Schwarz's comment implies. Over the decades, workers had developed a number of traditions associated with such holidays that had little to do with religious sentiment but were nonetheless rooted in the religious calendar. These included drinking bouts on the eve of holidays and visits to ancestral homes whence many workers had come seeking work in the factories. Of course, such activities were still possible, but were now made more difficult by one's workmates and family members having different days off.

While many Soviet officials relished the opportunity to deal religious practice and the Orthodox church a blow, they were not so sanguine about doing the same to the working-class family. It is true that the introduction of the *nepreryvka* coincided with numerous utopian projects for communal living designed to overcome the "backwardness" of the family and liberate women from traditional family bonds.[78] In practice, however, different days off for husbands and wives was a source of considerable disgruntlement among workers that, so it was feared, could undermine production. Here again, as with the three-shift system, central authorities could do little more than instruct and recommend. Ultimately, management arranged work schedules and had to adjudicate among competing requests from workers to have days off adjusted.

This was a relatively minor problem compared to that of ensuring that workers would still have access on their days off to cultural organizations, educational institutions, shops, baths, laundries, and other facilities. "Neither baths, day-care facilities, cafeterias, laundries, cultural establishments, clubs, nor the commercial network have gone over to the *nepreryvka*," a Vesenkha official told a December 1929 all-union conference on the continuous workweek. At the same gathering, Larin cited reports from Orekhovo-Zuevo that, while cultural and educational institutions had not adjusted, the Orthodox church had.[79] Delegates from the Urals, the Crimea, and the Groznyi oil-producing region spoke of "chaos," "confusion," and worker resistance as a result of the change.[80]

Yet the authorities persisted. By May 1930, *Za industrializatsiiu,* the organ of Vesenkha, could claim on the basis of a Workers' and Peasants' Inspectorate survey that unexcused absences on Sundays and religious holidays were down and that "the majority of enterprises covered by the enquiry show an increase in output per head."[81] The proportion of workers on continuous schedules rose, reaching 72.9 percent by October.[82] By this time, however, the basic premise of the continuous workweek was becoming questionable.

It was one thing to have the plant in continuous operation, but another to have machines operating continuously. In coal mining, which was then undergoing a process of "forced mechanization," the proportion of cutting machines and pneumatic picks that were out of action reached alarming rates, due chiefly to inadequate maintenance, the lack of spare parts, and the inexperience of cutters and pick operators. In cotton and shoe manufacturing, the main problem was a lack of raw materials. In other industries, it was the uneven distribution of workers among shifts and the constant changing of assignments necessitated by staggered days off.

Thus, as one Commissariat of Labor official pointed out in August 1930, 75 percent of the workforce at the Khar'kov Electrical Goods Factory was on the continuous workweek, but only 10 to 12 percent of the machinery was in continuous use. Elsewhere, he claimed, the *nepreryvka* had assumed a purely "formal" or "fictitious" character. For example, in Leningrad, the majority of enterprises formally committed to the continuous workweek actually operated on the basis of the interrupted five-day schedule, or a "surrogate *nepreryvka*."[83]

Faced with such massive noncompliance, the central authorities eventually retreated. In April 1931, Vesenkha approved a plan to convert the giant Stalingrad Tractor Works to an interrupted six-day schedule.[84] Two months later, in his "New Conditions, New Tasks" speech, Stalin decried the lack of personal responsibility in the use and care of machinery as "the illegitimate companion of the continuous work week." Arguing that it was better to adopt the interrupted six-day week than to perpetuate a nominal uninterrupted schedule, Stalin gave his imprimatur for many enterprises to abandon the continuous workweek system entirely.[85]

It would be wrong, however, to assume that the authorities had renounced their intention to intensify production. Quite the contrary was true. Time was still of the essence, and "Bolshevik" or "shock" tempo was the operative term. Fordism was imported along with American engineers, whose intolerance of wasted time became legendary. One of them, employed at the Stalingrad Tractor Works construction site, was quoted as saying in badly accented Russian, "We don't need the word 'tomorrow.' Throw it out. The machine will work today. People will work today. As for 'tomorrow'—this is never."[86] It was as if time itself was to be cheated. The Five-Year Plan in four years; *Time Forward!* (to cite the title of the most famous novel of the period)—these were the slogans used to mobilize both management and workers.

For all the emphasis on rationalization and the effective use of worktime, industrialization during the first Five-Year Plan was achieved primarily by greater labor inputs, that is, via the massive increase in the size of the industrial workforce. But there was a limit to how many unskilled peasants could be accommodated in industry. Once the plants built during the first Five-Year Plan began to come on line, the priority shifted toward the "passion for assimilating new technology." "This is now the main task," Stalin announced at the Central Committee's plenary session in January 1933.[87] Already by this point, a new labor policy was in place. It consisted of the extension of differentials among workers on piece rates and the establishment of various short-term, on-the-job training programs to encourage skill acquisition, and, at least in part to encourage labor discipline, the empowering of management to dismiss workers for a single day's unexcused absence.[88]

Officially reported indices of absenteeism and job turnover fell precipitously in 1933. This decline, which did not necessarily reflect the real situation, nonetheless served to highlight the problem of the poor use of worktime. During this period, the press was filled with articles complaining about the bad organization of work and lack of supervision that resulted in only a small fraction of the workday being used productively. Coal mining, where supervision was especially difficult to maintain and the transportation of people, equipment, and coal difficult to coordinate, was perhaps the worst offender. Face workers in the Donbass region reportedly worked an average of 4 hours and 20 minutes of their 6-hour shifts in 1933. This was better than roofers, who averaged only 3 hours and 50 minutes out of the 7 hours they were supposed to be on the job.[89]

Time and motion studies, with which Soviet officials had long been enamored, showed that losses or working time in the factories were caused by both worker indiscipline and stoppages over which the worker had no control. In the former category were unscheduled smoking breaks, chats with fellow workers, "excessive" resting, wandering about the shop for no apparent purpose, and leaving work early. The latter consisted in the main of waiting for machines to be adjusted and fetching spare parts, which often necessitated waiting in line. In addition, there was a large gray area in between these two categories, which is exemplified by the workday of a forge-and-press-shop worker at the Rostov-on-Don Agricultural Machinery Factory (Rostel'mash). Beginning his shift at 7:00 A.M., he spent 18 minutes stoking up his oven and 37 minutes waiting for it to heat up. He then worked for 188 minutes at his machine, after which he spent 20 minutes fetching parts, 21 minutes storing them, 74 minutes waiting for the oven to heat up again, 10 minutes moving details about, and 45 minutes adjusting his lathe, before cleaning up and leaving at 2:00 P.M.[90]

The point of the time and motion study was to provide norm setters with a "scientific" basis for determining output norms. Obviously, such norms were higher than so-called experiential norms, but it proved extraordinarily difficult to implement them. Part of the problem was the sheer number of norms involved—hundreds of thousands in some of the larger enterprises—and finding a sufficient number of qualified personnel who were willing to assume the responsibilities associated with this exacting but poorly remunerated and contentious task. Disagreements among authorities about which workers were to be timed, whether breaks to enable workers to relieve themselves should be included, and the permissibility of adding "laid on" time for difficult jobs complicated the task.[91]

Aside from these essentially technical difficulties, more basic and apparently intractable contradictions in the Soviet economic system militated against the application of scientifically based norms. These contradictions included (1) pressure from the upper levels of the bureaucracy for higher targets as opposed to enterprise management's tendency to underestimate productive capacity, (2) strictures against overexpenditure of the wage fund against the use of "loose" norms to attract or retain skilled workers, and (3) the interdependence of workers up and down the production line in contrast to mobilization techniques, such as shock work and socialist competition, that rewarded individual output, often at the expense of the smooth flow of production.

Until 1935, the Commissariat of Heavy Industry (Narkomtiazhprom) and other economic commissariats insisted on the application of scientifically based norms, while management and workers generally and successfully resisted them. With the advent of the Stakhanovite movement in that year, these positions were reversed.[92] The movement, inspired by Aleksei Stakhanov's feat of digging fourteen times his quota of coal in one six-hour shift, fundamentally challenged previous norm-determining practices, including time and motion studies. By altering the division of labor and applying other innovations to production techniques, the Stakhanovites at once discredited the experts and provided the pretext for substantial norm increases in the spring of 1936.

The massive literature that popularized the movement contained two recurrent themes bearing directly on worktime. One was the importance of arriving early (thus extending the actual workday by as much as a half hour) to set up, to make sure that there were adequate supplies of raw material and parts, and to delegate tasks to auxiliary workers.[93] The other was to make full use of worktime. As Stalin remarked in his speech to the All-Union Conference of Stakhanovites in November 1935, "The Stakhanovites . . . are . . . people with culture and technical knowledge, who demonstrate precision and accuracy in work, who are able to appreciate the time factor in work and who have learned how to count not only the minutes, but also the seconds."[94]

What Stakhanovites could not do was overcome the above-mentioned contradictions. Indeed, to a large extent, the Stakhanovite movement intensified them. Given that it was impossible to provide all production workers with the wherewithal to meet and surpass their output norms, imbalances between sections were inevitable, bottlenecks increased, and semifinished goods piled up with nowhere to go. While some workers were able to exceed their norms by two, three, and five times, enterprises as a whole were hard pressed to meet their targets. In the long run, most Stakhanovites found that they could not sustain their level of output or their wages, and this led to accusations of sabotage and wrecking against enterprise management and technical personnel. Sabotage there was, but it was just as likely to have been carried out by jealous or disgruntled workers as by hard-pressed foremen or shop supervisors.

During and especially after the Great Purges, revelations about the poor use of worktime were no less frequent than in the first half of the 1930s. Stakhanovites may have counted in seconds, but it was reported that, in the first half of 1938, iron-ore-cutting machinists in the Krivoi Rog basin productively used only 52.9 percent of their worktime, loading-machine operators only 50.8 percent, drillers 58.4 percent, and shovelers 60.1 percent.[95] During roughly the same period, stoppages accounted for 23 percent of worktime in the rolling mills.[96]

One of the unintended consequences of the Great Purges seems to have been a breakdown of discipline in the factories. While experienced managers dared not traduce workers for fear of being denounced, those newly promoted still had a great deal to learn.[97] Thus, according to *Zu industrializatsiiu,* the following situation existed at the Moscow Electrical Works (Elektrozavod) in August 1937:

Throughout the day, an unending stream of people spills over into the corridors of the factory, throughout the shops and onto the stairwells. This is the best indication of the level of discipline and organization of production. In the corridor of Elektrozavod, books are traded and ice cream sold. Half a factory, and half a department store![98]

Clearly, many workers took advantage of lax supervision. If, as was claimed in 1939, Krivoi Rog miners had become accustomed to working three or four hours a day and no more, then we should not be surprised that they spent only half of their nominal worktime productively.[99] Other press accounts detailed instances of workers arriving late, visiting and chatting with one another, disregarding foremen's commands, and leaving before the end of their shift. This situation, which the authorities would have found disturbing under normal circumstances, was intolerable in the context of growing international tensions. On December 28, 1938, Sovnarkom, the party's Central Committee, and VTsSPS issued a decree that went some way beyond the antitruancy legislation of November 1932. According to a clarifying decision of January 8, 1939, lateness by more than twenty minutes was to be construed as an unexcused absence punishable by reprimand, transfer to lower-paid work, and, for repeated offenders, dismissal. Managers who did not enforce these measures were subject to criminal prosecution, and numerous exemplary cases were published in the press.[100]

The impact of these acts should not be underestimated. It must be pointed out, however, that they were primarily designed to promote work discipline, not a more effective organization of production and hence efficient use of worktime. The official explanation for disorder in the factories focused on "backward" elements among workers, foremen's lack of authority, and higher management's "rotten liberalism". Systemic contradictions, however, structured much of the behavior that the central authorities condemned. Even after they had once again invoked scientific norm determination, the authorities were powerless to prevent local "adjustments," which were correlated more closely to the reality of the shop floor.[101]

That reality was an irregular pace of production, whereby periods of intense activity—"storming"—alternated with those in which workers stood around waiting for their machines to be repaired or foremen to come up with tools and instructions. This irregularity was exacerbated by the campaign methods of mobilization utilized by party and trade union organs, which usually coincided with the end of plan periods. Poor production quality was not only a consequence of such a system but perpetuated it in the sense that defective equipment broke down easily and was repaired with defective components.

As war approached, party and state officials promoted new forms of intensification, particularly in the armaments and machine construction industries. These included the combination of occupations and multiple machine movements, both of which were clearly intended to maximize the use of available capital resources and free male workers for conscription. At the same time, the party undertook to raise the status and authority of foremen and other low-echelon managerial personnel.

These efforts proved insufficient, and on June 26, 1940, the President of the Supreme Soviet issued a decree that replaced the standard seven-hour day (six in extractive industries) with an eight-hour day and a forty-eight hour week. The decree also made unexcused absence from work a criminal offense, punishable by up to six months of corrective labor at the place of employment and with reduced wages. The new law was amplified by instructions from the party that increased worktime should not mean increased pay (i.e., that hourly and piece rates should be reduced) and from VTsSPS to the effect that those sentenced to corrective labor should receive no sick-benefit contributions.[102] Although it would appear that this criminalization of labor truancy was enforced only sporadically, the eight-hour workday persisted until the late 1950s when the seven-hour day was gradually reintroduced.

## VII

Throughout the interwar years, the Soviet government sought to redefine and restructure the workday. Essentially, there are two ways of interpreting these efforts. One, most clearly expressed in Solomon Schwarz's classic book, *Labor in the Soviet Union,* stresses the political leadership's voluntarism. In Schwarz's view, the leadership was bent on overcoming Russia's historical backwardness through industrialization, and on achieving industrialization through squeezing the maximum out of the working masses by every means possible. The means ranged from deception—as in the alleged case of the introduction of the seven-hour day—to the use of various speed-up and stretch-out techniques, and, ultimately, the laws of 1938–1940, baldly characterized by Schwarz as a "cruel policy." [103]

The other approach, and the one adopted here, incorporates a wider range of actors and factors to explain policy directions and consequences. It interprets policy as being governed as much by circumstances that were not of the leadership's making as by a long-term agendas. Many of the policies discussed here, such as the bonus wage system of 1920 and the seven-hour workday, were introduced, at least in part, in response to immediate crises, and were modified when they proved unpopular and unworkable. The *nepreryvka* was effectively sabotaged by the high degree of absenteeism among workers and the failure of management to integrate repair and production time. Indeed, worker–management collusion, a consequence of the shortage of labor in general and skilled labor in particular, as well as high production targets, meant that control over worktime remained largely beyond the reach of central authorities. Neither the laws during the interwar period nor even the Great Purges succeeded in breaking this bond.

## NOTES

1. S. G. Strumilin, "Rabochee vremia v promyshlennosti SSSR (1897–1935 gg.)," in *Izbrannye proizvedeniia v piati tomakh* (Moscow, 1964), 3:363–368. See also Theodore Von Laue, "Russian Labor between Field and Factory, 1893–1903," *California Slavic Studies,* 3 (1964): 33–65.

2. Strumilin, "Rabochee vremia," pp. 364–365.

3. According to Central Statistical Administration data, the workday and workyear from 1913 to 1917 were slightly longer than indicated in Table 9-1, a difference that may be a function of the enterprises from which the data were drawn. Tsentral-

'noe statisticheskoe upravlenie (TsSU), *Fabrichno-zavodskaia promyshlennost' v period 1913–1918 gg.* (Moscow, 1926), pp. 162–163, table 16, and 164–173, table 18.

4. Strumilin, "Rabochee vremia," pp. 365–366; S. A. Smith, *Red Petrograd: Revolution in the Factories 1917–1918* (Cambridge, 1983), pp. 65–77.

5. The 238-day figure comes from Strumilin, "Rabochee vremia," p. 365; the 249-day figures is from TsSU, *Fabrichno-zavodskaia promyshlennost'*, pp. 162–163, table 16.

6. *Sobranie uzakonenii i rrasporiazhenii rabochego i krest'ianskogo pravitel'stva, 1917–1924*, (Moscow, 1917–1924), 1917, 1–10. (Hereinafter cited as *SU*.) See also Margaret Dewar, *Labour Policy in the U.S.S.R. 1917–1928* (London, 1956). pp. 17, 161.

7. The 1918 Labor Code can be found in *SU*, 1918, 87/88–905; and Dewar, *Labour Policy*, pp. 174–177.

8. See Section 100 of "The Program of the Communist Party of Russia," in N. Bukharin and E. Preobrazhenskii, *The ABC of Communism*, trans. Eden and Cedar Paul, (Ann Arbor, 1977), p. 392. See also Bukharin's and Preobrazhenskii's discussion of the need for a "normal workday," ibid., pp. 287–288, 351–352.

9. S. G. Strumilin, "Dinamika produktivnosti truda v Rossii," *Vestnik Truda* 5–6 (1924): 144–146. See also Maurice Dobb, *Russian Economic Development Since the Revolution* (New York, 1928), pp. 25–128; Alex Nove, *An Economic History of the U.S.S.R.* (Middlesex, England, 1984), pp. 46–82. For a discussion of the collapse and its effects on Moscow's industries and the working class, see William Chase, *Workers, Society and the Soviet State: Labor and Life in Moscow, 1918–1929* (Urbana, 1987), Chap. 1.

10. V. I. Lenin, *Polnoe sobranie sochinenii*, 5th ed., 55 vols. (Moscow, 1958–1965), 27:259.

11. On the changing composition of the Moscow workforce in 1918–1921, see Chase, *Workers*, Chap. 1.

12. *Pravda*, July 23, 1918, p. 4.

13. In Moscow in 1920, the average worker worked only 219 days. TsSU, *Statisticheskii ezhegodnik 1918–1920* (Moscow, 1921), Part 25, pp. 174–175, table 4.

14. On the food crisis in Moscow, see Chase, *Workers*, Chap. 1. See also E. O. Kabo, *Pitanie russkogo rabochego do i posle voiny: po statisticheskim materialam 1908–24 gg.* (Moscow, 1926); and S. G. Strumilin, "Ratsionalizatsiia truda i sverkhurochnye raboty," *Izbrannye proizvedeniia* 3 (1964): 48.

15. *Izvestiia tekstil'noi promyshlennosti i torgovli*, June 7, 1921, p. 11.

16. Strumilin, "Ratsionalizatsiia truda," p. 48.

17. *SU*, 1920, 36–172.

18. TsSU, *Statisticheskii ezhegodnik, 1918–1920,* Part 19, p. 99, table 17.

19. Strumilin, 'Ratsionalizatsiia truda," pp. 48–49.

20. For examples, see *Nationalizatsiia promyshlennosti v SSSR: sbornik dokumentov i materialov 1917–1920 gg.* (Moscow, 1954), pp. 256–257, 644–645; *Krasnyi arkhiv*, 106 vols. (Moscow, 1922–1941), 96:74; *Rabochii Klass sovetskoi Rossii v pervyi god diktatury proletariata: sbornik dokumentov i materialov* (Moscow, 1964),

pp. 148–150; *Uprochenie sovetskoi vlasti v Moskve i Moskovskie guberniia: dokumenty i materialov* (Moscow, 1958), pp. 241–253; and *Pravda,* July 4, 1918, p. 3.

21. TsSU, Vserossiiskai promyshlennaia i professional'naia perepis' 1918 g. (Moscow, 1926), Part 2:186–187; TsSU, *Statistika truda v promyshlennykh zavedeniiakh* (Moscow, 1922), Part 1:28; E. G. Gimpel'son, "Zarabotnaia plata; material'noe obespechenie rabochikh v 1917–1920 gg." *Istoricheskie zapiski* 87 (1971):70.

22. TsSU, *Statistika truda,* Part 1:28; Gimpel'son, "Zarabotnaia plata," pp. 70–78.

23. Lenin, *Polnoe sobranie,* 27:258.

24. Data on worktime by industry and/or union for this period can be found in TsSU, *Statisticheskii ezhegodnik, 1921* (Moscow, 1922), Part 3, pp. 214–217, table 3; TsSU, *Statisticheskii ezhegodnik 1922–1923* (Moscow, 1924), Part. 1, chap. 4, pp. 202–207, table 4-A, TsSU *Statistika truda,* p. 25, table 3; TsSU, *Statisticheskii ezhegodnik g. Moskvy i Moskovskoi gubernii 1924–1925 gg.* (Moscow, 1927), Part 4, p. 194, table 13. See also M. Katel, "'Rabochee vremia promyshlennykh rabochikh SSSR," *Vestnik truda,* May 1925, pp. 102–115; *Vestnik metalloprom* 10–12, pt. 2 (October–December 1922): 24; *Vestnik mettaloprom* 4–8 (April–August 1923): 65; *Organizatsiia truda* 6–7 (October 1924): 103.

25. *SU,* 1921, 76–634. See also Dewar, *Labour Policy,* pp. 90, 214.

26. For a discussion of unemployment's causes, dimensions, and consequences, see Chase, *Workers,* Chap. 4.

27. A. A. Matiugin, *Moskva v period vosstanovleniia narodnogo khoziastva (1921–1925 gg.)* (Moscow, 1947), pp. 67–71.

28. For discussions of NOT, TsIT, and *Liga Vremia,* see Kendall Bailes, "Alexei Gastev and the Soviet Controversy over Taylorism, 1918–1924," *Soviet Studies* 29, no. 3 (1977): 373–394; Zenovia Sochor, "Soviet Taylorism Revisited," *Soviet Studies* 33, no. 2 (1981): 246–264.

29. For a fuller discussion see Chase, *Workers,* Chap. 7.

30. Iu. I. Suvorov, *Bor'ba Kommunisticheskoi partii za povyshenie effektivnosti proizvodstva v oblasti promyshlennosti (iz opyta khoziaistvennoi deiatel'nosti Moskovskoi partiinoi organizatzii v 1925–1928 gg.)* (Iaroslav', 1972), pp. 28–37.

31. Chase, *Workers,* Chap. 6.

32. *Sobranie zakonov i rasporiazhenii rabochego i kresti'ianskogo pravitel'stva: Soiuz Sovetskikh Sotsialisticheskikh Respublik, 1924–1928* (Moscow, 1924–1928), 1927, pp. 13–134.

33. The increasing proportion of new (i.e., inexperienced and unskilled) workers in the factories at a time of mass unemployment resulted from the enactment of a free labor market in 1925 and the hiring of rural migrants by industrial managers desirous of keeping their labor costs low.

34. On the absentee rates, see also L. E. Mints, ed., *Voprosy truda v tsifrakh: statisticheskii spravochnik za 1927–1930 gg. (k XVI s"ezdu VKP(B))* (Moscow, 1930), p. 23. For specific examples, see *Moskovskii proletarii,* June 30, 1926, pp. 5–6, and July 28, 1926, pp. 11–12.

35. For examples of contemporary discussions of the problem, see G. Polliak,

"Nevykhody na rabota po dniam nedeli," *Statisticheskoe obozrenie* 4 (April 1927): 48–57; *Moskovskii proletarii*, June 30, 1926, pp. 5–6, and March 14, 1928, p. 2.

36. P. Petrochenko and K. Kuznetsova, *Organizatsiia i normirovanie truda v promyshlennosti SSSR* (Moscow, 1971), pp. 84–86.

37. I. Tolstopiatov, "Trudditsiplina i proguly," *Voprosy truda* 1 (1929): 21–25.

38. For a fuller discussion, see Chase, *Workers*, Chap. 7.

39. For example, see B. Markus, "Voprosy okhrany truda v tekstil'noi promyshlennosti (nachale 1927/28 goda)," *Voprosy truda* 2 (February 1928): 33–40.

40. For example, see *Moskovskii proletarii*, July 27, 1924, p. 6.

41. F. Aristov, "Nedochety v rabote Moskovskogo GOT i oblasti okhrany truda (po materialam MRKI)," *Voprosy truda* 5 (May 1928): 110–111.

42. Strumilin, "Biudzhet vremeni Russkogo rabochego v 1922 g.," in *Izbrannye proizvedeniia*, 3:190–203; and "Biudzhet vremeni rabochikh v 1923/24 g.," in ibid., pp. 203–232.

43. As noted in Anatole Kopp, *Town and Revolution: Soviet Architecture and City Planning 1917–1935*, trans. Thomas E. Burton (New York, 1970), pp. 152–155.

44. John Barber, "Notes on the Soviet Working-Class Family," paper presented at the Second World Congress for Soviet and East European Studies, Garmish-Partenkirchen, Federal Republic of Germany, 1980.

45. *Pravda*, October 16, 1927. For two very different accounts of how the manifesto was received, see Isaac Deutscher, *The Prophet Unarmed, Trotsky: 1921–1929* (Oxford, 1959), pp. 364–366; and A. P. Finarov, "Perekhod promyshlennykh predpriiatii na 7-chasovoi rabochii den'v 1928–1932 gg.," *Istoriia SSSR* 6 (1959): 108.

46. This point is emphasized by Solomon Schwarz, *Labor in the Soviet Union* (New York, 1952), p. 2670. See also his "The Seven-Hour Day in Soviet Russia," *International Labour Review* 9 (1929): 329–330. There were deliberations within the Supreme Council of the National Economy (Vesenkha), as indicated by E. H. Carr and R. W. Davies, *Foundations of a Planned Economy, 1926–1929*, 3 vols. (Harmondsworth, England, 1974), 1:529.

47. V. A. Zaitsev, "Rabochii den' i prospekt ego sokrashcheniia," *Planovoe khoziaistvo* 5 (1927): 59–72.

48. See for example, Schwarz, *Labor in the Soviet Union*, p. 260, where it is stated that "today (i.e.1952) there can be no doubt that the purpose was to play off the new reform against the left opposition within the CPSU." Also, Deutscher, *Prophet*, p. 364.

49. *Pravda*, October 16, 1927.

50. See tables in Carr and Davies, *Foundations*, 1:1013–1014.

51. These restrictions also applied to youths aged fourteen to eighteen. Three shifts were most common in oil production (92.1 percent of all workers), flour milling (84.2 percent), and coal mining (70 percent). See TsSu, *Rabochii den' v fabrichno-zavodskoi promyshlennosti v 1928 g.* (Moscow, 1928), pp. 7, 9, 15.

52. Carr and Davies, *Foundations,* 1:529.

53. *Pravda,* October 18, 1927.

54. Carr and Davies, *Foundations,* 1:486–487. In Moscow, the unemployment rate reached 20 percent in 1927. See Chase, *Workers,* Chap. 4.

55. V. V. Shmidt, *Na putiakh provedeniia 7-chasovogo rabochego dnia* (Moscow, 1929), p. 5.

56. Schwarz, "Seven-Hour Day," pp. 334–335.

57. Ibid., pp. 336–337; and Lev Edvard, *Semichasovoi rabochii den* (Moscow, 1930), pp. 32–34.

58. Schwarz, "Seven-Hour Day," p. 341.

59. Ibid., p. 339.

60. B. L. Markus, *Perekhod na semichasovoi rabochii den* (Moscow, 1928), pp. 37, 42–43.

61. For the Commissariat's ruling, see *Trud,* January 12, 1928. For evidence of the persistence of split shifts, see *Trud,* October 1, 1928.

62. *Trud,* January 7, 1928.

63. Ia. Kvasha and F. Shofman, *Semichasovoi rabochii den' v tekstil'noi promyshlennosti,* p. 141, quoted in Schwarz, "Seven-Hour Day," p. 351.

64. For hygenists' observations, see N. Rozenbaum, Kh. Rivlina, E. Belorets, and L. Seletskaia, "Vliianiia intensifikatsii truda na utomliaemost' tkachei," *Gigiena truda* 8 (1928): 12–15; N. E. Akim, "Okhrana truda na tekstil'nykh fabrikakh Moskovskoi gubernii s semichasovym rabochim dnem," *Gigiena, bezopasnost' i patologiia truda* (Hereinafter cited as *GBPT*) 5 (1929): 93–98; for working conditions, see B. Markus, "Iz praktiki osushchestvleniia semichasovogo rabochego dnia," *Bol'shevik* 8 (1928): 45; for living conditions, P. M. Dubner and I. L. Kremlev, *24 chasa v sutki* (Leningrad, 1931), p. 19.

65. Markus, *Perekhod,* 41–42.

66. Schwarz, "Seven-Hour Day," p. 352.

67. Akim, "Okhrana truda," p. 94.

68. *GBPT* 9 (1929): 117.

69. Ibid. 1 (1930): 104; 2 (1930): 119. See also the condemnation by N. Shvernik, chairman of VTsSPS, of the "criminally slipshod relation on the part of management to technical safety and the protection of labor," in *XVII konferentsiia VKP(b), Stenograficheskii otchet* (Moscow, 1932), p. 113.

70. Edvard, *Semichasovoi rabochii den',* p. 25.

71. Schwarz, *Labor in the Soviet Union,* p. 267; and N. Zhukov, *Sem' chasov, 1927–1932 gg. Itogi provedeniia 7-chasovogo dnia na predpriiatii* (Moscow, 1933), 1931.

72. I. V. Stolitskii, *Nepreryvnaia proizvodstvennaia nedeliaput'k ozdorovleniiu truda i byta* (Moscow, 1930), p. 2.

73. Schwarz, *Labor in the Soviet Union,* p. 271.

74. S. Schwarz, "The Continuous Working Week in Soviet Russia," *International Labour Review* 2 (1931): 158–161. For press commentary, see *Trud,* June 15, 18, and 26, 1929. For the characterization of Larin, see Carr and Davies, *Foundations,* 1:530.

75. Schwarz, "Continuous Working Week," p. 163; V. Liubimov, *Bol'she vnimaniia nepreryvke* (Moscow–Leningrad, 1931), pp. 6–10.

76. Iu. A. Schauer, *Chto nuzhno znat' rabochemu o nepreryvnom proizvodstve* (Moscow, 1930), pp. 30–33; and speech by I. Tolstopiatov in *Vsesoiuznoe soveschanie po nepreryvke 11–12 dekabria 1929 g.* (Moscow 1930), pp. 39–42. Tolstopiatov mentioned the existence of thirteen variations on the standard five-day workweek.

77. Schwarz, "Continuous Working Week," p. 173.

78. For a penetrating discussion of such projects, see Gail Lapidus, *Women in Soviet Society* (Berkeley, 1978), pp. 88–103.

79. *Vsesoiuznoe soveshchanie*, pp. 21–22, 64. The Vesenkha official was I. Kraval, head of the department of labor economics.

80. Ibid., pp. 34, 74, 79.

81. *Za industrializatsiiu* (Hereinafter cited as *ZI*), May 22, 1930.

82. Schwarz, *Labor in the Soviet Union*, p. 274.

83. *ZI*, August 1, 1930.

84. *ZI*, May 8, 1931.

85. J. V. Stalin, *Works*, 13 vols. (Moscow, 1952–1955), 13:62–82.

86. *ZI*, July 6, 1930.

87. Stalin, *Works*, 13:189.

88. See Robert Beattie, "'A Great Turn' That Never Happened? A Reconsideration of the Soviet Decree on Labor Discipline of November 1932," *Russian History/Histoire russe* (forthcoming), for the argument that this decree had more to do with the food crisis and attempts to limit the influx of hungry peasants than a labor crisis.

89. *Voprosy profdvizheniia* 2 (1934): 19.

90. *Voprosy profdvizheniia* 8–9 (1934): 75.

91. On these issues, see L. H. Siegelbaum, "Soviet Norm Determination in Theory and Practice, 1917–1941," *Soviet Studies* (1984): 52–57.

92. The reversal actually dates from May 1935, several months before Stakhanov's feat, which occurred on August 30–31. See *Sovet pri narodnom komissare tiazheloi promyshlennosti SSSR, pervyi plenum, 10–12 maia 1935 g.* (Moscow, 1935), pp. 172, 174, 230, 304.

93. See, for example, A. I. Redel'man and V. F. Novikov, *Stakhanovets-tokar Likhoradov* (Moscow, 1935), p. 26; *Organizatsiia upravleniia* 2 (1936): 12: A. Kh. Busygin, *Zhizn' moia i moikh druzei* (Moscow, 1939); and *Neizvedannymi putiami. Vospominaniia uchastnikov sotsialisticheskogo stroitel'stva* (Leningrad, 1967), p. 314.

94. *Labour in the Land of Socialism, Stakhanovites in Conference* (Moscow, 1936), p. 17.

95. P. Kuzentsov, "Normirovanie truda—na sluzhbu stakhanovskomu dvizheniiu," *Planovoe khoziaistvo* 1 (1939): 136.

96. E. Lokshin, "Stakhanovskoe dvizhenie v tiazheloi promyshlennosti," *Planovoe khoziaistvo* 2 (1938): 63.

97. On the rise of absenteeism and labor turnover, see *Pravda*, May 23 and July 19, 1937; February 8 and July 7, 1938. On the difficulties of promotees, see *Pravda*, November 1 and 4, 1938; December 4, 1938.

98. Quoted in O. A. Ermanskii, *Stakhanovskoe dvizhenie i stakhanovskie metody* (Moscow, 1939), p. 327.

99. *Problemy ekonomiki* 1 (1939), cited in Donald Filtzer, "The Formation of Modern Soviet Production Relations under Stalin: The Example of the Use of Work Time," paper presented at West European Conference on Soviet Industry and the Working Class in the Inter-War Years, University of Birmingham, 1981, p. 17.

100. For the decree of December 28, 1938, see *Kommunisticheskaia partiia sovetskogo soiuza v rezoliutsiiakh i resheniiakh s"ezdov, konferentsii i plenumov TsK*, 9th ed. (Moscow, 1985), 7:40–48. For a summary of the legislation and press reports, see Schwarz, *Labor in the Soviet Union*, pp. 102–106.

101. *Mashinostroenie*, January 18, 1939; *Industriia*, February 14, 1938, and February 4, 1939.

102. *Pravda*, June 27, 1940.

103. Schwarz, *Labor in the Soviet Union*, p. 110.

# 10

## The New Deal: The Salvation of Work and the End of the Shorter-Hour Movement

### *Benjamin Kline Hunnicutt*

### I

PREDICTING THE future is a hazardous business. Historical trends that trace lovely curves on the statistician's graph can reverse overnight. The experience of those who practiced forecasting during the Great Depression should serve as a warning to modern-day "futurists" that even the most obvious prediction can prove embarrassing.

Among the most confident of vaticinations in the 1930s was that hours of work would continue to decline, as they had for over a hundred years. According to American futurists of that time, before the present century was half over, fewer than 600 hours per year would be required of the average worker, less than 14 hours a week. Such renowned Englishmen as George Bernard Shaw and Julian Huxley made similar predictions. It was Huxley's view that a 2-hour workday was in the offing. Few, indeed, were those prescient enough to foresee that a century-long movement for shorter hours had reached a turning point and that the process would suddenly reverse, with hours of work getting longer for a decade and then remaining stable until the present day.[1]

For historians, Charles Beard and Marion C. Cahill, the outlook for the shorter hours movement was just as positive. Looking back, the historian saw a steady decline of working hours throughout the nineteenth century. The decline accelerated during the first dozen years of the twentieth century and then plummeted a record 8 percent from 1913 to 1920. Even though hours stabilized in the 1920s at forty-nine per week, that hiatus ended with the 1929 stock market crash, after which hours started to drop again, down to a weekly average of fewer than thirty-three by 1933. From the statistical record, the obvious conclusion was not merely that shortening the hours of labor was a continual process but that work reductions were accelerating.[2]

And more than numbers were involved. The historian in the 1930s knew full well that shorter hours had been the central concern of labor organizations during their formative years, the 1820s and 1830s, and had remained one of labor's two more important goals. The other, higher wages, had been frequently mentioned in conjunction with shorter hours by union leaders. And in the depression years, when labor was beginning to emerge as a national force, the interest in shorter hours had intensified.

Some of the most dramatic stories in American history had to do with labor's short-hour struggle: the strikes of 1886, the Haymarket disaster, and the steel strike of 1919. Added to them in the 1930s was labor's militant stand for national thirty-hour legislation as a remedy of relief from the depression, a stand accompanied by threats of a "universal strike" if hours legislation was not passed immediately.[3]

The historian of the 1930s also knew that the shorter-hour movement was more than a cause of labor. Before the Civil War, idealistic reformers had joined wage-earners to support the movement. Subsequently, shorter hours had held a prominent place in showcases of Progressive reform, such as the Populists' Omaha platform, Teddy Roosevelt's "Bull Moose" program, Woodrow Wilson's administration, and the 1932 Democratic campaign.[4]

Moreover, politicians had delivered state legislation that limited hours of work for women and children, and for male workers in hazardous occupations. Several states had passed hours laws, and state courts had ruled them constitutional. The U.S. Supreme Court had upheld these statutes, deciding that the states, through the exercise of their constitutional police powers, had the right to regulate hours if workers' safety and health were endangered. Courts even found that "Sabbath" laws, which regulated working hours on Sunday, were consistent with the state's police powers because laws gave workers time for "necessary rest and relaxation." Consequently, new "blue laws" were enacted in the 1920s. Court cases and laws regarding the hours of work had been occasions for the expression of some of the most progressive legal opinions, helping to establish a trend in the law founded on Louis D. Brandeis's "sociological principles," which nearly transformed American jurisprudence. Finally, the federal government, beginning in the antebellum period with Martin Van Buren's ten-hour executive order, had proceeded, step by step, to limit workers' hours in government jobs and on federal contracts, and had even moved to regulate industries in interstate commerce during Wilson's administration with the 1916 Adamson act.[5]

# II

The movement for shorter hours, then, for years a centerpiece of American reform, although ignored by the Republicans in the 1920s, in the dawn of the New Deal, seemed bound to continue and to be realized more fully. The historian seldom had stronger reasons to risk predicting the future from the perspective of the past.

Even more evidence existed. Businessmen, industrialists, and conservative politicians, traditional champions of long hours, seemed to have come around to support the shorter hour cause, albeit reluctantly and with conditions. These included that wages would be reduced proportionately, that shorter hours would be a temporary measure for the duration of the depression, and that the shortening of the workday would be voluntary. Even with these conditions, these groups had taken the first positive steps to adjust worktime during the depression, and Herbert Hoover's secretary of labor, William Doak, went so far as to observe that "industry, in general, favored" shorter hours.[6]

With no more intensive research than reading the daily newspapers, the historian of the 1930s would have known that major industrial firms cut back weekly hours to forty and then to thirty in 1930 and 1931. Kellogg's of Battle Creek, Sears Roebuck, General Motors, Standard Oil of New Jersey, Hudson Motors, and several cotton manufacturers took these measures as alternatives to laying off workers. In August 1932, the Industrial Conference Board (ICB) made a survey of 1718 business executives on the basis of which it estimated that 50 percent of American industry had shortened hours to save jobs. Typical of the reasons executives gave the ICB were that more workers could be employed and that wages, although lower per capita, would be more widespread and thus would promote confidence and consumer spending.[7]

H. I. Harriman, president of the U.S. Chamber of Commerce, addressing the nation over the CBS radio network, advocated the "application of spread work to all classes of workers . . . to white collar workers, commercial firms, banking, municipal and state government." He concluded that "it is better for all of us to be at work some of the time than for some of us to be at work all of the time while others are not at work at all.[8]

Even such a bastion of conservatism as the American Legion took a stand and organized for action. On August 24, 1932, it began its own work-sharing drive, what it called its "war against Depression," claiming that 3300 of its posts nationwide led their communities in the share-the-work effort.[9]

Historians of the 1930s surely thought it significant that Herbert Hoover began to favor voluntary efforts to "share-the-work." With his support of the chemical industry's program, Hoover incorporated shorter hours into his administration's depression policies and declared that it was part of his "nine point economic program," a step that William Doak, the Emergency Committee on Employment, and the Organizations on Unemployment Relief had been encouraging for over a year.[10]

From Hoover's early support, the political story unfolded rapidly. In June 1932, Hoover was pressed by the AFL to call a national convention on shorter hours. He chose instead to meet with a group of New England politicians and businessmen organized by Governor Winant of New Hampshire. Disapproving of labor's move to shorter-hour legislation, Hoover joined with business and supported voluntary efforts based in trade associations. These efforts came to fruition in August when the National Conference of Business and Industrial Committees created the Teagle Commission (named for its chairman, Walter Teagle) to study work sharing.[11]

The share-the-work drive opened in September 1932 and grew immediately into a national force with strong business support. Even though the National Association of Manufacturers (NAM) supported the drive primarily as a hedge against labor's push for national hours legislation, public response to the idea and business cooperation were impressive. Assessing the movement, the U.S. Department of Labor estimated that 25 percent of all employees "held jobs on the plan." On the basis of this estimate, Teagle claimed that 3 million to 5 million jobs were created.[12]

The movement built momentum in the 1932 campaign. Both major parties had a shorter-hour plank in their platforms. Hoover and Franklin Roosevelt vied with each other in their support of the share-the-work drive. Roosevelt pointed with pride to his efforts in New York State to lower hours and set minimum wages; Hoover countered with a rehearsal of his support for the national share-the-work drive. Prominent supporters were to be found along the entire range of the political spectrum, including labor supporter Monsignor John Ryan, Governor Gifford Pinchot, New York's Mayor Fiorello H. La Guardia, Roosevelt's later secretary of labor, Frances Perkins, automaker Henry Ford, U.S. Senators Robert Wagner and David Walsh, department store owner E. A. Filene, and millionaire Vincent Astor.[13]

The shorter-hour momentum continued after the election. But with the change in the political climate in Washington, public and congressional interest shifted from voluntary efforts to national legislation. After a few halfhearted overtures to the Teagle Commission in September 1933 and a lukewarm endorsement in October, the AFL Executive Council rejected the Teagle campaign with its pay cutting and drafted a bill that limited hours per week to thirty. The AFL had considered a constitutional amendment for hours regulation at their November convention, but had settled on legislation suggested to the organization by such groups as the National Citizen's League for Industrial Recovery and the National Grange. In December, Hugo Black introduced the AFL's bill to the 72nd Congress; among other provisions, it prohibited, in interstate or foreign commerce, all goods produced by establishments where workers were employed more than five days a week or six hours a day.[14]

Several AFL-affiliated unions had argued for a minimum-wage provision to be included in the bill. The AFL, however, concluded that such legislation would have less political support and would almost certainly be ruled unconstitutional. Moreover, most labor leaders opposed minimum-wage provisions, reasoning that a minimum wage could easily become a maximum wage. The best course of action seemed to be to enforce a nationwide reduction in the supply of labor. This would provide immediate "work relief." Then, as more people were put back to work at thirty hours, buyer confidence would return, purchasing power expand, and the economy recover. After the economy improved, labor could bargain effectively for higher wages in a condition of continued labor scarcity. Because of the excess of work supply—excess hours that were manifested as unemployment—hours reductions seemed to be the necessary first step to higher wages.[15]

The hearings held in Congress and the public debate on the bill attracted a good deal of attention. Old-fashioned reformers, hearing the echoes of their Progressive past, joined farm groups, intellectuals, educators, religious leaders, and sociologists in support of labor's argument about the economic benefit of shorter hours. In addition to practical discussions, some idealistic and "romantic" rhetoric was heard. Like labor leaders, supporters of the legislation felt obliged to defend the leisure time that would result from a thirty-hour week. In so doing, some revived an older vision of progress muted by the previous "business decade"; others offered new ideas about leisure's potential in the modern world.[16]

## III

Speculations about the bright possibilities of the "new leisure" filled the press, as incongruous during the depression as the plowing up of fields of corn and the burning of food for fuel in the Midwest.

Teagle's trademark phrase, "share the work," was accompanied by such terms as "technological unemployment," "economic maturity," "market gluts," "overproduction," "the shorter-hour cure for overproduction," "limited production," "secular stagnation," and Hugh Johnson's famous "Saturnalia of Destruction"—all pointing to a widespread feeling that the depression had been caused by too much production. Economic distress stemmed, not from a lack of industrial growth and production, but from too much. Growth had destabilized the economy. To some, this was an unmitigated disaster. To others, such as Monsignor Ryan, overproduction proved that the economy had grown to a point where human needs could be largely met and "a life of reasonable and frugal comfort" could be made available to all workers, if only the problem of distribution were solved.[17]

Two obvious solutions to overproduction, producing less and selling more, were offered. But the latter seemed to have been largely discredited. The president of the AFL, William Green, along with most other Americans, had heard the "new business gospel of consumption" throughout the 1920s. Its prophets had preached that enough new markets could be found, enough "luxuries" transformed into necessities by advertising and the spending example of the rich, that overproduction could be averted and workers could escape the scourge of unemployment. But for Green and many others, including some businessmen, the depression had shown this gospel and its prophets to have been false. Green, like most others in the labor movement, had never fully accepted the idea that industrial growth could go on indefinitely and new work could be found to replace jobs taken over by the machine. Labor's counterargument was that free time was the natural result of technological advance and the satisfaction of basic, "reasonable" human need. The depression had shown that technological displacement was a reality and that workers had a choice only as to the forms the new free time would take. Workers could have either increased unemployment or more leisure time. All the advertising and business "hype" in the world about new markets and perpetual economic growth could not change that hard fact.[18]

The shorter-hour cure for unemployment, proposed by labor in the 1920s to counter the "gospel of consumption," ruled the day in the early years of the depression. The rationale for the "cure" was that if production had become excessive and had resulted in pools of copper and other commodities, and glutted inventories of retail traders, then the best course of action was simply to work fewer hours and produce less. Necessary work would be spread around naturally by the market, and the worker would then have the blessing of leisure, not the curse of unemployment.

To be sure, economic balance required that wages be increased enough so that workers could buy what was produced. Shorter hours would act to redistribute wealth, producing a scarcity of labor in relation to demand, and thus give workers enough money to buy what they needed to live; a redistribution of wealth would take capital away from the rich, who were slow to spend on ever more lavish luxuries and who tended to oversave. Shorter hours would, in theory, direct capital to the production of necessities, of things readily consumed, and away from unneeded goods and services that required the efforts of armies of salesmen, "marketing experts," and advertisers. Thus shorter hours would be an economic counterweight, acting to draw down existing surpluses and then as a governor on future runaway overproduction of the wrong kinds of goods and services. Such was the reasoning behind the thirty-hour legislation that started to build momentum in the U.S. Congress.

By April 1933, Roosevelt had ignored the shorter-hour "thunder from the left'' as long as he could. After the Senate passed the thirty-hour bill without major modification on April 6, reports circulated widely that should the House version of the bill (introduced by William Connery of Massachusetts) reach the floor, it would pass with little opposition. Ernest K. Lindley characterized these developments as a ''revolution boiling up from the bottom.''[19]

Roosevelt, prodded to action, directed Secretary of Labor Frances Perkins to draft an administration response. In the meantime, Speaker of the House Henry T. Rainey vowed that the House would hold back the ''hotheads'' in the Senate and ''wait till all of the president's reconstruction legislation [was] passed'' before the thirty-hour proposal was taken up.[20]

Within a few days, Perkins prepared the administration's position. After a cabinet meeting on April 12, Perkins and Secretary of Commerce Daniel C. Roper announced the administration's support of thirty-hour legislation with some adjustments—''to make it flexible and workable.'' Perkins proposed that provisions for a minimum wage should be included, as well as stronger production controls, over and above simple reduction of hours. Perkins and Roper also reported that Roosevelt opposed the provision for an import ban and that they would try to have it removed. But, bowing to political realities, the administration accepted the basic purpose of the Black bill: to reduce unemployment by reducing work hours ''across the board,'' for as many workers as possible.

On April 13, Perkins appeared before the House Labor Committee to endorse the thirty-hour principle and present the administration's modifications and additions. Afterward, she announced that the committee and the administration were largely in agreement and that she would ''clear the way for passage.'' The main point of controversy was the import ban, which the House committee steadfastly supported. These developments prompted the *New York Times* and many other newspapers to predict prompt passage of the bill by the House and Roosevelt's signature within the month. William Green, after a visit with Perkins and Roper, was quoted as saying that passage and signing were sure things and that the nation was days away from a thirty-hour work week.[21]

This was the series of events that the historian in 1933 witnessed. These were the things that led prominent observers to expect as reasonable what utopian writers of the nineteenth century had contemplated only in their fantasy world: progressively shorter hours, the withering away of work, and the birth of a new kind of progress in the free realm of human leisure. Rhetoric, historical trends, and political realities combined to point to shorter hours. Those who earlier had tried to save work from leisure's erosion— businessmen and conservative politicians—had realized their error, put away their gospel of consumption and come to serve the cause. Finally, weekly worktime had decreased fifteen hours in less than four years; prospects seemed great for another, immediate, three-hour reduction. Surely the prediction of the fourteen-hour week was reasonable; perhaps even Huxley's two-hour day was not too extreme.

## IV

Why were the prophets so wrong in their predictions? Why at the moment when the shorter-hour process seemed irresistible did hours of labor reach their lowest point and begin to increase?

In fact, several hazards appeared in shorter hours' otherwise open waters— reefs that might have foretold different things to come. The gifted seer could point to Roosevelt's lukewarm endorsement of thirty hours, his behind-the-scenes manipulation of the bill in the Senate committees and on the House floor, and his firm opposition to import limitations; in addition, opposition to thirty hours legislation was building both within the administration and in the business world. In place of shorter hours, this opposition would create a new definition of progress: the American "right to work" and a "full-time job."

Even though most businessmen and industrialists had supported the Teagle campaign in September and October 1932, they began to draw back by December of that year, after which their support of shorter hours was more apparent than real. Business tended to support shorter hours only when introduced voluntarily and when both wages and hours were controlled by businessmen. When the shorter-hour movement resulted in legislation for the thirty-hour week, opposition emerged rapidly from behind the work-sharing façade.

Teagle found himself defending his campaign against charges made by businessmen that it was "communist inspired," especially when he suggested that the voluntary establishment of a thirty-hour workweek might be a long-term but necessary response to the depression. Because he alienated a number of business supporters and because of the Black bill's momentum, the U.S. Chamber of Commerce shelved the Teagle program early in 1933.[22]

Thereafter, the chamber and the NAM conducted what amounted to a rhetorical share-the-work movement, designed more to castigate "cut-throat" competition by firms (especially in the South) that worked their employees more than forty hours. A chamber committee headed by P. W. Litchfield, president of Goodyear Tire, issued a call in early April 1933 for a maximum workweek of not less than forty hours and warned that trying to legislate for fewer hours might have "disastrous" results (i.e., a temporary emergency measure might become permanent).[23]

Just before the Senate passage of the Black bill, a North American

Newspaper Alliance survey showed industry divided on the shorter-hour issue, but with an increasing majority in opposition to it. The overriding concern, reported by this survey, was that the legislation might result in hours
of work stabilizing permanently at current levels or even below them. Numerous businesspeople who were fully content to support a voluntary and
temporary share-the-work movement were horrified by the prospect that the
workweek might never recover from the depression, that the Black bill might
set shorter hours rigidly in place. Instead of looking at the increase in leisure
time as inevitable or as a potentially beneficial thing, businesspeople tended
to equate recovery with the *restoration* of longer working hours—if not to
the pre-1929 level of forty-nine hours, then at least to a standard eight-hour
day, five-day week.

After the Senate passed the Black bill, the House gave every indication
that it would follow suit, and Roosevelt, through Perkins, endorsed the thirty-
hour principle. Business opposition solidified, however; Hugh S. Johnson
observed that economists, businessmen, and industrialists "would turn back-
hand somersaults against the thirty hour week."[24]

Businessmen held emergency meetings in Philadelphia, Chicago, and
other cities; talk of "chaos and disaster" filled the air. James Emery, counsel for the NAM, testified that the bill "excites anxiety throughout American
Industry as a rigid and highly centralized regulation not of commerce but of
production." Perkins reported that after she had testified before the House
Labor Committee, "a flood" of objections and requests for exemptions had
inundated her office. The *New York Time* bristled with indignant letters and
sarcastic editorials. *Newsweek* announced: "Thirty Hour Week Startles Nation."[25]

Within the administration, there was surprise and consternation at this
vehement opposition. Raymond Moley remembered that "the Perkins substitute proved almost as great a shock to employers as the Black bill itself.
Miss Perkins and F.D.R. were aghast at the commotion it caused."[26]

The great outcry following Perkins's endorsement put Roosevelt on the
defensive and set him and his advisers looking around for ways to placate
the opposition. At first, Perkins tried to work out a compromise within the
framework of the Black and Connery bills. In addition to the minimum-
wage and regulation-of-production amendments, she floated proposals for
greater executive control of hours and wages in order to reduce the thirty-
hour bill's rigid provisions. Controls would be administered through the secretary of labor's office with operations delegated to a three-person board.
These proposals set off new howls of protests and accusations that Perkins
wanted to control all of America's business out of Washington. Perkins,
"amused and astonished" that her efforts to reconcile factions and make the
Black bill "flexible and workable" had been so misunderstood, explained

that she only wanted to make it possible to set hours over thirty and up to forty. She added, somewhat apologetically, "please remember that the Black bill is limited to two years."

But a change in the administration position was evident in the emphasis Perkins began to place on the minimum wage and the flexible regulation of hours by federal boards. A week after she endorsed the thirty-hour principle, she downplayed it as an unemployment remedy, referring to it with disapproval as "compulsory share-the-work." Instead, using phrases similar to those used by businessmen when trying to distance themselves from the Teagle campaign, she stressed the necessity of preventing "cut-throat" competition from firms that set hours above "reasonable levels."[27]

Meanwhile, Roosevelt and his advisers were struggling to put together their own comprehensive recovery program. Immediately following the Perkins endorsement of the Black bill, opposition to thirty hours and the principle of work sharing gained strength in the administration. Several members of the so-called Wagner group objected to the bill. Harold Moulton of the Brookings Institute, more than anyone else, was opposed and devoted great amounts of time to discounting the "shorter hour solution to unemployment." Donald Richberg and Alexander Sachs, using the same phrases, described the bill as "sharing the poverty . . . and fundamentally unsound." Richberg reported that "many in the administration" agreed with his point of view. Rexford Tugwell, while conceding that shorter hours might have to be used to limit production in "extreme cases," observed that if "we shall have to resort permanently to limitation of hours . . . [this] would not be progress . . . it would be an admission that we have created a Frankenstein which we are unable to control." Raymond Moley was careful to distance himself from the Perkins substitute, recalling that he "had nothing to do with it." He thought the whole idea "utterly impractical."[28]

As assistant secretary of state, Moley began work on proposals that had been accumulating in his office and contacted business leaders to find out what could be done to minimize the Black bill's potential damage. Alternative suggestions soon emerged from Moley's office in the form of a remarkably early and accurate *New York Times* report by Louis Stark. On April 14, Stark reported that the "administration's plans for *changes in the Black bill*" constituted a "mobilization of industry." Senator Robert Wagner had told Stark that the administration was considering federal regulatory agencies, similar to the old war boards, that would help "stabilize industry, . . . quicken and regulate it, . . . protect it against losses, . . . and rebuild, not just hold the line." Stark also reported that Roosevelt was considering an enlarged public works program as "a key to revival and industrial expansion," to be added as an amendment to the thirty-hour bill.

Throughout April, pressure mounted in the Senate among Roosevelt's strongest supporters for inclusion of a public works program in the Black measure. Led by Senators Wagner, Robert La Follette, and Edward Costigan, and supported by members of Roosevelt's cabinet and "Brain Trust," backers of a public works program vied with supporters of thirty-hour legislation in Congress. During a White House conference held on April 15, they asserted that together with a $2 billion public works program, the minimum-wage provision added to the Black bill would eliminate the necessity for a thirty hours limit. The senators agreed with administration representatives at the conference that all the "essential features" and "major goals" of the Black bill could be "effectively embodied" in public works legislation, increases in the Reconstruction Finance Corporation, and the expanded relief efforts provided by the Wagner bill.

Added to the opposition mounting in the Senate and within the White House, the State Department began rumblings on its own. The unwillingness of Massachusetts Representative William Connery, chairman of the House Labor Committee, and other committee members to compromise on the Black bill's import limitations alienated a number of people, including Secretary of State Cordell Hull, who looked forward to a reduction of trade barriers and toward freeing and expanding foreign trade to help end the American and world depression. Hull feared that a ban on foreign products (based on how many hours were worked) was impractical, and could mean an escalation in the trade wars that were already going on.[29]

Hence, within two weeks of Perkins's endorsement of the thirty-hour principle, the skeleton of Roosevelt's recovery program emerged. Moley described the suggested additions and amendments to the Black bill as "a hodgepodge of provisions [to] stimulate industry and [for] business–government planning . . . to satisfy the forces behind the Black bill." Included in the list were public works, the stimulation of spending through wage guarantees, the regulation of industry by federal boards, more liberal commercial policies, and efforts to expand foreign trade.[30]

Perkins tried to work with the House Labor Committee to restructure the Black bill along administration lines. But committee members, led by Connery and Welch from California, resisted her efforts. They were willing to accept a three-person board in the Department of Labor that would set maximum hours up to and even over forty hours a week and a minimum wage; but they would do so only if the administration would "withdraw its objections to the inclusion of foreign products" in the bill's commercial bans. This was something that Roosevelt and the State Department would not do. Finally, in response to Perkin's attempts to turn the Black bill into an administration vehicle and blunt the thirty-hour provision, the House Labor Committee suggested that the administration gather together all the amendments they were offering the committee and present them to Congress as a separate administration measure. Let the Black and Connery bills stand or fall on their own, on the thirty-hour principle.[31]

Roosevelt, his advisers and cabinet, then broke with the thirty-hour bill and with share the work, and began work on a National Industrial Recovery Act (NIRA). In early May, Senate Majority Leader Joseph Robinson reported that the Black bill was no longer "part of the President's program." But Roosevelt attempted to hold the political forces behind the Black bill together and marshal support behind his bill. The AFL's support was probably the most difficult to obtain. Roosevelt met with the AFL's Green on April 29 and May 2 and laid out parts of the NIRA for him. Gradually, Green and other labor officials were persuaded, lured by NIRA's Section 7a, which guaranteed union organization and collective bargaining and outlawed "yellow-dog contracts." The addition of a public works program sweetened the deal. Thus labor, succumbing to Roosevelt's charm and political acumen, fell in line behind the NIRA and temporarily withdrew pressure for thirty-hour legislation. Nevertheless, Green and other union leaders took a wait-and-see attitude; they held thirty hours in reserve, ready to employ it again if the NIRA did not live up to expectations. Even while praising Section 7a and public works, Green insisted that "thirty hours [was] imperatively necessary."[32]

Businessmen, with the threat of thirty hours hanging over their heads, fell raggedly into line as well (with the notable exception of the NAM). On May 3, Moley, Hugh Johnson, and Tugwell met with representatives of the Chamber of Commerce in Washington and worked out an acceptable compromise. The chamber was willing to accept 7a, with its concessions to labor, as the only workable compromise, the only way to turn back the Black and Connery bills.

Averell Harriman, then President of the U.S. Chamber of Commerce, relieved at escaping the thirty-hour threat, was moved to eloquence, calling Roosevelt's program the "Magna Carta for American industry and labor." With his political house in some degree of order, Roosevelt presented the NIRA to Congress on May 15, 1933.[33]

The NIRA was a compromise. As such, it represented a collection of different approaches to industrial stabilization, relief, and recovery. The issue of shorter hours was included, but competing programs had been formulated and set in place. These programs were to grow and finally replace shorter hours as an unemployment strategy. The NIRA's public works programs and the principle of creating new work by direct government spending and federal programs were the major competitors to shorter hours. They were alternatives to the notion of limited production in a "managed" economy. With the coming of the "second New Deal," these and similar policies designed to stimulate economic growth overshadowed the century-long process of shorter-hour reform.

## V

The Roosevelt administration began to circumvent share the work at the start of the National Recovery Administration (NRA). The NRA codes reduced actual working hours in only a few instances, such as cotton textiles and mining where hours averaged over forty-eight a week. Even though these few cases were important and highly visible, most of the industrial codes set maximum hours well above then-current averages. Over 90 percent of the NRA codes set hours at forty a week or longer, at a time when the average workweek in American industry was well under thirty-six hours. A case-by-case evaluation shows that average workweeks in particular industries were longer than code maximums only 14 percent of the time in the early months of the NRA, ranging to a high of 18 percent at its end. Moreover, during the life of the NRA, actual hours (seasonally adjusted) in industries covered by the codes increased in most cases, up an average of 3 percent from 1933 to 1935. In those few industries that experienced a decline in hours of work, most had average workweeks below thirty-seven hours with a code maximum of forty or more, so the codes could hardly be said to have been a major factor in these declines.[34]

Labor was well aware of this trend toward a forty-hour standard and was troubled by the NRA's obvious inability or unwillingness to reduce work hours substantially. In September 1933, the AFL began to demand immediate code revisions, but such calls had little impact. Consequently, the AFL opened a new offensive. In a speech before the Metal Trades Department of the AFL, Green issued what news reporters called "a vital ultimatum to the recovery administration" in a strongly worded attack on the NRA and a call for the reintroduction of the Black–Connery bills.[35]

But throughout 1934, until right before the congressional elections, the administration and its supporters in Congress blocked the 73rd Congress versions of the Black–Connery bills. With his opposition to thirty hours, Roosevelt placed himself in the position of siding with business and depending on continued and expanded economic growth to reduce unemployment levels. Yet, through the summer, unemployment remained high. Labor kept up the pressure, and by mid-August, shorter hours emerged as a key issue in the off-year elections.[36]

The AFL conducted a noisy convention in San Francisco in early October, stridently demanding the passage of Black–Connery and threatening "universal," nationwide strikes if thirty-hour legislation was held up any longer. Calling thirty hours the AFL's "paramount purpose," and noting the "disillusionment of labor with the workings of section 7a," Green warned that "all congressional candidates were being asked to give their views on the Black/Connery bill and that these replies would be broadcast to the voters." The convention committed labor to "use all means at its disposal to gain the thirty hour week; economic and political." And if the election did not return a Congress willing to grant this demand, then national strikes, what Green termed "class war practically," would be the likely result.[37]

Roosevelt held fast to the course set by the administration in 1934—that is, to the standard of forty hours. It was a risky stand. The political consequences were liable to be fearsome given the militance and increasing political prominence of labor.[38]

In masterful fashion, Roosevelt engaged Black–Connery on two main fronts. First, he took the initiative during the election campaign and committed his administration to the creation of new work opportunities as the way to reemployment—a direct alternative to work sharing. He presented new programs such as the Works Progress Administration (WPA) that created jobs for the unemployed and stimulated business activity, adding his social security plan to protect those who could not be reemployed. Second, just as he had done in 1933 and 1934, he took a reactive stand to thirty-hour bills throughout 1935, offering bits and pieces of the NIRA to labor as discrete pieces of legislation, as pressure built in Congress for passage of Black–Connery.

As the so-called second New Deal began, Roosevelt abandoned the project of controlling production and lost patience with business voluntarism. He was convinced by advisers such as Harry Hopkins to act directly to provide jobs and stimulate economic activity. Leaving his suspicions about market maturity and limited growth behind, Roosevelt began to use public works, liberal monetary policy, larger government payrolls, and deficit budgets to stimulate production and consumption to promote reemployment. Such projects as the WPA demonstrated that Roosevelt had begun to assume that the federal government had the obligation to provide work if the private sector could not. But government was the employer of last resort. The first line of attack would be stimulation of private industry and business. Then, whatever slack remained, what Hopkins called "idle time," would be taken up by constructive government projects, not "wasted" by the redistribution of that "slack" though shorter hours. Hence Roosevelt, at the prodding of his advisers, consistently opposed thirty-hour legislation, offering his own programs in a series of alternatives.

In his annual message to Congress on January 4, 1935, Roosevelt vowed to replace the dole, cash handouts, and degrading "marketbaskets" with constructive work programs. Slums needed to be cleared, parks and recrea-

tion facilities built, rural areas provided with electricity and adequate housing, and forests reseeded. So many things needed doing; so many were
looking for a job. The obvious solution was for government to bring the two
together, the worker and the work. The burden of care for the chronically
unemployed, would fall again on local agencies. But able-bodied persons on
relief would be given what they most needed: work. Roosevelt also pledged
to support the omnibus social security plan, which included unemployment
insurance and retirement programs. Together, work relief and social security
constituted the new unemployment policy and replaced most of what had
been tried the previous two years under industrial stabilization.[39]

On April 8, 1935, Congress authorized \$5 billion through the Emer-
gency Relief Appropriations Act for work relief. On May 6, Roosevelt
launched the WPA, appointing Harold Ickes as head of the planning division
and Harry Hopkins as administrator (and the man with the real power).[40]

Following Hopkins's lead, Roosevelt began to support WPA projects
that provided the maximum work creation for the minimum amount of federal spending. "Light projects" that were as labor intensive as possible were
favored over longer-term, heavy construction projects, which were preferred
by Ickes and the PWA. The majority of large construction projects were
postponed in favor of projects "which tapped unemployment pools; which
could move promptly; which could be completed in a relatively short period
of time; and which would use more man-power and less materials."[41]

By 1935, Harry Hopkins and the WPA chairman of the Division of Ap-
plications and Information, Frank C. Walker, had lost what few qualms they
had about "national goals" or "transcedent purposes" for public works. In
May, Walker observed that the WPA had advanced beyond old-fashioned
notions of "utility, engineering, and soundness" and had introduced "a new
conception of public works." From then on, WPA projects would be undertaken "on the simple basis that they will provide employment. . . . A new
yardstick must be applied to all works projects and the emphasis on all
engineering and economic soundness must be subordinated . . . to the acute
unemployment problem." The primary object was simply to get people off
the relief rolls and back to work.[42]

For Hopkins and Walker, work needed no transcendent purpose. Work
was worthwhile on its own, aside from product or result. It was the end for
which other parts of the economy and government were the means. Without
work, people suffered more than the simple absence of income. They suffered extreme emotional, social, mental, and "spiritual" distress. The whole
of the personality deteriorated. Work skill was the first to go, followed by
community esteem, family respect, "pride, courage, self-respect, ambition,
and energy." For the individual, work was life's center, a point of reference
and stability without which existence was confusion. Men and women found

"no substitute for work to keep themselves sound in body and mind." And
for the state, work was one of its principal reasons for being and a primary
way to maintain national identity, order, and cohesion. Work "conserves
[human beings] as a national asset, the lack of work lets them sink into a
national liability." In Hopkins's mind, maintaining "the right to work" was
the state's first responsibility to its citizens and absolutely essential for the
survival of democracy.[43]

Hopkins's views on public works and his management of the WPA
dovetailed with what Marriner S. Eccles, new governor of the Federal Reserve Board, said and did about monetary policy. After the banking bill
cleared Congress and was signed by the President on August 24, 1935,
Eccles was able to exert effective control over monetary policy and, for the
first time, use the Federal Reserve Board as a tool for the implementation
of an administration's economic policies. In Eccles's words, that policy could
be summed up as one of "easy money."

But Eccles, departing from economic orthodoxy, argued that "easy
money" would not cause inflation. Like Hopkins and Ickes, Eccles built his
case on the fact that so much idleness existed in the economy. Following
his colleagues' lead, Eccles argued that since so much potential wealth was
being lost because of "idle time" and "surplus labor," the Federal Reserve
Board should make money more readily available to underwrite increased
production. Like Hopkins, he equated increased production with the creation
of new work. The way to reemployment was to be found in the liberalization
of discount rates, reserve requirements, and definitions of eligible paper to
be used for loads. The large amount of idle time that already existed in the
economy would act as a buffer, absorbing the new "liquidity." Idle men
and women would be put to work with the newly available funds, producing
new goods and services—real wealth that would give substance to the banks'
paper promises.[44]

To advocates of share the work, Eccles pointed out that both "unjusti-
fied" wage increases and hours reductions "limit and actually reduce production." As such, they were "not in the interests of the public or in the
real interests of the workers themselves." He argued that shorter hours "re-
tard and restrict production" and thus were a prime cause of inflation—of
too many dollars chasing too few goods (given his monetary policies). "Surplus labor" should be employed to create new wealth, not drawn down and
wasted by shorter hours. He was not willing to admit that existing labor,
machine, and capital surpluses could be alleviated by share the work. The
free time of the depression equaled unemployment to Eccles. It was idleness
and waste. It needed to be reemployed by economic growth. Otherwise, this
free time would continue to cost billions in lost wealth to the nation—and

Eccles's monetary policies would turn out to be as inflationary as his critics feared.[45]

In all three areas that concerned him as governor of the Federal Reserve Board—monetary reform, tax policy, and the deficit—Eccles centered his attention on "idle hours" and the "wasted time" of unemployed Americans. He went out on a limb, insofar as the conventional wisdom of the time was concerned, supporting policies that built on the potential that "reemployed" idle time had to pay back the deficit, make good the bank's paper extensions, and make the tax structure an engine for economic growth rather than a barrier to individual effort. These views came to be more and more important in setting the "second New Deal's" political and legislative course after mid-1935.

## VI

In spite of these positive steps to achieve reemployment by the creation of new work, the thirty-hour bill continued to haunt Roosevelt. As 1935 began, Black and Connery reintroduced their original bills in the Senate and House respectively. The *New York Times* reported in early February that "the thirty-hour bill is the piece of legislation most feared by industry in the current session" Even though many businessmen agreed with the Chamber of Commerce that Roosevelt would oppose Black–Connery and that without his endorsement it could not get through Congress, the fear remained in most conservative and anti-New Deal circles that such strong sentiment for the bill was developing that the administration would be forced later to give in to the rest of labor's legislative agenda.[46]

In late March, the bill was reported out of the Senate Labor Committee just at the time that Congress was dragging its heels on renewal of the NIRA. Senator Black admitted that his bill "was closely connected with NRA" and that if congressional leaders were not ready to renew the agency and support tougher industrial codes, then the sterner measure of thirty-hours legislation would result. Connery, on the House side, shared Black's confidence, commenting that "sentiment for the thirty hour week is predominant in both the House and the Senate . . . if we could get it on the floor it would pass the House 'in a minute.' "[47]

Louis Stark wrote in the *New York Times* that whereas labor was dead serious about Black–Connery and would be happy to have the legislation pass, still the reporting of the bill out of the Senate Labor Committee and its simultaneous appearance on the House floor were signs that labor, together with several congressmen, had a larger strategy. In addition to pushing thirty hours as a way of increasing support for the NRA's renewal in

Congress, labor was using thirty hours as a stalking horse to force the administration to support the Wagner bill, in the form that labor endorsed, and the Guffey Coal Stabilization bill. Labor's strategy became more apparent when pressure mounted in the Senate to tack thirty hours on to the NRA renewal in order to block the Clark resolution, which would have limited the NRA's life to ten months instead of the two years that labor supported.

Labor's strategy worked. The NIRA was renewed in early May for two years. Even though Roosevelt continued to oppose the Wagner bill, saying that he preferred the protections of Section 7a, Frances Perkins threw her support behind the stronger version of the Wagner bill, which kept the National Labor Relations Board (NLRB) in the Department of Labor. And with the tacit approval of the administration, the bill passed the Senate on May 16. The whole legislative picture was thrown into confusion, however, with a series of Supreme Court decisions on May 27, "Black Monday."

Among the decisions, the *Schechter* poultry case had the greatest impact on the New Deal's industrial and labor legislation, virtually destroying the NIRA. Instead of trying to revise the NIRA to make it constitutional, Roosevelt attempted to save components of the act. Abruptly, he threw his full support behind the Wagner bill, which rapidly became law on July 5. In addition, he approved the Connally Act, which regulated the oil industry along the lines of the NRA codes (but more effectively). The administration also supported passage of the Guffey–Snyder Coal Conservation Act in August and was able to get social security legislation through Congress and signed the same month.

Thus, labor saw its entire legislative program enacted in less than two months after the *Schechter* decision—all except for one item. The explosion of activity by the administration in July and August eclipsed the congressional move to renew the NRA in the form of the Black–Connery bill.

As several reporters had predicted before the 1934 election, Roosevelt had pulled another political trick out of his hat. He had put together the sort of "permanent industrial policy, coupled with a social security program of unemployment insurance and old-age pensions," that reporters predicted would be necessary to make "the thirty-hour agitation look small in comparison." And in so doing, Roosevelt had well and truly launched the "second New Deal."[48]

Roosevelt displayed his well-known political agility throughout these events. But he was more than a political opportunist when it came to his opposition to the shorter-hour cure for unemployment. He was not doctrinaire in this matter, and was willing to accept parts of the share-the-work strategy in the retirement provisions of social security legislation and the Fair Labor Standards Act of 1938 as pragmatic measures; but by 1935, he and his advisers had developed ideological and policy alternatives to share the work that they consistently put forth as better unemployment remedies, even at a considerable political price.

While the Black-Connery forces would have divided a stable "lump of labor," Roosevelt was consistently more interested in increasing total work effort and creating new jobs. While supporters of shorter hours dreamed of increased leisure as a basis for individual freedom and progress, the administration envisioned government acting to assure everyone the "right to work" a "full-time job"—looking to secure work, not to find freedom from work.

The political contest that raged over Black–Connery reflected an ideological division of the first importance; it was a conflict between two views of progress and ideas about the fate of work during the depression. With the ascendancy of Roosevelt's views about the importance of economic recovery and vitality, visions of increased leisure as the basis of culture and a healthy social order faded. With the coming of the "right to work," made certain by government support, the politics of shorter hours faded. With the emergence of the second New Deal, the shorter-hour process in the American economy ran up against its first successful adversary. The salvaging of work from the steady erosion of shorter hours began.

In an April 1958 letter to Arthur Schlesinger, Leon Keyserling stressed the fact that Roosevelt came to Washington without a "systematic economic program." The "highly experimental, improvised and inconsistent" programs of the first New Deal defy categorization. They were the product of diverse "schools of reformers" who had been promoting programs that Roosevelt, higgledy-piggledy, picked up. According to Keyserling, the PWA, CWA, NIRA, etc., were not parts of a systematic plan or overall purpose. It was the "desire to get rid of the Black bill" that promoted the administration to draw up such things as the NRA "to put in something to satisfy labor." This point has also been made by other notables in Roosevelt's administration.

But thirty-hour legislation continued throughout the depression to goad Roosevelt to action. Black–Connery was introduced in each depression Congress until it passed, in highly modified form, as the Fair Labor Standards Act (FLSA) in 1938, with virtually all of its work-sharing teeth pulled. The FLSA's hours limitation was never lower than industrial averages and never functioned to decrease work "across the board," which was the distinguishing mark of Black–Connery. Hence, thirty-hour legislation continued to function as a sort of reverse polestar, enabling Roosevelt to chart his course by the simple expediency of sailing directly away from it. Roosevelt's instinctive reaction against thirty hours matured to positive approaches to industrial stabilization and reemployment built on work creation, not work spreading; programs were founded on industrial growth and increased spending as the wellsprings of progress. In the process, he and his administration discarded the century-old notion that increased leisure had the potential for social and individual advance.[49]

Roosevelt committed the federal government to assuring American workers a forty-hour week, and in so doing he institutionalized a bias against free time in any form—leisure or unemployment. Since the depression, few Americans have thought of free time as a natural, continuous, and positive result of economic growth and increased productivity. Instead, leisure has been seen as a drain on the economy, a wage liability, and an abandonment of economic progress.

## VII

Certainly, the end of the shorter-hour movement has many dimensions and causes that must be explored. But the narrative presented in this chapter suggests two important points, one social and the other political. During the depression, free time took the form of massive unemployment. Instead of accepting labor's thirty-hour-week remedy, Roosevelt and the majority of Americans saw this free time as a tragedy that had to be eliminated by increasing economic activity—stimulated by government spending if necessary. The concept of free time as a natural part of economic advance and a foil to materialistic values was abandoned.

Changes in attitudes found concrete forms in federal law and policy established during the depression that continue today. Hence the end of the shorter-hour movement is to be explained partially in political terms. Since the depression, public policy has been designed to maintain "adequate demand" and "full employment." Government deficit spending, liberal Treasury policy, increased government payrolls, and expanded public works projects have been employed whenever the private sector has shown signs of stagnation.

Beginning with Roosevelt's inauguration and continuing through such efforts as the Fair Labor Standards Act of 1938, the Employment Act of 1946, the Commission on Money and Credit in 1961, and, one might even argue, Ronald Reagan's spending policies, governmental programs to deal with unemployment have been constant. Their premise has been, in the words of the Unemployment Act of 1946, "the continuing policy of the federal government . . . to promote maximum employment, production, and purchasing power." In practical terms, policies have been, and continue to be, designed to remedy unemployment by the federal government's acting as a "permanent stabilizing force in the economy," spending whatever is necessary to stimulate the economy to "full employment" and "full production."[50]

The shorter-hour cure for unemployment has been forgotten for over forty years partly because of the public policy described above. Share the work and increased leisure have simply not had a political constituency since the Great Depression. Leisure has been neither an important social nor political issue. Decisions made during the depression about the danger of increased free time and the importance of economic growth and "full employment" have become articles of modern faith and political dogma.

The ending of shorter hours is indicative of a monumental change in American and Western notions about work and the direction for progress. For over a century, reductions in working hours were considered, almost universally, to be a desirable outcome of industrialization. Some of the most idealistic dreams of a generation of reformers centered on the expectation that worktime would decline, that workers could increasingly escape work's bondage. But labor's call for "the progressive reduction in the hours of labor" has been replaced by the more general call for more work and more jobs. Communists, social democrats, socialists, and capitalists agree: the more work, the better. Those who, like Herbert Marcuse, continue to call for a steady reduction of worktime have become the true radicals. Work stands today at the center of life; it is the self-justifying end of progress and economic development for which the rest of the economic, political, and social machinery have been subordinated and brought into service. Work today has many of the earmarks of a modern religion, and increased leisure is a prime candidate for the modern heresy.

## NOTES

1. *New York Times,* August 5, 1930, p. 6, and November 17, 1930, p. 1. Unlike other broadly based reform measures that have prospered in this century, the shorter-hour movement reached a historical plateau nearly forty years ago. For accounts of this phenomenon, see J. D. Owen, "Workweeks and Leisure: An Analysis of Trends, 1948–75," *Monthly Labor Review* 48 (1976): 3–8. Owen claims that there has been "no increase in leisure" since the depression. For others who have commented on this development, see Y. Barzel and R. McDonald, "Assets, Subsistence, and the Supply Curve of Labor," *American Economic Review* 63 (1973): 621–633; D. H. Dalton, "The Age of the Constant Workweek: Hours of Work in the United States Since World War II," Ph.D. dissertation, University of California, Berkeley 1972; T. A. Finegan, "Hours of Work in the United States: A Cross Sectional Analysis," *Journal of Political Economy* (1962): 452–470; Benjamin Hunnicutt, "The End of Shorter Hours," *Labor History* 25 (Summer 1984): 373–404; Ethel Jones, *An Investigation of the Stability of Hours of Work per Week in Manufacturing 1947–1970,* Research Monograph No. 7 (Athens, Ga., 1970), *passim;* S. Linder, *The Harried Leisure Class,* (New York, 1970), p. 135; H. Northrup, "The Reduction in Hours," in C. Dankert *et al., Hours of Work* (New York, 1965), *passim;* G. C. Winston, "An International Comparison of Income and Hours of Work," *Review of Econom-*

*ics and Statistics* 48 (1966): 28–39; and J. Zuzanek, "Society and Leisure," *Journal of Leisure Research* 6 (1974): 294–304.

Another curious fact about the end of the shorter-hour movement is that the workweek and workday did all their shrinking during a period of relative stability in the workforce, that is, during a time when the percentage of the population in the workforce was fairly constant. More recently, when that percentage has grown and more people have been working in the labor market than ever before, hours of work have stabilized. Since the percentage of people who work has grown so large so fast, a case can be made that Americans, as a group, work more hours per capita than at any time in this century since World War I. U.S. Bureau of the Census, *Historical Statistics of the United States from Colonial Times to the Present* (Washington, D.C., 1975), p. 127.

2. *New York Times,* October 5, 1933, pp. 2, 3; M. C. Cahill, *Shorter Hours: A Study of the Movement Since the Civil War* (New York, 1922), pp. 14–19, 43–46, 156–159, 211; S. Chase, "Leisure in a Machine Age," *Library Journal* 41 (August 1931): 629–632; R. S. Lynd and H. M. Lynd, *Middletown* (New York, 1929), pp. 11, 53, 80, 81, 225, 226, 301–310, 495–497; G. A. Lundberg, M. Komarovsky, and M. A. McInerny, *Leisure: A Suburban Study* (New York, 1934), pp. 21–25; P. H. Douglas, *Theory of Wages* (New York, 1934), Chap. 12. For recent descriptions of the history of the workweek, see J. Owen, *The Price of Leisure* (Montreal, 1970), pp 62–67; J. S. Zeisel, "The Work Week in American Industry," *Monthly Labor Review* 81 (January 1958): 23–29; U.S. Bureau of the Census, *Historical Statistics;* J. Kreps, *Lifetime Allocation of Work and Income* (Durham, N.C., 1971), pp. 17–24; E. B. Jones, "New Estimates of Hours and Work per Week and Hourly Earnings, 1900–1957," *Review of Economics and Statistics* 45 (November 1963): 374–385; U.S. House of Representatives, *Hours of Work, Hearings before the Select Subcommittee on Labor of the Committee on Education and Labor,* 88th Cong., 1963, pp. 73–104.

3. J. R. Commons *et al., History of Labor in the United States,* 3 vols. (New York, 1918–1935), 1:170–172, 384–386, 479, 546; 3:97–113: See also S. Perlman, *A History of Trade Unionism in the United States* (New York, 1950; originally published 1921), pp. 4, 45, 46; and C. and M. Beard, eds., *Whither Mankind* (New York, 1928), Chap. 8 *et passim.*

4. F. T. deVyver, "Five-Day Week," *Current History* 33 (November 1930): 223–227; "History of Movement for Shorter Hours in Industry and the Five-Day Week," *New York Times,* June 2, 1929; Cahill, *Shorter Hours,* pp. 11–58, 250–256; *New York Times,* July 5, 1892, and August 8, 1912. For recent analyses, see R. Hofstadter, *The Age of Reform* (New York, 1955), p. 242; L. Wolman, "Hours of Work in American Industry," *National Bureau of Economic Research* 71 (1938): 20; N. Pollack, *The Populist Response to Industrial America* (Cambridge, Mass., 1962), pp. 28–31.

5. R. McCloskey, *The American Supreme Court* (Chicago, 1960), pp. 153–156; and Alpheus Thomas Mason, *The Supreme Court from Taft to Warren* (New York, 1958), p. 6.

6. *New York Times,* August 2, 1932; "Spread-Work Plans Gain Ground on the

Employment Front," *Business Week* 11 (October 1932); "American Industry and the Five-Day Week," *Congressional Digest* (1932): 225; L. C. Walker, "The Share-the-Work Movement," *Annals of the American Academy* 165 (January 1933): 13.

7. *New York Times,* August 5, 1932, and January 16, 1937; "Cereals: Six-Hour Day Helps Kellogg Company Do More Work," *Newsweek* 9 (September 1936): 27; "Humanizing Machines—II, Kellogg's Six-Hour Day," *Forum and Century* 96, no. 3 (1933): 97.

8. *New York Times,* August 14, 1932.

9. *New York Times,* August 25, 1932.

10. W. S. Gifford, letter to President Hoover from Walter S. Gifford, director of the President's Organization on Unemployment Relief, Box 319 (August 3, 1932), and "Report of the President's Organization on Unemployment Relief," Box 339; both in Herbert Hoover's Presidential Papers, Hoover Library, West Branch, Iowa. See also "Spread-Work Plans Gain Ground on the Employment Front," "Spreading-Work Program of President's Conference of August 26, 1932," *Monthly Labor Review* 35 (October 1932): 790–792; "President Hoover's Economy Proposal: Five Day Week Staggered Furlough Plan," *Congressional Digest* 9 (May 1932): 130; *New York Times,* August 2, 1932; and W. J. Barrett, "Present Plans for Spreading Employment," *Congressional Digest* 11 (October 1932): 232.

11. *New York Times,* July 21, 22, 24, 25, and August 2, 1932; J. G. Winant, "New Hampshire Plan," *Review of Reviews* 86 (November 1932: 24; O. McKee, Jr., "New Hampshire Does Her Bit," *National Republic* 20, no. 6 (October 1932): 3.

12. *New York Times,* December 10, 1932, and January 15, 1933; "Job Sharing: 5 Million Helped by Work-Spreading, Teagle Committee Estimates," *Business Week* 14 (February 1, 1933); "Nation-Wide Drive for the Five-Day Week," *Literary Digest* 115 (1933): 3–4; "Spread-Work Plans Gain Ground."

13. *New York Times,* May 16 and 21, June 21 and 30, September 22, and October 5, 1932; W. Graf, *Platforms of the Two Great Political Parties: 1932 to 1944* (Washington, D.C., 1944), pp. 336, 354; R. F. Himmelberg, *The Great Depression and American Capitalism* (Boston, 1968), p. 41.

14. *New York Times,* October 7, 1933; "Labor's Ultimatum to Industry: Thirty-Hour Week," *Literary Digest* 114 (December 10, 1932): 3–4; "A.F. of L. Opens War for Its 30-Hour Week, *Newsweek* 1 (July 22, 1933): 6, *New York Times,* July 17 and October 12 1932, September 28, October 10 and 23, 1933, and December 13, 1934; "Labor Will Fight," *Business Week* 14–15 (December 14, 1932): 32; "The Labor Army Takes the Field: A Shorter Work Week to Make Jobs," *Literary Digest* 115 (April 15, 1933): 6.

15. F. T. Carlton, "Employment and Leisure," *American Federationist* 39 (1932): 1256–1260; U.S. House of Representative, Committee on Labor, *Hearings on H.R 14105,* 72nd Cong., 2nd sess., 1933, pp. 1–23: For a review of the AFL's attitude toward work sharing, see the following issues of the *American Federationist:* January 1931, p. 22; February 1931, p. 145; April 1931, p. 401; June 1931, p. 677; September 1931, p. 1056; December 1931, p. 1455; April 1932, p. 382; May 1932, p. 504; September 1932, p. 985: For continuous support of Black–Connery, see the

following issues of the *American Federationist:* January 1933, p. 13; February 1933, p. 179; April 1933, p. 347; May 1933, p. 458; November 1933, p. 1174; January 1935, p. 12; February 1935, p. 132; December 1936, p. 1244; October 1937, p. 1052; November 1938, p. 1176. See also S. Miller, Jr., "Labor and the Challenge of the New Leisure," *Harvard Business Review* 11 (1933): 462–667; and W. Green, "Leisure for Labor—a New Force Alters Our Social Structure," *Magazine of Business* 56 (August 1929): 136–137.

16. *New York Times,* January 6, 8, 12, 19, and 20, 1933; U.S. House of Representatives, Committee on Labor, *Hearings on H.R. 158 and H.R. 4557,* 73rd Cong., 1st sess. 1933, *passim;* U.S. House of Representatives, Committee on Labor, *Hearings on H.R. 7202, H.R. 416, and H.R. 8492,* 73rd Cong., 2nd sess., 1934, *passim;* D. C. Fisher, "The Bright Perilous Face of Leisure," *Journal of Adult Education* 5 (1933): 237–243; L. C. Walker, *Distributed Leisure: An Approach to the Problems of Overproduction and Underemployment* (New York, 1931), pp. 21–52; "Reduction of Working Hours and the Advantages of Leisure," *Review of Reviews* 82 (1932); A. Pound, "Out of Unemployment into Leisure," *Atlantic Review* 146 (December 1930): 784–792; B. Russell, "Reeducation of Working Hours and the Advantages of Leisure," *Review of Reviews* 82 (1932): 48–54; G. B. Cutten, *Challenge of Leisure* (Columbus, Ohio, 1933), *passim;* A. O. Dahlberg, *Jobs, Machines, and Capitalism* (New York, 1932), *passim;* C. D. Burns, *Leisure in the Modern World* (New York, 1932), *passim;* W. H. Hamilton, "Challenge of Leisure," *New Republic* 74 (1933): 191–192; T. D. Eliot, "Reevaluating Our Leisure in Our Civilization," *Christian Register* 113 (1934): 758–759; F. Franklin, "Uses of Leisure," *Saturday Review of Literature* 9 (November 5, 1932): 222; "New Leisure," *Nation* 137 (November 29, 1933): 610–611; W. S. Coffin, "Too Little Culture for Leisure," *American Magazine of Art* 24 (June 1933): 299–300; E. E. Calkins, "Lost Art of Play," *Atlantic Monthly* 106 (1933): 438–446; A. B. Brown, "Education for Leisure," *Hibbert Journal* 31 (1933): 440–450; M. P. Coleman, "Leisure and the Arts," *Library Journal* 59 (1934): 60–61; R. Aiken, "A Laborer's Leisure," *North American Review* 232 (1931): 268–273; "New Leisure, Its Significance and Use," *Library Journal* 58 (May 15, 1933): 444; W. Pangburn, "Leisure Time and Education Opportunities and Needs," *Recreation* 27 (1934): 499–500; A. N. Pack, *The Challenge of Leisure* (New York 1934), *passim;* J. Destree, "Popular Arts and Workers' Spare Time," *International Labor Review* 27 (1933): 184–206; A. Daniels, "Responsibility of the College in Education for Leisure," *Schools and Society* 41 (1935): 706–707; H. S. Dimock, "Can We Educate for Leisure?" *Religious Education* 29 (1934): 120–124; J. H. Finley, "What Will We Do with Our Time?" *National Municipal Review* 22 (1933): 416–417; E. E. Hoyt, "The Challenge of the New Leisure," *Journal of Home Economics,* (October 1933 p. 688; E. T. Lies, "Education for Leisure," *National Education Association Journal* 21 (1932): 253–254; E. T. Lies, *The New Leisure Challenges the Schools* (Washington, D.C., 1933), *passim;* E. T. Lies and R. L. Duffus, *The Arts in American Life* (New York, 1933), *passim;* L. P. Jacks, "The Coming Leisure," *New Era* 13 (1932): 349–351; B. A. McClenahan, "Preparation for Leisure," *Sociology and Social Research* 18 (1933): 140–149; J. T. Palmer, "New Leisure—Blessing or Curse?" *School Executive Mag-*

*azine* 54 (1935): 198–199; W. A. Orton, *America in Search of Culture* (Boston, 1933), *passim;* W. S. Coffin, "Art and Leisure," *Art Digest* 7 (1933): 10; W. B. Bizzell, "Learning and Leisure," *School and Society* 39 (1934): 65–72; E. E. Calkins, "New Leisure: A Curse or a Blessing?" *Recreation* 26 (April 1934): 22–27; N. M. Butler, "Leisure and Its Uses, *Recreation* 28 (May 1934): 219–222.

17. H. P. Fairchild, "Exit the Gospel of Work," *Harper's,* April 1931, pp. 566–573; F. S. Cohen, "The Blessing of Unemployment," *American Scholar* 2 (1933): 203–214; F. H. Allport, "This Coming Era of Leisure," *Harper's* 163 (November 1931): 641–652; "In the Driftway: American Vice of Busyness," *Nation* 132 (January 28, 1931): 98–99; "Coming: The Age of Leisure," *Literary Digest* 112 (January 16, 1932): 26; "Not Less, but More: Thirty-Hour-Week," *Saturday Evening Post* 207 (February 9, 1935): 26; R. Payne, *Why Work: or the Coming of Leisure* (Boston, 1939), *passim;* H. A. Overstreet, *A Guide to Civilized Loafing* (New York, 1934), *passim;* "Machine and Leisure," *Industrial Arts and Vocational Education* 26 (1937): 416–417; "A.F. of L. Opens War," p. 6; "The Six-Hour Day," 69 (January 1933): 33; "Union Wage and Hour Policies and Employment," *American Economics Review* 30 (June 1940): 290; C. E. Dankert, "Efficiency and Unemployment," *Canadian Forum* 12 (February 1932): 169; Pound, "Out of unemployment," p. 784; "Unemployment and the Thirty-Hour Week," *Journal of the National Education Association* 22 (February 1933): 59.

18. W. Green, "Leisure for Labor," *Magazine of Business* 54 (August 1929): 136–137; H. L. Slobodin, "Unemployment or Leisure—Which?" *American Federationist* 37 (1930): 1205–1208; W. Green, "Shorter Hours," *American Federationist* 38 (January 1931): 22; M. Lynch, "The Shorter Workday: The Complete Argument," *American Federationist* 33 (March 1926): 291; W. Green, "The Five-Day Week to Balance Production and Consumption," *American Federationist* 33 (October 1926): 1299; M. Woll, "Labor and the New Leisure," *Recreation* 27, (1933): 418; L. P. Jacks, "Today's Unemployment and Tomorrow's Leisure, *Recreation* 25 (1933): 678; A. J. Lindsay, "Unemployment: The 'Meanwhile' Problem," *Contemporary Review* 143 (June 1933): 687.

19. *New York Times,* April 6, 1933; Arthur M. Schlesinger, *The Coming of the New Deal* (Boston, 1959), p. 95; G. Turner, "The New Leisure of the New Deal," *Catholic World* 138 (November 1933): 168.

20. *New York Times,* April 8, 1933; *Newsweek,* April 15, 1933, pp. 8, 21.

21. Arthur Link, *American Epoch* (New York, 1963), pp. 390–395; *New York Times,* April 12, 13, and 14, 1933.

22. "What Price Leisure," *Business Week,* August 3, 1932, p. 36; *New York Times,* November 1, and December 10, 1932; "Work-Spreaders Will Make Jobs Now, Face the Issues Later," *Business Week,* October 12, 1932; "Work-Spreaders Will Have to Spread It Thin," *Business Week,* October 26, 1932, p. 6.

23. *New York Times,* April 2, 1933.

24. "Six-Hour Day: Cornell Crystallizes Some Conclusions on Industry's Attitude," *Business Week,* May 10 1933, p. 4.

25. *New York Times,* April 12, 15, and 20, 1933; *Newsweek,* April 15, 1933, p. 8.

26. Raymond Moley, *After Seven Years* (New York and London, 1939), p. 186.

27. *New York Times,* April 20, 1933.

28. Rexford Guy Tugwell, *The Battle for Democracy* (New York, 1935), p. 265; Alexander Sachs, "The National Recovery Administration Policies and the Problem of Economic Planning," in *Recovery Program,* ed. Clair Wilcox, Herbert Fraser, and Patrick Murphy Malin (New York, 1934), pp. 107–191; Donald R. Richberg, *My Hero; The Indiscreet Memoirs of an Eventful but Unheroic Life* (New York, 1954), pp. 163–167; H. G. Moulton, "In Defense of the Longer Work Week," *Annals of the American Academy* 184 (March 1936): 64; H. G. Moulton and Maurice Leven, "The Thirty-Hour Week," *Scientific Monthly* 40 (March 1935): 257.

29. *New York Times,* April 15 and 19, 1933. For Cordell Hull's reaction, see *New York Times,* April 20 and 25, 1933.

30. *New York Times,* April 19 and 26, 1933.

31. *New York Times,* April 19, 1933.

32. *New York Times,* May 3, 1933.

33. *New York Times,* May 21, 1933.

34. Charles Frederick Roos, *Hours of Work, NRA Economic Planning,* (Bloomington, Ind., 1937), p. 105.

35. *New York Times,* September 29, 1933.

36. *New York Times,* April 26, July 8, October 28, and December 3, 1934; "In the Driftway," p. 73; "Wages, Hours, and Recovery," *Business Week,* March 3, 1934, p. 24; "Hours and Wages," *Business Week,* October 20, 1934, p. 5; "Labor's Day: NRA Policy Hearings," *Business Week,* February 9, 1935, p. 6; "Washington Notes," *New Republic,* December 1934, p. 81.

37. *New York Times,* October 9 and December 13, 1934.

38. *New York Times,* October 14 and November 22, "Washington Notes: Battle of the Session: The 30-Hour Week Bill—Apostle Alfred P. Sloan—Senators on the Spot," *New Republic* 81 (December 16, 1934): 191.

39. *New York Times,* January 6, 1935.

40. Link, *American Epoch,* pp. 395–405.

41. Harry Hopkins, "They'd Rather Work," *Collier's* 96 (November 16, 1935).

42. *New York Times,* May 17, 1935; "Washington Notes," *New Republic* 82 (May 8, 1935): 365.

43. Harry L. Hopkins, *Spending to Save: The Complete Story of Relief* (Seattle and London, 1936), pp. 183–184.

44. Arthur M. Schlesinger, *The Politics of Upheaval* (Boston, 1960), pp. 292–301.

45. Marriner S. Eccles, "Government Spending Is Sound," speech over NBC, reprinted in *Vital Speeches* 5 (January 23, 1939): 272–275; S. J. Wolf, "Eccles Would Save Capitalism by Reform," *Literary Digest* 119 (January 5, 1935): 5; Rudolph L. Weissman, ed. *The Public Papers of Marriner S. Eccles: Economic Balance and a Balanced Budget* (New York, 1940), pp. 84–85; *New York Times,* March 16, 1937; "Federal Reserve: M. S. Eccles, Mormon and Liberal, Succeeds Black as Governor," *Newsweek* 4 (November 17, 1934): 34.

46. *New York Times,* February 6, 1935; "Politics, Either Way: 30-Hour Bill

Won't Die Unaided," *Business Week,* February 2, 1935, p. 40; W. Green, "Would a Thirty-Hour Week Increase Employment? Pro," *Congressional Digest* 14 (April 1935): 112.

47. *New York Times,* March 19 and April 3, 1935.

48. *New York Times,* October 14, 1934.

49. Schlesinger, *Politics of Upheaval,* pp. 690–692; "In the Driftway," p. 73; "Wages, Hours, and Recovery," *Business Week,* March 3, 1934, p. 24; "What Price Leisure?" p. 36; "Hours and Wages," p. 5; "Labor's Day: NRA Policy Hearings," p. 6; "Washington Notes," *New Republic* 81 (1934): 191; U.S. House, *Hearings on H.R.* 14105, pp. 1–23; *New York Times,* April 29 and May 3, 1933, October 28 and November 22, 1926 and December 3, 1934; H. W. Dodds, "The Problem of Leisure in an Industrial Age: The Significance of Work," *Vital Speeches of the Day* 4 (August 1938): 619.

50. Arthur M. Okum, ed., *The Battle against Unemployment: An Introduction to a Current Issue of Public Policy* (New York, 1965), vii–viii; Albert Rees, "Dimensions of the Employment Problem," in *A Symposium on Employment* (Washington, D.C., 1964), *passim;* Heilbroner, *Economic Problem,* (Englewood Cliffs, N.J., 1970), pp. 140–170.

# Index

245